BLACK WOMANIST ETHICS

American Academy of Religion Academy Series

edited by
Susan Thistlethwaite

Number 60
BLACK WOMANIST ETHICS
by
Katie G. Cannon

Katie G. Cannon

BLACK WOMANIST ETHICS

Scholars Press
Atlanta, Georgia

BLACK WOMANIST ETHICS

by
Katie G. Cannon

© 1988
American Academy of Religion

Library of Congress Cataloging-in-Publication Data

Cannon, Katie G.
  Black womanist ethics.

  (American Academy of Religion academy series ; no. 60)
  Bibliography: p.
  1. Christian ethics. 2. Afro-American women—Conduct
of life. I. Title. II. Series.
BJ1275.C33 1988   241'.08996073   87-38120
ISBN 1-55540-215-1 (alk. paper)
ISBN 1-55540-216-X (pbk. : alk. paper)

Printed in the United States of America
on acid-free paper

Dedicated to my mother,
CORINE LYTLE CANNON,
WHO TAUGHT ME HOW TO WORK AND DREAM,
AS WELL AS HOW TO PRAY.

TABLE OF CONTENTS

Contents

ACKNOWLEDGMENTS

I am grateful to many people who have contributed to the completion of this project. Some have provided the essential financial substance—'the daily bread'; others have contributed the beauty, goodness and truth' which flow throughout this document; and still others have put their hand in mine, propping me up on every leaning side when the road was rough and the going was critically tough.

I thank Professor Beverly Wildung Harrison, the primary inspiration behind my work in Christian Ethics. Her critical questions and organizational suggestions greatly improved my professional style. In skillful and creative ways, she always gives back as rain, the ideas I put forth as mist.

I would also like to thank the other members of my dissertation committee, Roger Shinn, Thelma Adair, Esther Stine and Cornel West who took time out to read various drafts of the manuscript and to make helpful comments in the final stages of this work.

I offer Constance Marie Baugh a heart-full of gratitude for her support and encouragement throughout this enterprise. She has kept me forever mindful of the sacredness of this task.

Martha Springs Porcher deserves thanks, in that she taught me how to recognize the beauty of Blackness in the commonplace and the greatness of Blackness in the common people.

Thanks to the following persons, each of whom knows the unique value of the laurels bestowed: Victoria Byerly, Carolyn S. Hopley, Jean Huffman, Ann Yeargin, Verlie Coleman, Betsy Halpern, Betty Bolen, Dorothy Gist, Emily V. Gibbes, Carter Heyward, Susan Harlow, Amelie Ratliff, Marian Martin, Vivian McFadden, Angelin Jones Simmons, Theodora B. Washington, Delores Dixon, Janet Walton, Anna Taylor, Jean Norton, Marcia Storch, Pamela Bowers, Elisabeth Schüssler Fiorenza and Nikita Allen.

I am indebted to my family; they continue to serve as my cloud and my fire—my parents, Esau and Corine Cannon; my sisters, Sara Cannon Fleming, Doris Cannon Love, and Sylvia Denise Moon; my brothers, James Ernest Cannon, John Wesley Cannon and Jerry Lytle Cannon—may our tribe increase.

INTRODUCTION

Origins of the Study

I first began pondering the relationship between faith and ethics as a schoolgirl while listening to my grandmother teach the central affirmations of Christianity within the context of a racially segregated society. My community of faith taught me the principles of God's universal parenthood which engendered a social, intellectual and cultural ethos, embracing the equal humanity of all people. Yet, my city, state and nation declared it a punishable offense against the laws and mores for Blacks and whites "to travel, eat, defecate, wait, be buried, make love, play, relax and even speak together, except in the stereotyped context of master and servant interaction."[1]

My religious quest was one of trying to relate the Christian doctrines preached in the Black Church to the suffering, oppression and exploitation of Black people in the society. How could Christians who were white, flatly and openly, refuse to treat as fellow human beings Christians who had African ancestry? Was not the essence of the Gospel mandate a call to eradicate affliction, despair and systems of injustice? Inasmuch as the Black Church expressed the inner ethical life of the people, was there any way to reconcile the inherent contradictions in Christianity as practiced by whites with the radical indictments of and challenges for social amelioration and economic development in the Black religious heritage? How long would the white church continue to be the ominous symbol of white dominance—sanctioning and assimilating the propagation of racism in the mundane interests of the ruling group?

In the 1960s my quest for the integration of faith and ethics was influenced by scholars in various fields who surfaced the legitimate contributions of Afro-Americans which had been historically distorted and denied. Avidly I read the analysis exposing the assumptions and dogmas that made Blacks a negligible factor in the thought of the world. For more than three and a half centuries a "conspiracy of silence" rendered invisible the outstanding contributions of Blacks to the culture of humankind. From cradle to grave the people in the United States were taught the alleged inferiority of Blacks in every place in society.

When I turned specifically to readings in theological ethics, I discovered that the assumptions of the dominant ethical systems implied that the doing of Christian ethics in the Black community was either immoral or amoral. The cherished ethical ideas predicated upon the existence of freedom and a wide range of choices proved null and void in situations of oppression. The real-lived texture of Black life requires moral agency that may run contrary to the ethical boundaries of mainline Protestantism. Blacks may use action guides which have never been considered within the scope of traditional codes of faithful living. Racism, gender discrimination and economic exploitation, as inherited, age-long complexes, require the Black community to create and cultivate values and virtues in their own terms so that they can prevail against the odds with moral integrity.

For example, dominant ethics makes a virtue of qualities that lead to economic success—self-reliance, frugality and industry. These qualities are based on an assumption that success is possible for anyone who tries. Developing confidence in one's own abilities, resources and judgments amidst a careful use of money and goods in order to exhibit assiduity in the pursuit of upward mobility have proven to be positive values for whites. But, when the oligarchic economic powers and the consequent political power they generate, own and control capital and distribute credit as part of a legitimating system to justify the supposed inherent inferiority of Blacks, these same values prove to be ineffectual. Racism does not allow Black women and Black men to labor habitually in benefical work with the hope of saving expenses by avoiding waste so that they can develop a standard of living that is congruent with the American ideal.

Theoretical and analytical analyses demonstrate that to embrace work as a "moral essential" means that Black women are still the last hired to do the work which white men, white women and men of color refuse to do, and at a wage which men and white women refuse to accept. Black women, placed in jobs that have proven to be detrimental to their health, are doing the most menial, tedious and by far the most underpaid work, if they manage to get a job at all.

Dominant ethics also assumes that a moral agent is to a considerable degree free and self-directing. Each person possesses self-determining power. For instance, one is free to choose whether or not she/he wants to suffer and make sacrifices as a principle of action or as a voluntary vocational pledge of crossbearing. In dominant ethics a person is free to make suffering a desirable moral norm. This is not so for Blacks. For the masses of Black people, suffering is the normal state of affairs. Mental anguish, physical abuse and emotional agony are all part of the lived truth of Black people's straitened circumstances. Due to the extraneous forces and the entrenched bulwark of white supremacy and male superiority which pervade this society, Blacks and whites, women and men are forced to live with very different ranges of freedom. As long as the white-male experience continues to be established as the ethical norm, Black women, Black men and others will suffer unequivocal oppression. The range of freedom has been restricted by those who cannot hear and will not hear voices expressing pleasure and pain, joy and rage as others experience them.

In the Black community, the aggregate of the qualities which determine desirable ethical values regarding the uprightness of character and soundness of moral conduct must always take into account the circumstances, the paradoxes and the dilemmas that constrict Blacks to the lowest range of self-determination. Forced to the lowest rungs of the social, political and economic hierarchy, Black existence is deliberately and openly controlled.

> . . . how we travel and where, what work we do, what income we receive, where we eat, where we sleep, with whom we talk, where we recreate, where we study, what we write, what we publish . . .[2]

The vast majority of Blacks suffer every conceivable form of denigration. Their lives are named, defined and circumscribed by whites.

Black faith and liberation ethics are extremely useful in defying oppressive rules or standards of "law and order" which unjustly degrade Blacks in the society. They help Blacks to purge themselves of self-hate, thus asserting their own human validity. The ethical values that the Black community has construed for itself are not identical with the body of obligations and duties that Anglo-Protestant American society requires of its members. Nor can the ethical assumptions be the same, as long as powerful whites who control the wealth, the systems and the institutions in this society continue to perpetuate brutality and criminality against Blacks.

These early concerns, coupled with in-depth research and study helped me to demolish internalized myths about Black inferiority, to criticize whole bodies of literature which imply evaluations of Blacks by standards not relevant to oppressed people, and to locate irrefutable evidence of moral sensibility within Black life and culture, thus bringing me to this present work, originally entitled "Resources for a Constructive Ethic for Black Women With Special Attention to the Life and Work of Zora Neale Hurston."

Black women are the most vulnerable and the most exploited members of the American society. The structure of the capitalist political economy in which Black people are commodities combined with patriarchal contempt for women has caused the Black woman to experience oppression that knows no ethical or physical bounds.

> As a black, she has had to endure all the horrors of slavery and living in a racist society; as a worker, she has been the object of continual exploitation, occupying the lowest place on the wage scale and restricted to the most demeaning and uncreative jobs; as a woman she has seen her physical image defamed and been the object of the white master's uncontrollable lust and subjected to all the ideals of white womanhood as a model to which she should aspire; as a mother, she has seen her children torn from her breast and sold into slavery, she has seen them left at home without attention while she attended to the needs of the offspring of the ruling class.[3]

The focus of this dissertation is to show how Black women live out a moral wisdom in their real-lived context that does not appeal to the fixed rules or absolute principles of the white-oriented, male structured society. Black women's analysis and appraisal of what is right or wrong and good or bad develops out of the various coping mechanisms related to the conditions of their own cultural circumstances. In the face of this, Black women have justly regarded survival against tyrannical systems of triple oppression as a true sphere of moral life.

The Black woman's collection of moral counsel is implicitly passed on and received from one generation of Black women to the next. Black females are taught what is to be endured and how to endure the harsh, cruel, inhumane exigencies of life. The moral wisdom does not rescue Black women from the bewildering pressures and perplexities of institutionalized social evils but rather, exposes those ethical assumptions which are inimical to the ongoing survival of Black womanhood. The moral counsel of Black women captures the ethical qualities of what is real and what is of value to women in the Black world.

Methodologies Used in the Study

The methodologies used in this study are diverse. The initial chapters employ an historical method and attempt a reconstruction of the Black woman's history in the United States. By tracking down the central and formative facts in the Black woman's social world, I have identified the determinant and determining structures of oppression in the Black woman's moral situation.

The subsequent chapters depart from most work in Christian and secular ethics. The body of data is drawn from less conventional sources but probes more intimate and private aspects of Black life. The Black woman's literary tradition has not previously been used to interpret and explain the community's socio-cultural patterns from which ethical values can be gleaned. In doing so, I have found that this literary tradition is the nexus between the real-lived texture of Black life and the oral-aural cultural values implicitly passed on and received from one generation to the next. The ethical character of Black folk culture is strongly and unmistakably present in Zora Neale Hurston's life and literature. Even though it is not explicitly stated or elaborated in a moral or philosophical system, Hurston's writings guide and enrich an ethical perspective which would otherwise be impoverished by a false objectivity. There are many ways to read Hurston's texts but I can demonstrate that my interpretation of this literature is neither isolated nor idiosyncratic.

Further, I acknowledge the uncharted waters of this method. It starts with experience instead of with theories of values or norms. However, I believe that basic experiential themes and ethical implications can lead to norms lived out in the realities of day-to-day experience.

My goal is not to arrive at my own prescriptive or normative ethic. Rather, what I am pursuing is an investigation (a) that will help Black women, and others who care, to understand and to appreciate the richness of their own moral struggle through the life of the common people and the oral tradition; (b) to further understandings of some of the differences between ethics of life under oppression and established moral approaches which take for granted freedom and a wide range of choices. I am being suggestive of one possible ethical approach, not exhaustive.

I make no apologies for the fact that this study is a partisan one. However, it is not merely a glorification of the Black female community, but an attempt to add to the far too few positive records concerning the Black woman as a moral agent. For too long the Black community's theological and ethical understandings have been written from a decidedly male bias. The particular usefulness of this method should enable us to use the lives and literature of Black women to recognize through them the contribution to the field of ethics that Black women have made. One test will be whether those who know this literary tradition find that I have done justice to its depth and richness. The second test is whether Black women recognize the moral wisdom that they utilize. The third test is whether Black feminists who have given up on the community of faith will gain new insights concerning the reasonableness of theological ethics in deepening the Black woman's character, consciousness and capacity in the ongoing struggle for survival. If these criteria are met, then I will have reached my objective.

Summary of the Study

In chapter I, I analyze the historical context in which Black women have found themselves as moral agents. The existential situation of Afro-American women cannot be understood and explained adequately apart from this historical background. The history of the Black woman in the United States generates the conditions for the patterns of ethical behavior and moral wisdom which have emerged in the Black female community. One year before the Pilgrims arrived on the Mayflower, at least three women were among the twenty Blacks on the Dutch frigate which landed at Jamestown, Virginia. These first African inhabitants of the English colonies were not slaves but were sold into indentured servitude.

More than two and a half centuries of chattel slavery, followed by another century of forced segregation, have shaped the context in which Black women then—and still to this day—make moral judgments and ethical choices. Throughout the history of the United States, the interrelationship of white supremacy and male superiority has characterized the Black woman's moral situation as a situation of struggle—a struggle to survive in two contradictory worlds simultaneously, "one white, privileged, and oppressive, the other black, exploited and oppressed."[4]

> The struggle has been against sexism, which all women have experienced. It has been also against racism, which black men and women have experienced. The struggle has been compounded because at times white women created barriers to achieving the goal of equality for black women. Other times black men stood as obstacles to the development of their women. For the most part, racism has been the greatest obstacle to the black woman's struggle.[5]

Thus, an untangling of the Black woman's history sheds light on the values and virtues that guide the Black woman's struggle for survival.

In chapter II, I analyze further the moral situation of the Black woman in the twentieth century. Beginning with the 1910 mass exodus of Black people from rural to urban settings and from South to North, Back women continued to find the concrete immediacies as the only arena for understanding and assessing their reality. As long as the circumstances and conditions in which Black women's moral sensibility originated have not passed away, then Black women will embrace a set of ethical virtues that allow them to live with dignity on their own terms.

In chapter III, I discuss the Black woman's literary tradition as a valid source for the central rubrics of the Black woman's odyssey. It is my thesis that the Black woman's literary tradition is the best available literary repository for understanding the ethical values Black women have created and cultivated in their ongoing participation in this society. To prevail against the odds with integrity, Black women must asess their moral agency within the social conditions of the community. Locked out of the real dynamics of human freedom in America, they implicitly pass on and receive from one generation to the next moral formulas for survival that allow them to stand over against the perversions of ethics and morality imposed on them by whites and males who support racial imperialism in a patriarchal social order. The Black woman's literary tradition documents the "living space" carved out of the intricate web of racism, sexism and poverty. The literary tradition parallels Black history. It conveys the assumed values in the Black oral tradition. And it capsulizes the insularity of the Black community. Black women writers function as

8 Black Womanist Ethics

continuing symbolic conveyors and transformers of the values acknowledged by the female members of the Black community. In the
quest for appreciating Black women's experience, nothing surpasses
the Black woman's literary tradition. It cryptically records the specificity of the Afro-American life.

In chapters IV and V, I turn more specifically to examining the
matrix of virtues which emerge from the real-lived texture of the
Black community as these are expressed in the life and work of Zora
Neale Hurston (1901[?]–1960). Special attention to Hurston's work is
in order because, of all the women in the Black literary tradition
who have contributed to the concrete depiction of Black life, Zora
Neale Hurston is "par exemplar." As the most prolific Black woman
writer in America from 1920 to 1950, Zora Neale Hurston's life and
literature are paradigmatic of Black culture and Black women's lives.

As an outstanding novelist, journalist, folklorist, anthropologist and critic, Zora Hurston possesses a sharp accuracy in
reporting the positive sense of self that exists among poor, marginal
Blacks, "the Negro farthest down."[6] The primary impetus for all her
writings was to capture the density of simple values inherent in the
provincialism of Blacks who work on railroads, live in sawmill
camps, toil in phosphate mines, earning their keep as common
laborers. In her short story, "John Redding Goes to Sea," Hurston
describes the microcosmic world of her main characters:

> No one in their community had ever been farther than
> Jacksonville. Few, indeed had ever been there. Their own
> gardens, general store, and occasional trips to the county
> seat—seven miles away—sufficed for all their needs. Life was
> simple indeed with these folks.[7]

Hurston's extreme closeness to the sensibilities of her unlettered
characters, along with her meticulous collection of folklore, legends,
superstitions, music and dance of the common people enabled her
work to serve as a rich repository of resources helpful in delineating
the moral counsel cultivated throughout the various periods of Black
history in the United States. In a letter to Langston Hughes in 1929,
Hurston summed up her deep dedication and abiding commitment
to recording Black life.

> For I not only want to present the material with all the
> life and color of my people, I want to leave no loop-holes for the
> scientific crowd to rend and tear us. I am leaving the story
> material almost untouched. I have only tampered with it where

the story teller was not clear. I know it is going to read different, but that is the glory of the thing, don't you think?[8]

In chapter VI, the conclusion of the study, I attempt to answer the following question: are the fundamental dispositions that Black women possess as they transcend their oppression and transform their lives part of the faith tradition which the Black Church confesses and teaches? In other words, to what extent have writers of Black theology included the affective sensibilities of Zora Neale Hurston's characters in their delineation of action guides for liberation? What is the correlation between the action-norms formulated within the existing framework of the Black religious heritage and the continuing social matrix in which Black people find themselves as moral agents?

It may surprise some readers that I have selected Howard Thurman and Martin Luther King, Jr. as the two theologians whose work provides the most relevant theological resources for deepening moral wisdom in the Black community. These two pre-liberation theologians initiate and envision in new ways the fundamental truth claims operative in the contemporary Black community. By identifying out of their work the key themes which correlate with the situation of oppressed people, I present their grounding for moral agency which can serve to broaden ethical adequacy in the Black community.

Furthermore, both Howard Thurman and Martin Luther King, Jr. addressed precisely those individuals in the Black community who were central to Zora Neale Hurston's depiction of Black life and experience. Their concrete expositions of the Christian faith correspond with the efficacious ways that "the Negro farthest down" deals with the contingencies in the real-lived context. As theologians, Thurman and King concentrate on the nature and significance of humanity and how oppression makes a difference in the notions Blacks use to see and to act in situations that confront them.

Preliminary Exploration of the Study: Zora Neale Hurston, Howard Thurman and Martin Luther King, Jr.

To those unfamiliar with Zora Neale Hurston, the Black Religious Heritage and Black Theology, some introductory comments are in order.

ZORA NEALE HURSTON

Between the middle of the Harlem Renaissance and the end of the Korean War, Zora Neale Hurston wrote four novels, two books of folklore, an autobiography and more than fifty short stories and essays. In 1934, Zora Neale Hurston was praised by the *New York Herald Tribune* for being in "the front rank" of all American writers. In 1935–36 she was the recipient of two Guggenheim Research Fellowships. During this time Hurston was offered a Rosenwald Fellowship to study for her doctorate in anthropology and folklore at Columbia University. However, within a month, the officers reneged on the offer because they found Hurston's degree plan unacceptable. Two important honors were bestowed on Hurston in 1943: Howard University presented her the Alumni Award for distinguished post-graduate work in literature and the *Saturday Review* presented her with the Anisfield-Wold Award for her autobiography, *Dust Tracks on the Road*. It was heralded as "the best book on race relations and as the best volume in the general field of fiction, poetry or biography which is of such character that it will aid in the sympathetic understanding and constructive treatment of race relations."

In both her life and work Hurston embodies a sensitized candor, in relation to the subtle, invisible ethos as well as the expressed moral values emanating from within the cultural institutions in the Black community. Unlike most of the other writers of her time, Hurston emphasized the unique cultural heritage and wholeness of Black life. She refuted the stereotypes which depicted Blacks as minstrels, vindictive militants, mere ciphers who reacted only to an omnipresent racial oppression. Under the tutelage of Franz Boas of Columbia University, the first anthropologist to attack the pseudoscientific theories of racial inequality and white supremacy,[9] Hurston took a combative stance, insisting that anatomical differences do not denote inferiority or decrease the qualities of "human beingness" among people of color.

> Negroes were supposed to write about the Race Problem. I was thoroughy sick of the subject. My interest lies in what makes a man or a woman do such-and-so, regardless of his color. It seemed to me that the human beings I met reacted pretty much the same to the same stimuli. Different idioms, yes. Circumstances and conditions having power to influence, yes. Inherent difference, no.[10]

Thus, Hurston uses a common folk expression to sum up this understanding of individuality:

"God made people duck by duck."[11]

Hurston boldly asserted this as her core message in the controversial essay of 1928, "How It Feels to Be Colored Me."

> But I am not tragically colored. There is no great sorrow damned up in my soul, nor lurking behind my eyes. I do not mind at all. I do not belong to the sobbing school of negrohood who hold that nature somehow has given them a lowdown dirty deal and whose feelings are hurt about it. . . . No, I do not weep at the world. I am too busy sharpening my oyster knife.[12]

Mary Helen Washington agrees that this is the point of departure in Hurston's life and in all of her work.

> She [Zora Neale Hurston] saw black lives as psychologically integral—not mutilated half-lives, stunted by the effects of racism and poverty. She simply could not depict blacks as defeated, humiliated, degraded, or victimized, because she did not experience black people or herself that way.[13]

Zora Hurston always looked first and foremost to the Black experience as the source of her living texts. She used "folk language, folkways and folk stories" as symbols to measure the intrinsic values of the Black oral-aural cultural tradition. In order to refute assumptions of genetic racism and to vindicate the Black community in the face of the oppressive slander of white supremacy, Hurston used a presentational method to document the culture, history, imagination, and fantasies of Black people.

Hurston depicted the inaudible stoutheartedness of Black folks. She was aware of the bad housing, overworked mothers, underworked fathers, functional illiteracy, malnutrition, that prevailed and continues to prevail, in the Black community. However, she maintained that Black life was more than defensive reactions to the oppressive circumstances of anguish and desperation perpetrated by the "Western Commercial of White and Male Supremacy." Hurston invested her energies in staying in touch with the rich, colorful creativity that emerged and re-emerges in the Black quest for human dignity. The cultural traditions that Hurston wrote about tend to represent statements of belief about the world, its creation, people's connectedness and estrangement within the insular community. The characters are women, men and children who know how to grasp the affirmative side of life amidst a system of brutalization. They learn early how to find personal fulfillment in the basic push-pull ambivalence of the do-it-yourself-or-do-without reality.

Out of a zeal to reject the false and degrading stereotypes promulgated in Anglo-American culture, Hurston wrote about Black life

> . . . as it existed apart from racism, injustice, Jim Crow—where people laughed, celebrated, loved, sorrowed, struggled—unconcerned about white people and completely unaware of being "a problem."[14]

It is in this sense that Alice Walker identifies Zora Hurston as the prime symbol of "racial health."[15]

As a Black-woman-artist, who was subjected to the violence of whites, of male superiority, and of poverty, Zora Neale Hurston offered an especially concrete frame of reference for understanding the Black woman as a moral agent. Karla Holloway describes Hurston's moral agency as being both the mirror and lamp, both the visual image and the mechanism that illuminates that image.[16] Hurston's own beingness is both the subject and object of her work. Thus, Hurston's life and work serve as a prophetic paradigm for understanding the modes of behavior and courses of action which are passed from generation to generation by the most oppressed segments of the Black population.

Robert Bone has also underscored Hurston's interest in the female condition generally, and Black womanhood in particular:

> . . . the loves, joys, frustrations and tragedies which attend the female condition complicate it and endow it with such rich possibility.[17]

Barbara Christian also elaborates this prophetic focus in Hurston's work:

> Hurston was so closely concerned with the peculiar characteristics of the relationship between the black woman and her community that she rarely moved outside it. Perhaps the intensity of her view is related to the position the black woman holds within her community, for she has, since its beginnings, been entrusted with its survival and enrichment.[18]

Beginning in early childhood, Hurston embraced a set of values which allowed her to prevail against the odds with integrity. Through the Black community's oral tradition Hurston learned how to live on Black terms—how to resist, to oppose and to endure the immediate struggles over and against terrifying circumstances.

During her middle years Hurston incarnated a personality of harmonious complex opposites. In the most comprehensive and thorough biography of Hurston so far written, Robert E. Hemenway describes the reconciling polarities of Hurston's personality as "fiercely flamboyant yet incredibly secretive, self-centered yet kind, a Republican conservative yet an early black nationalist—a sophisticated writer who was never afraid to be herself."[19] Joyce O. Jenkins says that Hurston's personality was one carved out of a pragmatic philosophy of life, wherein Hurston made up her own rules, refusing to be bound by what she ought to do and think.[20]

During the later years of her career, Hurston's life serves as a "cautionary metaphor" symbolizing what happens to women of color in a capitalist society who have no money of their own. Henry Louis Gates argues that economic limits determined Hurston's choices more than violence or love.[21]

> Miss Hurston wrote well when she was comfortable, wrote poorly when she was not. Financial problems, poor book sales, grants and fellowships too few and too paltry, ignorant editors and a smothering patron produced the sort of dependence that directly influenced, if not determined her style. . . . [S]he was frequently without money, sometimes pawning her typewriter to buy groceries, surviving after 1957 on unemployment benefits, substitute teaching and welfare checks.[22]

Hurston's own code of living forms a basis for her female characterizations. In other words, Hurston and her female characters are Black women who learn to glean directives for living in the here-and-now. In their tested and tried existential realities, the majority of these women refuse to get caught up in the gaudy accoutrements of the middle strata sham. Against the vicissitudes of labor exploitation, sex discrimination and racial cruelties, they embrace an ingenuity which allows them to fashion a set of values on their own terms as well as mastering, radicalizing and sometimes destroying pervasive, negative orientations imposed by the larger society.

Zora Neale Hurston and her fictional counterparts are resources for a constructive ethic for Black women, wherein they serve as strong resilient images, embodying the choices of possible op-

---

tions for action open within the Black folk culture. For Hurston, women who live in the circle of life must discern the genuine choices available or else they will be characterized by one or more of the following folk metaphors: "mule," "spit cut," "rut in the road," "chewed-up" and "discarded sugar cane," and "wishbone."

As moral agents struggling to avoid the devastating effects of structural oppression, these Black women create various coping mechanisms that free them from imposed norms and expectations. The moral counsel of their collective stories accentuates the positive attributes of Black life. Through the mode of fiction, they articulate possibilities for decision and action which address forthrightly the circumstances that inescapably "color" and shape Black life. As the bodily, conditional and psychical representatives of the majority of the members of the Afro-American female population, Hurston and her characters serve as the consciousness that calls Black women forth so that they can break away from the oppressive ideologies and belief systems that presume to define their reality.

As Ellease Southerland has noted, Hurston's work brings together a religion of opposites, and when these opposites are made to coincide, there is the power of new life.[23] This transcendent spirit of new life provides a hard-won sense of self-understanding in the midst of extreme constraints and projects a positive valuation of the Black woman's humanity even when life itself is threatened. Sherley A. William in writing the foreword for the most recent edition of Hurston's classic, *Their Eyes Were Watching God*, makes this same point:

> And when we (to use Alice Walker's lovely phrase) go in search of our mother's gardens, it's not really to learn who trampled on them or how or even why—we usually know that already. Rather, it's to learn what our mothers planted there, what they thought as they sowed, and how they survived the blighting of so many fruits.[24]

The re-enactment of female experiences, "holding up proverbial mirrors" within the social fabric of the Black community, conveys the moral wisdom of the contemporary Black woman. Hurston's character, Mentu, in *Moses, Man of the Mountain*, cryptically describes the proverbial mirroring in this manner: "You are right to listen to proverbs. They are short sayings made out of long experiences."[25]

It may surprise some readers that a study in Black theological ethics would focus on Zora Neale Hurston. To be sure, she did not write as an exponent of the Black religious experience, but rather, the religious heritage that is central in the Black community is latent throughout her work. All of Hurston's leading protagonists are religious people who express their loves, frustrations and tragedies in the context of their faith or lack thereof. Hurston did not develop the religious devotion of her characters but portrayed it in much the same way that she reported the situation of the McDuffy couple in the "Eatonville Anthology":

> Mrs. McDuffy goes to church every Sunday and always shouts and tells her "determination." Her husband always sits in the back row and beats her as soon as they get home. He says there's no sense in her shouting, as big as a devil as she is. She does it to slur him. Elijah Moseley asked her why she didn't stop shouting, seeing she always got a beating about it. She says she can't "squench the spirit." Then Elijah asked Mr. McDuffy to stop beating her seeing that she was going to shout anyway. He answered that she just did it for spite and that his fist was as hard as her head. He could last as long as she. So the village let the matter rest. [26]

In using the Black community as a narrative device, Hurston reports how even the Bible was made over on the front porch of Joe Clarke's general store. "Stories of creation became colorful explanations for the realities of day-to-day life; black people became black, Zora learned, by misunderstanding God's commandment in Genesis to 'get back'."[27]

At the beginning of her writing career, Zora Hurston submitted a play to the 1926 *Opportunity* contest entitled *The First One*.[28] This was her first attempt to fictionalize biblical saga, wherein she used the folkloric process to "Afro-Americanize" the legend of Noah's son, Ham. A number of Hurston's works deal with biblical imagery: *Jonah's Gourd Vine, Their Eyes Were Watching God, Moses, Man of the Mountain, Under Fire and Cloud*, "The Seventh Veil," and "The Woman in Gaul."

The inclusion of sermons was also quite common in Hurston's fiction and folklore. Her most famous sermon, "The Wounds of Jesus," which dramatized the crucifixion, was disclaimed by the *New York Times* as "too good, too brilliantly splashed with poetic imagery to be product of any one Negro preacher."[29] On May 8, 1934, Zora Hurston wrote to James Weldon Johnson expressing her disappointment with the white critic's ignorance of the place and power of religion in the Black community.

> He means well, I guess, but I never saw such a lack of information about us. It just seems that he is unwilling to believe that a Negro preacher could have so much poetry in him. When you and I (who seem to be the only ones even among Negroes who recognize the barbaric poetry in their sermons) know that there are hundreds of preachers who are equalling that sermon weekly. He does not know that merely being a good man is not enough to hold a Negro preacher in an important charge. He must also be an artist. He must be both a poet and an actor of a very high order, and then he must have the voice and figure. He does not realize or is unwilling to admit that the light that shone from GOD'S TROMBONES [sic] was handed to you, as was the sermon to me in *Jonah's Gourd Vine*.[30]

In exploring the religious themes in Hurston's work, Joyce O. Jenkins concludes that for all of Hurston's characters "faith in God does not necessarily prove to be redemptive for those who are believers."[31] In *Their Eyes Were Watching God*, Hurston describes non-redemptive suffering:

> All gods dispense suffering without reason. Otherwise they would not be worshipped. Through indiscriminate suffering men know fear, and fear is the most divine emotion. It is the stones for altars and the beginning of wisdom. Half gods are worshipped in wine and flowers. Real gods require blood.[32]

In her autobiography, Hurston talks about the meaning of prayer:

> Prayer is for those who need it. Prayer seems to me a cry of weakness, an attempt to avoid, by trickery, the rules of the game as laid down. I do not choose to admit weakness. I accept the challenge of responsibility. Life, as it is, does not frighten me, since I have made peace with the universe as I find it, and bow to its laws.[33]

Zora Neale Hurston immersed herself in the Black folk life. She accurately reported the rites, manners and customs that related Blacks to, and set Blacks apart from, their social milieu during the first half of this century. However, when Hurston summarized her personal views of religion, it is quite evident that her own stance is

radically different from the faith affirmations implied in her characters. Hurston concluded:

> But certain things seemed to me to be true as I heard the
> tongues of those who had speech, and listened at the lips of
> books. It seems to me to be true that heavens are placed in the
> sky because it is the unreachable. The unreachable and there-
> fore the unknowable always seem divine—hence, religion.
> People need religion because the great masses fear life and its
> consequences. Its responsibilities weigh heavy. Feeling a
> weakness in the face of great forces, men seek an alliance with
> omnipotence to bolster up their feeling of weakness, even
> though the omnipotence they rely upon is a creature of their
> own minds. It gives them a feeling of security. . . . It seems to
> me that organized creeds are collections of words around wish.
> I feel no need for such. However, I would not, by word or
> deed, attempt to deprive another of the consolation it affords.
> It is simply not for me.[34]

In my further explication of the moral counsel implicit in
Hurston's life and work, I found Mary Burgher's description of Black
women writers to fit precisely Zora Neale Hurston's life and literature. For that reason, I have chosen to use Burgher's characterization as the organizing principles of chapters IV and V. Three phrases
serve as keys to interpret Hurston's life and literature: ". . . the
Black woman's daring act of remaking her *lost innocence into invisible dignity*, her *never-practiced delicacy into quiet grace*, and her
forced responsibility into unshouted courage[35] (author's italics).

Theological Ethics and the Black Religious Heritage

Briefly surveying the Black religious heritage, we find that the
Black Church is the crucible through which the systematic faith
affirmations have been revealed.[36] The Black Church came into
existence as an invisible institution in the slave community during
the seventeenth century.[37] Hidden from the eyes of the
slavemasters, Black women and men developed an extensive religious life of their own. Utilizing West African religious concepts in a
new and totally different context and syncretistically blending them
with orthodox, colonial Christianity, the slaves made Christianity
truly their own.[38] C. Eric Lincoln puts it this way:

The blacks brought their religion with them. After a time they accepted the white man's religion, but they have not always expressed it in the white man's way. It became the black man's purpose—perhaps it was his *destiny*—to shape, to fashion, to re-create the religion offered him by the Christian slave master, to remold it nearer to his own peculiar needs. The black religious experience is something more than a black patina on a white happening. It is a unique response to a historical occurrence that can never be replicated for any people in America.[39]

The systematic thoughts and religious beliefs of the antebellum Black Church served as a double-edged sword. Confidence in the sovereignty of God, in an omnipotent, omnipresent, and omniscient God, helped slaves accomodate to the system of chattel slavery. With justice denied, hopes thwarted and dreams shattered, Black Christians believed that it was God who gave them emotional poise and balance in the midst of their oppression. In the prayer meetings and song services, in the sermons and spirituals, the slaves found refuge in a hostile white world. Howard Thurman argues that it was this stance that caused Blacks who were enslaved to make worthless lives . . . worth living.[40] " Being socially proscribed, economically impotent, and politically brow-beaten," Benjamin Mays writes, "they sang, prayed, and shouted their troubles away."[41]

The Black Church also made the slaves discontent with their servile condition. The Black religious experience equipped slaves with a religion that called them to engage in acts of rebellion for freedom. Much of the theology of the period called for slaves to eliminate the soruces of their oppression.[42] The faith assertions of the Black Church encouraged slaves to reject any teachings that attempted to reconcile slavery with the gospel of Jesus Christ. Slave religion was dominated by a tradition of defiance which emphasized the communal struggle for survival.[43] George Rawick, in *From Sundown to Sunup*, points out:

It was out of the religion of the slaves, the religion of the oppressed, the damned of this earth, that came the daily resistance to slavery, the significant slave strikes, and the Underground Railroad, all of which constantly wore away at the ability of the slave masters to establish their own preeminent society.[44]

During the Reconstruction Era, the Black Church continued to assume its responsibility for shaping the expository and critical thought that would help the adherents of the faith understand the interplay of historical events and societal structures. Not buried from sight were the pains and lessons from bondage.[45]

The teachings of the Church continued to develop out of the socioeconomic and political context in which Black people found themselves. The theology after emancipation focused on Christians working to help the social order come into harmony with the Divine Plan. In every sphere where Blacks were circumscribed and their legal rights denied, the Black Church called its members to a commitment of perfecting social change and exacting social righteousness here on earth. Unwavering faith in God provided Black Christians with patience and perserverance in the massive struggles for their human and constitutional rights.

Hence, the after-effects of slavery and their consequences called the Black Church forth as the community's sole institution of power. Whether urban or rural, the Black Church was the only institution totally controlled by Blacks. It was the only place outside the home where Blacks could express themselves freely and take independent action. The Church community was the heart, center and basic organization of Black life. And, those who were the religious leaders continued to give distinctive shapes and patterns to the words and ideas that the Black community used to speak about God and God's relationship to an oppressed people.

During the migratory period (1914–1925), the Black Church served as a bulwark against laws, systems and structures which rendered Black people as nonentities. As Black people moved from South to North and from rural to urban areas seeking relief from stifling circumstances, the Black Church was the citadel of hope. The Black religious experience renewed hope and spiritual strength, touching the lives of the weary travelers in all their ramifications.

Segregation laws and practices cut Blacks off and prohibited their participation in most of the societal institutions—eliminating Blacks from the body of politics, educational distinctions, judicial justice and economic opportunities. Hence, the Church was used for almost every·sort of activity—a center for civic activities, a concert hall for artists and choirs, a lecture room for public spirited individuals, and boarding quarters for migrant people who had nowhere else to go. During this colossal movement of Black people, the Church continued to serve as the focal point for the structure of Black life in community.

Joseph R. Washington sums up the unique history and tradition of the Black Church in this manner:

> In the beginning was the Black church, and the Black church was with the Black community, and the Black church was the Black community. The Black church was in the beginning with the Black people; all things were made through the Black church and without the Black church was not anything that was made. In the Black church was life, and the life was the light of the Black people. The Black church still shines in the darkness and the darkness has not overcome it.[46]

Enoch Oglesby concurs:

> Though unsystematized in terms of concrete ethical methodology and not always conforming to the alleged rational criteria of its white counterpart, the black church, without doubt, contains, I believe, some significant ethical canons which gave hope, historically speaking, to a destitute people, and moral courage to press against the dehumanizing system of chattel slavery.[47]

HOWARD THURMAN

Howard Thurman, the author of twenty books, forty-five articles, and over eight hundred tapes of sermons, lectures, meditations and interviews on religion, has distinguished himself as the most prolific Black writer on religion.[48] Due to his strong bias against the scientific systematizing of religious beliefs, Thurman resisted being called a theologian. Yet his ardent following consisted of religious and historical scholars who characterized Howard Thurman as "the most articulate interpreter of the Christian understanding of existence among Black American church persons.[49] As one of the most popular religious figures of the twentieth century, Howard Thurman "has brought new standards to Black worship and theology."[50] Joseph R. Washington, Jr., in his book *Black Religion*, calls Thurman "the most provocative innovator in the spiritual realm yet produced by the [Negro] folk. . . . Thurman has come as close as any Negro to being a theologian."[51]

The central metaphor that shapes the conception of moral existence and sets Howard Thurman's general ethical orientation is a vision of "community relatedness." Thurman's theological ethics comes out of "the conscious and direct exposure of the individual to God."[52] Fragmented, unfulfilled individuals align their separated lives with all of life, so that as newly empowered individuals, they form community which will allow them to bring insights and concerns of the Christian faith to bear on altering the most oppressive situations in society. In illuminating the nature of God and the moral responsibility of humans, Thurman's ethics move in two concentric circles. The compact inner circle is the mystical religious experience and the surrounding supervening circle is the inherent relatedness of inclusive community. Thurman rules out laws, principles, norms, fixed ends and the like as models for moral agency; ethics emerges from mystical consciousness which obligates individuals to transform the social environment. First, we are to commend our spirits to God.[53] Next, we work to tranform the powers and principalities which destroy the personality so that justice, equality and human rights will be safeguarded for all.[54] The essence of Thurman's theological ethics is that the religion of Jesus is a "technique of survival for the oppressed."[55] Each person's life must be defined, nurtured and transformed, wherein the self is actualized, affirming the inward authority which arouses greater meaning and potential with each mystical experience.

Howard Thurman believes that moral-ethical insights emerge from religious experiences. Faithful living, the day-to-day activity that guides and gauges conduct of individuals as they shape their social reality, is a result of direct exposure to the Divine Personality. All interactions either encourage wholeness or brokenness. All experiences either nourish religious exposure to truth or snuff it out. Oneness with God progresses from outward life to the inward life, to outward life in community.[56] The mystical experience with God provides resources which order, focus and define precepts and actions which can be used to transform socio-political structures that denigrate and inhibit the realization of wholeness that God brings to all life.

MARTIN LUTHER KING, JR.

Martin Luther King, Jr., systematic theologian, eloquent Black preacher and leader of the mass civil rights movement in the United States, expressed the essential structure of his ethics as the inseparability of Christian faith and ethical principles.[57] Ervin Smith maintains that the foundation of King's ethical formulation is that "there is no real commitment to God in the absence of social

responsibility for the community. At the same time, community
efforts or social actions are likely to be directionless and, in the long
run counterproductive, if they are not grounded in the prior love of
God."[58] King argues that life's most persistent and urgent question
is "What are you doing for others?" Repeatedly in his writings and
sermons, King emphasizes the Christian's social responsibility to
work toward social change which would usher in the beloved community. Martin Luther King's imperative was for a radical criticism
of the existing social order. His thesis was that Christians are morally
bound to cooperate with the forces of good and equally bound to
refuse cooperation with evil. Evil was defined as those actions,
thoughts and ideologies that resulted in alienation from God and
from neighbor. Followers of Christ are called to resist oppression, to
oppose authorities and laws that rob humans of their birthright of
freedom and dignity.

Throughout King's theology one finds justice and love as the
justifying rules and judgments for determining what is morally right
and wrong, good and bad. His theological ethics interrelate these
two norms. It is almost impossible to discuss one in isolation from
the other. Kenneth Smith and Ira Zepp, in *Search for the Beloved
Community*, observe that King did not systematically delineate his
understanding of the relationship between love and justice; they are
simply inseparable themes in his writings. As King grappled with
the relevance of these norms in the struggle for social justice, he
explains the interrelatedness of the two:

> It is not enough to say "We love Negroes, we have many
> Negro friends." They [i.e., white liberals] must demand justice
> for Negroes. Love that does not satisfy justice is no love at all. It
> is merely a sentimental affection, little more than what one
> would feel for a pet. Love at its best is justice concretized.[59]

King goes even further to acknowledge that in order for love and
justice to be properly understood, they must be integrally related
with power.

> What is needed is a realization that power without love is
> reckless and abusive and that love without power is sentimental
> and anemic. Power at its best is love implementing the de-
> mands of justice. Justice at its best is love correcting everything
> that stands against love.[60]

King's understanding of life is articulated in Hegel's dialectical principle, "Truth is found neither in the thesis nor the antithesis, but in an emergent synthesis which reconciles the two."[61] King believes that God is the ground of all reality and the moral principle of the universe. He says, "The universe, because this divine power is at the center, must have a moral order to it—it must involve certain principles that are themselves right and good."[62] Love and justice are the primary principles which King holds in creative synthesis in the process of salvation. These norms translate faith into social action which allows us to receive humanity in full stature. For King, the Christian religion demands responsibility to act on behalf of social reform. "Any religion that professes to be concerned with the soul of men and is not concerned with the slums that damn them, the economic conditions that strangle them and the social conditions that cripple them is a dry-as-dust religion."[63] Otis Turner argues that the critical point that King makes is that love without justice or justice without love is fundamentally inadequate. "One without the other leads to conditions which fail to meet the needs of human existence."[64]

King uses the word "toughmindedness" for justice and "tenderheartedness" for love. Justice alone leads to despotism, love alone leads to impotence and weakness. But the two are mutually complementary and mutually interdependent as a creative synthesis of opposites in fruitful harmony. King points out that toughmindedness is a quality that perceives and acts in accordance with truth. It is the strength and the dignity needed in order to face bullies, guns, dogs, tear gas and vicious mobs. Toughmindedness allows one to stand up amid a system that oppresses her/him and develop an unassailable and majestic sense of one's own value.

> There is little hope for us until we become toughminded enough to break loose from shackles of prejudice and half truth, and downright ignorance. The shape of the world today does not permit us the luxury of softmindedness. A nation or civilization that continues to produce softminded men purchases its own spiritual death on an installment plan.[65]

Tenderheartedness (love) is the spiritual faculty that supports the birthright of freedom and human dignity for all. It does not debase the person. Nor does it impede the growth of the personality. The loss of this quality is the basic cause of racism. Hardheartedness reduces human beings to "things," treats women and men as "its" without the slightest twitch of conscience. King believes that love fused with justice and undergirded with constructive coercive power is the ultimate solution to the problem of evil.

Notes

/1/   Pierre L. Van Den Berghe, *Race and Racism: A Comparative Perspective* (New York: Wiley, 1967), p. 77.
/2/   W. E. B. DuBois, *Dusk at Dawn* (New York: Harcourt Brace and Co., 1940).
/3/   Frances M. Beal, "Slave of a Slave No More: Black Women in Struggle," *The Black Scholar* 12 (November/December 1981): 16–17; reprinted from vol. 6 (March 1975).
/4/   Ernestine Walker, "The Black Woman" in *The Black American Reference Book*, ed. Mable M. Smythe (Englewood Cliffs, N.J.: Prentice Hall, Inc., 1976), p. 344.
/5/   Sharon Harley and Rosalynn Tarborg-Penn, eds., *The Afro-American Woman, Struggles and Images* (Port Washington, N.Y.: Kennikat Press, 1978), p. ix.
/6/   Zora Neale Hurston, *Dust Tracks on a Road* (Philadelphia: J. B. Lippincott Co., 1942; reprint ed., 1971), p. 177. For Hurston's elaboration of "the Negro farthest down," read chapter 10, "Research" and chapter 12, "My People! My People!"
/7/   Hurston, "John Reading Goes to Sea," *Opportunity* 4 (January 1926), p. 17.
/8/   Zora Neale Hurston to Langston Hughes, 30 April 1929, James Weldon Johnson Collection, Yale University, New Haven.
/9/   Franz Boas, *The Mind of Primitive Man* (New York: Macmillan Co., 1911), and *Race, Language and Culture* (New York: Macmillan Co., 1940).
/10/   Hurston, *Dust Tracks on a Road*, p. 206.
/11/   Ibid, p. 213.
/12/   Hurston, "How It Feels to Be Colored Me," *The World Tomorrow* (May 1928), p. 17.
/13/   Mary Helen Washington, "A Woman Half in Shadows," Introduction to *I Love Myself When I Am Laughing . . . A Zora Neale Hurston Reader*, ed. Alice Walker (Old Westbury, N.Y.: The Feminist Press, 1979), p. 17.
/14/   Mary Helen Washington, Ibid.
/15/   Alice Walker, "Zora Neale Hurston—A Cautionary Tale and a Partisan View," Foreword to Robert Hemenway, *Zora Neale Hurston, A Literary Biography* (Urbana: University of Illinois Press, 1977), p. xii.
/16/   Karla F. C. Holloway, "A Critical Investigation of Literary and Linguistic Structures in the Fiction of Zora Neale Hurston" (Ph.D. dissertation, Michigan State University, 1978).
/17/   Robert Bone, "Zora Neale Hurston," in *The Black Novelist*, ed. Robert Hemenway (Columbus, O.: Charles E. Merrill Co., 1970), pp. 126–133.

/18/ Barbara Christian, *Black Women Novelists: The Development of a Tradition, 1892–1976* (Westport, Conn.: Greenwood Press, 1980), p. 60.

/19/ Robert Hemenway, *Zora Neale Hurston, A Literary Biography* (Urbana: University of Illinois Press, 1977), p. 5.

/20/ Joyce O. Jenkins, "To Make A Woman Black: A Critical Analysis of the Women Characters in the Fiction and Folklore of Zora Neale Hurston" (Ph.D. dissertation, Bowling Green State University, 1979).

/21/ Henry Louis Gates, "Soul of a Black Woman," *New York Times Book Review* (19 February 1978), pp. 13, 30–31.

/22/ Gates, p. 31.

/23/ Ellease Southerland, "Zora Neale Hurston: The Novelist-Anthropologist's Life/Works," *Black World* 25 (August 1974), p. 20.

/24/ Cited by Sherley A. Williams, Foreword to Zora Neale Hurston, *Their Eyes Were Watching God* (Urbana: University of Illinois Press, 1978)

/25/ Zora Neale Hurston, *Moses, Man of the Mountain* (Philadelphia: Lippincott Co., 1938; reprint ed.: Chatham, N.J.: The Chatham Bookseller, 1967).

/26/ Zora Neale Hurston, "The Eatonville Anthology," *The Messenger* 7 (September-November 1936): 262 ff. Hurston also develops this same story line in "Sweat," *Fire!!* 1 (November 1926): 40–45. For a general discussion of the religious implications in the life and work of Zora Neale Hurston, see the following: Lloyd W. Brown, "Zora Neale Hurston and the Nature of Female Perception," *Obsidian: Black Literature in Review* 4, iii (1978): 39–45; James W. Byrd, "Zora Neale Hurston: A Novel Folklorist," *Tennessee Folklore Society Bulletin* 21 (1955): 37–41; Lillie P. Howard, "Marriage: Zora Neale Hurston's System of Values," *College Language Association Journal* 21 (December 1977): 256–258; Ann L. Rayson, "The Novels of Zora Neale Hurston," *Studies in Black Literature* 5 (Winter 1974): 1–10; Barbara Smith, "Sexual Politics and the Fiction of Zora Neale Hurston," *Radical Teacher* 8 (May 1978); S. Jay Walker, "Zora Neale Hurston's *Their Eyes Were Watching God:* Black Novel of Sexism," *Modern Fiction Studies* 20 (Winter 1974–75): 519–527.

/27/ Robert Hemenway, *Zora Neale Hurston: A Literary Biography* (Urbana: University of Illinois Press, 1977), pp. 12–13. See also, Hugh M. Gloster, "Zora Neale Hurston, Novelist and Folklorist," *Phylon* 3 (Second Quarter 1943): 153–156; Evelyn Thomas Helmick, "Zora Neale Hurston," *The Carrell* II (June–December 1970): 1–19; Blyden Jackson, "Some Negroes in the Land of Goshen," *Tennessee Folklore Society Bulletin* 19 (December 1953): 103–107; Marion Kilson, "The Transformation of Eatonville's Ethnographer," *Phylon* 33 (Summer 1972): 112–119; Valerie Gray Lee, "The Use of Folktalk in Novels by Black Women Writers," *College Langauge Association Journal* 23 (1977): 266–272; Clyde Taylor, "Black Folk Spirit and the Shape of Black Literature," *Black World* 21 (August 1972): 31–40.

/28/ This was Zora Hurston's second play. Her first one, *Color Struck*, won second prize in the 1926 *Opportunity* contest. It is published in *Ebony and Topaz*, ed. Charles Johnson (New York: National Urban League, 1927), pp. 53–57.

/29/ John Chamberlain, "Books of the Time," review of *Jonah's Gourd*

Vine, by Zora Neale Hurston, in the *New York Times,* 1934, n.p.
/30/   Zora Neale Hurston to James Weldon Johnson, 8 May 1934, James
Weldon Johnson Collection, Yale\University, New Haven.
/31/   Joyce Jenkins, "To Make A Woman Black," p. 17. There is also a
discussion in James Rambeau, "The Fiction of Zora Neale Hurston," *Markham Review* 5 (1976): 61–64; Southerland, pp. 20–30; Erlene Stetson,
"Their Eyes Were Watching God: A Woman's Story," *Regionalism and the
Female Imagination* 4 (1978): 30–36; Mary Helen Washington, "The Black
Woman's Search for Identity: Zora Neale Hurston's Work," *Black World*
(August 1972), pp. 68–75.
/32/   Zora Neale Hurston, *Their Eyes Were Watching God* (Philadelphia: J.
B. Lippincott Co., 1937), p. 215.
/33/   Zora Neale Hurston, *Dust Tracks on A Road,* p. 286.
/34/   Hurston, Ibid, pp. 286–287; see also, Emma L. Blake, "Zora Neale
Hurston: Author and Folklorist," *Negro History Bulletin* 29 (April 1966):
149–150, 164; Florence Borders, "Zora Neale Hurston: Hidden Woman,"
Callaloo: A Black Southern Journal of Arts and Letters 2, ii (1979): 89–92;
Addison Gayle, Jr., "Strangers In a Strange Land," *Southern Exposure* 3, 1
(1975): 4–7; Fannie Hurst, "Zora Hurston: A Personality Sketch," *The Yale
University Library Gazette* XXXV (1961): 17–22; June Jordan, "On Richard
Wright and Zora Neale Hurston: Notes Toward a Balancing of Love and
Hatred," *Black World* 23 (April 1976): 4–8; John Oliver Killens, "Another
Time When Black Was Beautiful," *Black World* 20 (November 1970): 20–36.
/35/   Mary Burgher, "Images of Self and Race in the Autobiographies of
Black Women," in *Sturdy Black Bridges,* ed. Roseann Bell, et al. (New
York: Anchor Books, 1979), p. 113.
/36/   James H. Cone, "Black Power, Black Theology and the Study of
Theology and Ethics," *Theological Ethics* 6 (Spring 1970): 202–215; Paul
Deats, Jr., *Toward a Discipline of Social Ethics* (Boston: Boston University
Press, 1972); Herbert O. Edwards, "Toward a Black Christian Social Ethic,"
The Duke Divinity School Review (Spring 1975), also in *The Interdenomina-
tional Theological Center Journal* 4 (Spring 1976): 97–108; Vincent Harding,
"The Religion of Black Power," in Donald Cutler, ed. *The Religious Situa-
tion: 1968* (Boston: Beacon Press, 1968); Beverly W. Harrison, "Anger as a
Work of Love: Christian Ethics for Women and Other Strangers," *Union
Seminary Quarterly Review* 36 (Supplementary Issue 1981): 41–57; Beverly
W. Harrison, "Liberation Theology and Social Ethics: Some Theses for
Discussion," *Methodology Seminar,* November 29, 1977; Major J. Jones,
Christian Ethics for Black Theology (Nashville: Abingdon Press, 1974); J.
DeOtis Roberts, "Black Theological Ethics: A Bibliographical Essay," *The
Journal of Religious Ethics* (Spring 1975): 69–109; J. DeOtis Roberts,
"Christian Liberation Ethics: The Black Experience," *Religion and Life* 48
(Summer 1979): 227–235; James Sellers, *Theological Ethics* (New York: The
Macmillan Co., 1966); Charles Freeman Sleeper, *Black Power and Chris-
tian Responsibility* (Nashville: Abingdon Press, 1968); James F. Smurl,
Religious Ethics: A Systems Approach (Englewood Cliffs, N.J.: Prentice-
Hall, 1972); *The Journal of Religious Ethics* 1 (Fall 1973): 5–63; Daniel Day
Williams, *What Present-Day Theologians Are Thinking,* revised ed. New
York: Harper & Brothers, 1959), especially pp. 114–115; Preston Williams,

"The Ethical Aspects of the 'Black Church/Black Theology' Phenomenon," Boston University School of Theology, January 1969.

/37/ W. E. B. DuBois, *The Negro Church* (Atlanta: Atlanta University Press, 1903); Lawrence W. Levine, *Black Culture and Black Consciousness: Afro-American Folk Thought From Slavery to Freedom* (New York: Oxford University Press, 1977); C. Eric Lincoln, ed., *The Black Experience in Religion* (New York: Anchor Press/Doubleday, 1974); Benjamin E. Mays and Joseph W. Nicholson, *The Negro's Church* (New York: Russell and Russell, 1933); Emmanual L. McCall, compiler, *The Black Christian Experience* (Nashville: Broadman Press, 1972); Albert J. Raboteau, *Slave Religion: The "Invisible Institution" in the Antebellum South* (New York: Oxford University Press, 1978); Joseph R. Washington, Jr., *Black Sects and Cults* (New York: Anchor Press/Doubleday, 1973); Carter G. Woodson, *The History of the Negro Church* (Washington: The Associated Publishers, 1921); Carter G. Woodson, *The Negro Church*, reprint ed. (Washington: The Associated Publishers, 1972).

/38/ E. Franklin Frazier exhorts readers of *The Negro Church in America* and *The Negro in the United States* to recognize the fact that the enslaved Africans had their culture and religious tradition "practically stripped." Frazier argues that it would be difficult to establish any relation between African religious practices and the Black Church which has developed in the U.S. The following scholars document the opposite point of view: St. Clair Drake, *The Redemption of Africa and Black Religion* (Chicago: Third World Press, 1970); Melville Herskovits, *The Myth of the Negro Past* (New York: Harper & Brothers, 1941); Henry H. Mitchell, *Black Belief: Folk Beliefs of Blacks in America and West Africa* (New York: Harper and Row, 1975); Harry V. Richardson, *Dark Glory, A Picture of the Church among Negroes in the Rural South* (New York: Published for Home Missions Council of North America and Phelps-Stokes Fund by Friendship Press, 1947); William C. Suttles, Jr., "African Religious Survivals as Factors in American Slave Revolts," *Journal of Negro History* 56/2 (April 1971).

/39/ C. Eric Lincoln, Foreword to William R. Jones, *Is God a White Racist?* C. Eric Lincoln series on Black religion (Garden City, N.Y.: Anchor Press/Doubleday, 1973), pp. vii–viii.

/40/ Howard Thurman, *Deep River and the Negro Spiritual Speaks of Life and Death* (Richmond, Ind.: Friends United Press, 1975), p. 135.

/41/ Benjamin Mays, *The Negro's God, As Reflected in His Literature* (Boston: Chapman & Grimes, Inc., 1938; reprint ed., Westport, Conn.: Greenwood Press, 1969), p. 26.

/42/ Vincent Harding, "Religion and Resistance Among Ante-bellum Negroes, 1800–1860," in August Meier and E. Rudwick, eds., *The Negro in the Making of America*, vol. 1 (New York: Atheneum, 1969), pp. 179–197; Robert S. Lecky and H. Elliott Wright, eds., *Black Manifesto: Religion, Racism and Reparations* (New York: Sheed & Ward, 1969); Wilson Moses, *Black Messiahs and Uncle Toms: Social and Literary Manipulations of a Religious Myth* (University Park: Pennsylvania State University Press, 1982); Timothy L. Smith, "Slavery and Theology: The Emergence of Black Christian Consciousness in Nineteenth Century America," *Church History* 41/4

/43/ W. M. Brewer, "Henry Highland Garnet," *Journal of Negro History* 31/1 (January 1928): 36–52; N. C. Cannon, *The Rock of Wisdom* (Moorland Library, Howard University, 1833); Timothy Mather Cooley, *Sketches of the Life and Character of the Rev. Lemuel Haynes* (New York: Harper & Brothers, 1837); John C. Diamond, "David Walker's Appeal: A Theological Interpretation," *The Journal of the Interdenominational Theological Center* III (Fall 1975); S. X. Floyd, *Life of Charles T. Walker* (Nashville: National Baptist Publishing Board, 1902); Earl Ofar, *"Let Your Motto Be Resistance": The Life and Thought of Henry Highland Garnet* (Boston: Beacon Press, 1972); Daniel A. Payne, "Protestation of American Slavery," ed. D. C. Strange, *Journal of Negro History* 51/1 (January 1967): 59–64; David Walker, "Walker's Appeal, in Four Articles," in *Black American Literature*, ed. Ruth Miller (Beverly Hills, Cal.: Glenco Press, 1971), pp. 119–124; Charles Wesley and Richard Allen, *Apostle of Freedom* (Washington: The Associated Publishers, 1935; reprint ed., 1969).

/44/ George Rawick, *The American Slave: A Composite Autobiography, From Sundown to Sunup* (Westport, Conn.: Greenwood Press, 1972), p. 51. Much of the radical theology for liberation is recorded in the spirituals and work songs of the slaves: James H. Cone, *The Spirituals and the Blues* (New York; The Seabury Press, 1972); R. Nathaniel Dett, ed., *Religious Folk Songs of the Negro* (Hampton, Va.: Hampton Institute Press, 1927); James W. Johnson and J. R. Johnson, *The Books of American Negro Spirituals* (New York: The Viking Press, Inc., 1925); John Lovell, Jr., "The Social Implications of the Spirituals," *Journal of Negro Education* 8/4 (October 634–643; Howard Thurman, *Deep River and the Negro Spiritual;* John W. Work, *American Negro Songs and Spirituals* (New York: Bonanza Books, 1940).

/45/ Yosef Ben-Jochannan, *The Black Man's Religion* (New York: Alkebu-lan Books Associates, 1974); James Edward Blackwell, *The Black Community: Diversity and Unity* (New York: Dodd, Mead, 1975); Melvin Drimmer, compiler, *Black History Reappraisal*, ed. and with commentary by Melvin Drimmer (Garden City, N.Y.: Doubleday, 1968); Martin R. Delany, *The Condition, Elevation, Emigration and Destiny of the Colored People of the United States* (Philadelphia: 1852; reprint ed., New York: Arno Press, 1968); Mary Ellison, *The Black Experience: American Blacks Since 1865* (New York: Barnes and Noble, 1974); Charles S. Johnson, *Shadow of the Plantation* (Chicago: University of Chicago Press, 1934); Charles Eric Lincoln, *The Negro Pilgrimage in America* (New York: Bantam Books, 1967); Milton C. Sernett, *Black Religion and American Evangelism: White Protestants, Plantation Missions, and the Flowering of Negro Christianity 1787–1865* (Metuchen, N.J.: Scarecrow Press, Inc., and the American Theological Library Association, 1975).

/46/ Joseph R. Washington, Jr., *Black Religion: The Negro and Christianity in the United States* (Boston: Beacon Press, 1964).

/47/ Enoch H. Oglesby, *Ethics and Theology from the Other Side: Sounds of Moral Struggle* (Washington: University Press of America, Inc., 1979), p. 4.

/48/ Lerone Bennett, Jr., "Howard Thurman: 20th Century Holy Man,"

Ebony, February 1978; Jean Burden, "Howard Thurman," *Atlantic,* October 1953; Jan Corbett, "Howard Thurman: A Theologian for Our Time," *The American Baptist,* December 1979; Mozella G. Mitchell, "The Dynamics of Howard Thurman's Relationship to Literature and Theology" (Ph.D. dissertation, Emory University, 1980); Luther E. Smith, Jr. *Howard Thurman: The Mystic as Prophet* (Washington: University Press of America, Inc., 1981); Elizabeth Yates, *Howard Thurman: Portrait of a Practical Dreamer* (New York: John Day, 1964).

/49/ John D. Mangram, in Samuel L. Gandy ed., *Common Ground: Essays in Honor of Howard Thurman* (Washington: Hoffman Press, 1976), p. 65.

/50/ Ralph G. Turnball, *A History of Preaching,* vol. 3 (Grand Rapids, Mich.: Baker Book House, 1974), p. 206.

/51/ Joseph R. Washington, Jr., *Black Religion* (Boston: Press, 1964), pp. 105, 111.

/52/ Howard Thurman, *The Creative Encounter: An Interpretation of Religion and the Social Witness* (Richmond, Ind.: Friends United Press, 1954), p. 20; see also Thurman's *The Centering Moment* (New York, Harper & Row, 1969); *The Inward Journey* (Richmond, Ind.: Friends United Press, 1961); "Mysticism and Jesus," lecture V given at the University of the Redlands, May 1973; further background reading: Rufus M. Jones, *Studies in Mystical Religion* (London: Macmillan & Co., 1923), and Alan Watts, *Behold the Spirit: A Study in the Necessity of Mystical Religion* (New York: Vintage Books, 1947).

/53/ Howard Thurman, *Deep Is the Hunger: Meditations for Apostles of Sensitiveness* (Richmond, Ind.: Friends United Press, 1951), p. 163.

/54/ Howard Thurman, "Good News for the Underprivileged," *Religion in Life,* Summer Issue 1935, pp. 403–409.

/55/ Howard Thurman, *Jesus and the Disinherited* (Nashville: Abingdon-Cokesbury Press, 1949), p. 29.

/56/ Howard Thurman, *The Growing Edge* (New York: Harper & Brothers, 1956).

/57/ L. Harold DeWolf, "Martin Luther King, Jr., as Theologian," *Journal of the Interdenominational Theological Center* 4 (Spring 1977): 1–11; Paul Garber, "King Was a Black Theologian," *Journal of Religious Thought* 31 (Fall–Winter 1974–75): 16–32; "Black Theology: The Latter Day Legacy of Martin Luther King, Jr.," *Journal of the Interdenominational Theological Center* 2 (Spring 1975): 100–113; Herbert Warren Richardson, "Martin Luther King—Unsung Theologian," in *New Theology,* no. 6, eds. Martin E. Marty and Dean G. Peerman (London: Collier-Macmillan, 1969); Lois D. Wasserman, "The Legacy of Martin Luther King, Jr.," *Negro History Bulletin* 38 (December 1974); S. M. Wilhelm, "Martin Luther King, Jr., and the Black Experience," *Journal of Black Studies* 10 (September 1979): 3–19.

/58/ Erwin Smith, *The Ethics of Martin Luther King, Jr.* (New York: The Edwin Mellen Press, 1981), p. 151.

/59/ Martin Luther King, Jr., *Where Do We Go From Here: Chaos or Community?* (New York: Harper & Row, 1968), pp. 89–90.

/60/   Ibid., p. 37.

/61/   Martin Luther King, Jr., *Strength To Love* (New York: Harper & Row, 1963), p. 1.

/62/   William R. Miller, *Martin Luther King* (New York: Weybright & Talley, 1968), p. 18.

/63/   Martin Luther King, Jr., *Stride Toward Freedom: The Montgomery Story* (New York: Harper & Row, 1958), p. 29.

/64/   Otis Turner, "Nonviolence and the Politics of Liberation," *Journal of the Interdenominational Theological Center* (Spring 1977): 50.

/65/   King, *Strength To Love*, p. 4.

CHAPTER I

THE BLACK WOMAN'S MORAL SITUATION, 1619–1900

The Moral Situation of the Black Woman in Slavery

Under slavery the Black woman had the status of property, her master had total power over her and she and her children were denied the most elementary social bonds—family and kinship. These *a priori* components of slavery[1] capture the Black woman's moral situation from the mid-seventeenth century to the Civil War.

THE BLACK WOMAN AS PROPERTY
Traditionally, scholars, historians and researchers have used the word "slave" to connote "male" with race superseding gender as the focal point.[2] However, in this section of my study, the attention will be given to the special situation of the female slave. The Black woman was defined as "brood sow" and "work-ox." Concession was given to her gender only when it was expedient for the slaveowner.

> . . . when it was profitable to exploit them as if they were men, they were regarded, in effect, as genderless, but when they could be exploited, punished and repressed in ways suited only for women, they were locked into their exclusively female roles.[3]

After the Civil War settlement, the Constitution of the United States, a politically comprised "compact between the northern bourgeoise and the southern slave-owning aristocracy,"[4] assessed the male slave for apportionment purposes at three-fifths of a white man. Black women were not counted and considered as human beings at all. The definition of humanity was restricted to white males only.

The state laws viewed Black women, no less than men, as chattel—mere property.[5] As a slave, the Black woman was subjected to the ownership of another. Her human life was estimated in terms of money, property and capital assets. She was a commodity to be bought and sold, traded for money, land or other objects. Even in very rare situations where there was paternalistic kindness by the slaveholder, the Black woman was denied the development that would have enabled her to function as a free moral agent.

At slave auctions, the Black woman was treated no differently from men. She was stripped naked, exposed to the public and dehumanized with pokes, probes and rude examinations. Considered to be subhuman, the bondwoman's monetary value was precisely calculated by her capacity to produce goods and services, combined with her capacity to breed, to reproduce "a herd of subhuman labor units."[6]

Even with massive slave importation from Africa, the Black woman's fecundity was exploited.[7] A continuing supply of exploitable labor was a lucrative factor in the capitalist slave economy. Slaves were needed to produce the vital southern export crops as well as contribute to the wealth derived from northern shaping enterprises. Without a continuing labor force of slaves, the colonial United States could not have become the capitalist metropolis that it did.

THE BLACK WOMAN AS "BROOD-SOW"

As "brood-sow" or "suckler" the Black woman

> . . . was forced to give birth as often as once a year. Her body was misused, and quite often she was old before her time. Not only was she forced to have children rapidly, but she was given very little time to regain her own strength and only two weeks to care for her children. After that time, the slave woman had to return to work.[8]

Jacqueline Jones' article, "My Mother Was Much of a Woman: Black Women, Work, and the Family Under Slavery," describes Black breeder-laborers in this way:

> One North Carolina slave woman, the mother of fifteen children, used to carry her youngest with her to the field each day and "when it get hungry she just slip it around in front and feed it and go right on picking or hoeing . . ." symbolizing in

one deft motion the equal significance of the productive and
reproductive functions to her owner.[9]

Neither pregnant women nor new mothers were exempt from
hard labor. The slave narratives of Moses Grandy included the
stories of women who were unable to nurse their infants regularly
and depicts the pain they endured.

> On the estate I am speaking of, those women who had
> sucking children suffered much from their breasts becoming
> full of milk, the infant being left at home. They therefore could
> not keep up with the other hands: I have seen the overseer beat
> them with raw hide, so that the blood and milk flow mingled
> from their breasts.[10]

THE BLACK WOMAN AS "WORK-OX"

"Compulsory labor overshadowed every other aspect of
women's existence,"[11] says Angela Davis. In all areas of slave labor,
the Black woman was present. As a "work-ox" the Black woman was
subjected to hard, steady, often strenuous labor. From sunup to
sundown she either worked alongside the male slaves in the cotton,
tobacco, rice and sugarcane fields or catered as a domestic, from
before dawn to late at night, to the demands made by the mistress
and other members of the master's family.[12] Kenneth Stampp notes:

> [T]he slavewoman was first a full-time worker for her
> owners, and only incidentally a wife, mother and home-
> maker.[13]

The Black woman was required to go to the field and to work in a
variety of industrial occupations with Black men. She worked as a
common laborer on the pine forests, turpentine, tar, pitch and rosin
plantations. She worked alongside males in mines extracting coal,
lead and gold. This compulsory labor forced the Black woman into
anomalous marginal positions in relation to the evolving ideology of
femininity. "Where work was concerned, strength and productivity
under the threat of the whip outweighed consideration of sex,"[14]
argues Davis.

The Black woman also worked as a domestic servant where she
was always "on call."[15] She juggled the cleaning, laundering, cooking, ironing, wood-hewing and water carrying, as well as caring for
the slaveowner's children. Responsible for seeing to the comforts of

the white household, the Black woman not only worked as "mammy" to white children but also served as "confidante" to their supposedly fragile mothers. As a slave, the Black woman was forbidden by stringent literary laws to receive an education, yet, when orders and commands were given of great detail by master or mistress, she was expected to "take mental shorthand in a flash" or suffer dire consequences.

In the antebellum literature the Black woman who worked as a domestic was praised as the contented, qualified woman to raise white children and at the same time portrayed as a member of subspecies due to the neglect of her own children.

> She is black in color as well as race and fat with enormous breasts that are full enough to nourish all the children of the world; her head is perpetually covered with her trademark kerchief to hide the kinky hair that marks her as ugly. Tied to her physical characteristics are her personality traits: she is strong, for she certainly has enough girth, but this strength is used in service of her white master and as a way of keeping her male counterparts in check; she is kind and loyal, for she is a mother; she is sexless, for she is ugly; and she is religious and superstitious, because she is black. She prefers the master's children to her own, for as a member of a lower species, she acknowledges almost instinctively the superiority of the higher race.[16]

As is so often the case, the reality of the Black woman domestic was the diametrical opposite of the myths. The Black woman "manifested irrepressible talent in humanizing" her environment.[17] Having only from midnight to daybreak to provide love and affection for her own offspring, the Black woman returned at night with leftovers, throwaways, discarded shells of the white employer's rubbish to her small, crude, squalid dwelling where she made a home for her family. Oftentimes she took into her quarters Black children whose parents had been sold away from them or they from their parents with the full knowledge that she could expect to have her own offspring with her for a few years, at the most.

THE SLAVEOWNER'S TOTAL CONTROL
OVER THE SLAVEWOMAN

As a slave, the Black woman was subjected to the threefold penalization of legal servitude, sexual exploitation and racial discrimination.

Legal Servitude

The evolving nature of the institution of chattel slavery required different forms of dehumanization in the seventeenth century from what slavery eventually became in the nineteenth century. Throughout all these periods, viewing the slave as human was simply understood as an obstacle to slave maximization. Slave codes and the treatment of slaves varied widely among the states. Slaves had no protection from masters who subjected them to arbitrary cruelty and brutal indignities. Slaveowners were free to promulgate slave laws as they saw fit. Hundreds of slaveowners bought and sold slaves, overworked them, beat and tortured them and sometimes even put them to death. The owner could inflict pain and death with the entire coercive power of the state behind him or her. Due to the indeterminant line among most slavemasters, between necessary correction and savage cruelty, the killing of Black people was generally not considered a crime.

> The absoluteness of force in the master's hand was a matter of public display. Strung up to trees, staked out on the ground, held down by others, stripped to the bare flesh, slaves were beaten with every variety of instrument from whip to blunt weapons. They were subjected to pain so that it not only seared their own flesh but their cries would make the skin of others crawl. They were branded, maimed, dismembered, and killed in full view of others. Such force was not only deterrent; it was a ready and dramatic show of authority, a reminder of the juxtaposition of unmitigated power against unrelieved helplessness. There was hardly a slave who did not as an adult suffer the lash. . . . Slavery was maintained by the monopoly of power in the master's hands.[18]

George Frederickson reports that even when the killing of a slave by a master finally became a crime, in the nineteenth century, the refusal to accept the testimony of other slaves—usually the only witness to such a proceeding—made this and other laws prescribing human treatment virtually unenforceable. There was no bureaucratic or corporate group willing to diffuse the slavemaster's authority.

Despite the considerable variations in the treatment of slaves, one common element everywhere was that chattel slavery was strictly racial—for Blacks only. Beginning with the law in Virginia in the 1660s, any person with African blood was a slave and all Africans who entered the American colonies came under the slave laws. In the 1730s, laws were passed prohibiting the freeing of slaves in the United States. Thus the status of a slave became a lifetime status. No objective circumstances such as education, skill, dress, or manner could modify this racist fundamental arrangement. State laws adopted the principle of *partus sequitur ventrem*—the child follows the condition of the mother regardless of the race of her mate. Absolving all paternal responsibilities, this principle institutionalized and sanctioned sexual prerogatives and the rape of Black women by white men. Hence, the Black woman became the carrier of the hereditary slave status. This legal status extended to her children and her children's children, a lifetime of abject servitude, supposedly to the infinity of time.

SEXUAL EXPLOITATION

Slavocracy was the rude transformation of African people into marketable objects. Slaves were rightless and lacking in responsibility. Slave women were answerable with their bodies to the sexual casualness of "stock breeding" with Black men and to the sexual whims and advances of white men. Being both a slave and female, the Black woman survived wanton misuse and abuse.

> [T]he systems of slavery and caste encouraged white and black males sexually and socially to exploit black women. Thinking of profits or believing in the inferiority of Afro-Americans, some slave masters encouraged or ignored black male advances to black females, regarding the mating of slaves much in the same way they did that of their livestock.[19]

According to Winthrop Jordan, American "slave owners acquired valuable young Negroes not only by forcing their slaves to mate, but doing little to interfere with a system which gave every encouragement to early and frequent sexual intercourse among slaves."[20]

Both Angela Davis and Jacqueline Jones argue that Black women and men were social equals in slavery as a result of the capitalist system.

> All slaves were barred by law from owning property or acquiring literacy skills, and although the system played favorites with a few, black females and males were equal in the sense that neither sex wielded economic power over the other. Hence property relations—"the basic determinent of the sexual division of labor and of the sexual order" within most

societies—did not affect male-female interaction among the slaves themselves.[21]

However, Ernestine Walker and Bell Hooks provide evidence for a different point of view. Walker lifts up stories from the slave narratives of Charles Bell wherein slave women are often beaten and maltreated by very irritable husbands.[22] Hooks puts it this way:

> Sexist historians and sociologists have provided the American public with a perspective on slavery in which the most cruel and dehumanizing impact of slavery on the lives of black people was that black men were stripped of their masculinity, which they then argue resulted in the dissolution and overall disruption of any black familial structure.
>
> [T]he black male slave was primarily exploited as a laborer in the fields; the black female was exploited as a laborer in the fields, a worker in the domestic household, a breeder, and as an object of white male sexual assault.[23]

Virtually all the slave narratives contain accounts of the high incidence of rape and sexual coercion. White men, by virtue of their economic position, had unlimited access to Black women's bodies. Sexual victimization of Black women by white men was accepted as inevitable almost as soon as Black women were introduced into America. At the crux of the ideology that Black women were an inferior species was the belief that Black women, unlike white women, craved sex inordinately.

> The rape of black women by white men or the use of their bodies for pleasure could be rationalized as the natural craving of the black women for sex, rather than the licentiousness of the white men.[24]

La Frances Rodgers-Rose in *The Black Woman* describes the sexual exploitation of the Black slavewoman in this manner:

> [T]he Black woman had to withstand the sexual abuse of the white master, his sons and the overseer. A young woman was not safe. Before reaching maturity, many a Black woman had suffered the sexual advances of the white male. If she refused to succumb to his advances, she was beaten and in some cases tortured to death.[25]

E. Franklin Frazier tells a story in *The Negro Family in the United States* about a slave who wrote that he and two others were once ordered to strip a slave girl naked, then hold her while the master's son, whose advances she had repulsed, flogged her with a bullwhip. At the finish she was near death.[26] The mixed blood of thousands upon thousands of African peoples' descendants is incontrovertible proof of sexual contact between white slavemasters and Black slave women. The rape of Black women by white men tends to be glossed over in the traditional literature on slavery. It is oftentimes hidden among the merciless taboos surrounding miscegenation.

> The antimiscegenation laws were intended, of course, to proscribe the sexual turf of the Black male. At the same time, the Black woman in slavery remained behind the pale of civil-rights or legal protection, and coexistence with the antimiscegenation laws in the southern states was the legalization of her rape.[27]

RACIAL DISCRIMINATION

The relationship of Black slave women with white free women was often volatile. The white female was charged with the responsibility of being "the repository of white civilization." She was the only one who could guarantee the purity of the white race and also the only one who could give birth to the white man's legitimate heirs; therefore it was believed that she must be lifted up and protected from racial contamination at all cost. This antebellum patriarchal concept made the white woman actually and symbolically the white man's greatest treasure.

> The "ethnic purity" of the whites must be maintained. White women had no holier duty, no more sacred mission, than that of transmitting in its integrity the heritage of ethnic endowment gained by the race through thousands of generations of struggle.[28]

Even when white women grew weary of their illusive pedestaled image as delicate, ornamental, timid virgins, their internalization of the rhetoric of patriarchy, which dominated the culture, as well as their racial privileges which compensated for their gender disadvantages, caused them repeatedly to embrace this image as the ideal.[29]

Key to the racial discrimation that the Black woman experienced was the vindictiveness of white women. The white woman's frustration at her own property-status which reduced her to a non-human existence, was often vented in violent behavior against black women.

> Since her authority was limited, many a white woman wielded it with a vengeance in the sphere where it was un-limited: running her house.[30]

Jacqueline Jones gives this description:

> Chastisement for minor infractions came with swift se-verity; cooks who burned the bread and children who stole cookies or fell asleep while singing to the baby suffered every conceivable form of physical abuse, from jabs with pins to beatings that left them disfigured for life.[31]

The Black woman became the correlate to the white lady. Her function was to perform the unavoidable and tedious tasks which were thought to be demeaning to civilized ladies.

> Regarded as mere objects of male pleasure and a demon-stration of male wealth, they frequenty treated their servants with cruel and capricious contempt in a pathetic effort to reclaim some semblance of their own dignity and worth. In this way, their upper-class bias and racist bigotry were combined with their actual degradation to pit woman against woman in a vicious cycle of subjugation that left Black women battered and impoverished.[32]

The Denial of Social Bonds for the Black Woman

The Black slavewoman, reduced to subservient marginality, was moveable property. Due to economic transactions, slaves were constantly being stripped of familiar social ties in order for their owner to maximize his profit. All of the slave's relationships existed under the shadowy threat of a permanent separation. As a deraci-nated outsider[33] in society, the Black woman lived with constant fear, and most of the time she had to endure the reality of having her husband and her children sold away from her under conditions that included the likelihood that she would never see them again. Rela-tionships between wives and husbands, blood kin and friends were broken up due to the interstate migration of slave labor. Countless slave families were forcibly disrupted. "This flow of enslaved Afro-

Americans must count as one of the greatest *forced* migrations in world history."[34] Frederick Douglass describes the denial of social bonds in this precise fashion:

> The idea of removal elsewhere, comes, generally, in the shape of a threat, and in punishment of crime. It is therefore, attended with fear and dread. A slave seldom thinks of bettering his condition by being sold, and hence he looks upon separation from his native place, with none of the enthusiasm which animates the bosoms of young freemen, when they contemplate a life in the far west, or in some distant country where they intend to rise to wealth and distinction. Nor can those from whom they separate, give them up with that cheerfulness with which friends and relations yield each other, when they feel that it is good for the departing one that he is removed from his native place. Then too, there is correspondence, and there is, at least, the hope of reunion, because reunion is *possible*. But, with the slave, all those mitigating circumstances are wanting. There is no improvement in his condition *probable*,—no correspondence *possible*,—no reunion attainable. His going out into the world, is like man going into the tomb, who, with open eyes, sees himself buried out of sight and hearing of wife, children and friends of kindred tie.[35]

Tainted by this paternalistic variety of racism, whites differentiated between the basic democratic rights and patterns of family life they claimed for themselves and those they considered as just treatment for their human merchandise. The conclusion of most Black writers about this period in history is thus:

> In nothing was slavery so savage and so relentless as in its attempted destruction of the family instincts of the negro [sic] race in America. Individuals, not families; shelters, not homes; herding, not marriages, were the cardinal sins in that system of horrors. Who can ever express in song or story the pathetic history of this race of unfortunate people when freedom came, groping about their scattered offsprings with only instinct to guide them, trying to knit together the broken ties of family kinship?[36]

The moral situation of the Black woman in the first two centuries of the American colonies' existence can be summed up in the inescapable theological debates and pseudoscientific discussions— either Black people were human beings and could not be property, or they were property and something less than human.[37]

> Black and white were constantly presented as antipodes,
> negative and positive poles on a continuum of goodness. In the
> minds of whites, Negroes stood as the antithesis of the
> character and properties of white people.[38]

All of life was graded according to an elaborate hierarchy, inherited
from the Middle Ages, known as the "great chain of being." Blacks
were assigned a fixed place as inferior species of humanity. The
common property of white culture were certain preconceptions
about the irredeemable nature of Black women and Black men as
"beings on an inferior order,"[39] a species between animal and
human. White colonists, caught in the obsessive duality of understanding the slave as property rather than a person, concurred with
racist ideology that proclaimed Blacks as lazy, cunning, lewd, im-
pure, naturally inferior, full of animality and matriarchal proclivities,
incapable of life's higher thoughts and emotion, and thus incapable
of equality with whites.

> The pitch of this ideology is not so much that the colored
> people are inferior as that they must remain inferior. Slaves can
> have no social organization of their own, no rights independent
> of their master's personal wishes; they can have neither status,
> function, nor social and geographical mobility like a caste; they
> cannot be permitted to contradict or dispute any question with
> the master. They are immediately and perpetually manipulable
> as instruments of production and must remain completely be-
> low the level of conscious organization and direction of com-
> munity life.[40]

Slave traders, in travels, reported that:

> . . . the black female was sexually aggressive and some-
> times mated with orangutang males, while the black male,
> because of his nature, hankered uncontrollably after the next
> link in the chain, the white woman.[41]

The Moral Situation of the Black
Woman After the Civil War

The institution of chattel slavery was destroyed in the "most
momentous event of the nineteenth century,"[42] the Civil War, from
1861 to 1865. Emancipation removed the legal and political slave

status from approximately four million Black people in the United States,[43] which meant that, in principle, Blacks owned their person and their labor for the first time.

During the periods of Emancipation and Reconstruction, Congress ratified the Thirteenth (December 18, 1865), Fourteenth (July 21, 1868), and Fifteenth (March 30, 1870) Amendments to the U.S. Constitution, granting Afro-Americans equal rights of freedom, due process and the vote for Black men only.[44] From 1865 to 1872 the Union-controlled government supported the Bureau of Refugees, Freedmen, and Abandoned Lands as the legal foundation to promote the general welfare of poverty-stricken ex-slaves.[45] The Bureau tried to find food, clothing, shelter and medical supplies for the former slaves; they tried to negotiate labor arrangements with white landowners; and even though their own courts were poorly organized with only the barest forms of due process of law, they tried to protect Afro-Americans from hostile white courts, legislators and vigilante intimidation. W. E. B. DuBois noted in the *Souls of Black Folk* that one of the few things untainted by sordid greed and vainglory in American history was the work done by the Freedmen's aid societies in starting one hundred colleges and secondary schools for Blacks.[46]

A few Black spokesmen participated in the political processes; they occupied local, state and federal offices during the initial stages of emancipation.[47] A small cadre of ex-slaves achieved prominence in the areas of education, law and business.[48] Once free, Blacks who had mastered specialized artisan skills became independent carpenters, blacksmiths, weavers and seamstresses. Thousands of Blacks purchased land and proved successful in experiments of land redistribution and yeomanry projects.

Unfortunately, however, for the vast majority of Afro-Americans, the traditional practices of racial and gender subordination subjected them to incredible suffering after the war. The general patterns of *de facto* social segregation and disenfranchisement of Blacks, "which were integral to the *raison d'etre* of the peculiar institution," continued as the norm. The chief cornerstone of the "moral" justification of slavery which was the supposedly inherent inferiority of the Black race, became more passionately entrenched in the defense of white supremacy in the postwar years.[49] White southerners accepted the abolition of slavery as one of the consequences of their military defeat and surrender at Appomattox in 1865 but they were totally unwilling to grant Black women and men respect as equal human beings with rights of life, liberty and property. The "rightness of whiteness" counted more than the basic political and civil rights of any Black person. "Southern whites of every class did everything in their power to resurrect the *ancien regime*," says Manning Marble.[50]

For instance, in 1866, Dr. C. K. Marshall from Mississippi echoed the undisguised racist hope of the majority of white southerners for the complete extinction of Blacks (as a consequence of inferiority):

> In all probability . . . on the morning of the first of January, 1920, the colored population in the South will scarcely be counted.[51]

Inveterate racial hostility grew much more than it had before the war. The thoughts and actions of most whites were engulfed in white supremacist ideology. Southern apologists received widespread acceptance from many Northerners who had opposed slavery on the ground of an indivisible United States while avidly supporting racial subordination. Alexis de Tocqueville concluded in his study, *Democracy in America,* that:

> Race prejudice seems stronger in those states that have abolished slavery than in those where it still exists, and nowhere is it more intolerant than in those states where slavery was never known . . .
>
> In the South the master has no fear of lifting the slave up to his level, for he knows that when he wants to he can always throw him down into the dust. In the North the white man no longer clearly sees the barrier that separates him from the degraded race, and he keeps the Negro at a distance all the more carefully because he fears lest one day they be confounded together.[52]

Thus, white Northerners joined white Southerners in resolutely opposing social and political equality for Blacks.

Racism became more pervasive in American society. Many academic historians, sociologists, anthropologists, educators, theologians and writers all fell in step with a heightened propaganda campaign. These scholars dredged up every conceivable argument to justify the natural inferiority of Blacks and the natural role of subordination of Blacks to whites.

> The leading and most respected literary journals of the
> country reflected the view that blacks were inferior and did not
> possess rights which should be protected by government. In
> the last two decades of the nineteenth century such journals as
> *Harper's, Scribner's* and the *Atlantic Monthly* strained their
> own ample ingenuity by portraying blacks in the most un-
> favorable light. . . . Invariably they were described as ugly. In
> articles, stories, anecdotes, poems and cartoons, Negroes were
> portrayed as superstitutious, dull, stupid, imitative, ignorant,
> happy-go-lucky, improvident, lazy, immoral, and criminal.[53]

Institutional slavery ended but virulent and intractable hatred
which supported it did not.

So, after seven years, the Freedmen's Bureau was effectively
curtailed and finally dismantled, leaving Afro-Americans with dead-
letter-amendments and nullified civil rights acts, with collapsing
federal laws and with increasing white terrorist violence. Beyond
the small gains and successes of a few Blacks, the optimism of ex-
slaves for full citizenship was soon extinguished. The Reconstruction
left Black people susceptible to exploitation in all areas of their lives.
They were "just above slavery and far short of full citizenship."[54]

An ethical analysis of the economic, political and social institutions that replaced slavery is crucial to the discussion of the moral
situation of Black women. Presumed as free agents for the first time
in the United States, Afro-American women suffered the direct
consequences of the economic social impoverishment due to the
political panoply of state laws requiring a fixed, rigid system of
segregation; and Afro-American women bore the brunt of the stag-
gering compounded elements of race, class and gender discrimination. Jeanne Noble describes it this way:

> While freedom brought new opportunities for black
> men, for most women it augmented old problems.[55]

During the post-emancipation period, racism and male supremacy continued to intersect patriarchal and capitalist structures
in definitive ways. Black women, young and old, were basically on
their own. Perhaps deserted or perhaps never married, hundreds of
thousands of Black women walked from plantation to plantation
poignantly searching for lost and stolen children. Due to the more
than 38,000 deaths of Black soldiers who fought in, serviced and led
guerrilla actions for the Union army and navy during the Civil War

and the estimated 5,000 Black men killed during the ten years following the war, large numbers of Black women found themselves widowed.[56] Hordes of ex-slaves fled as aimless refugees when the Union military armies penetrated the South. Other women were fortunate enough to cross the greatest chasm one can imagine, from slavery to freedom, with their families intact. Whether a Black woman began her career as a free woman, as an autonomous family supporter or as a co-partner with her spouse, the Black woman began her life of freedom with no vote, no protection and no equity of any sort.

BLACK WOMEN AS SHARECROPPERS

The Black woman continued to experience the traditional white-Black, master-servant relationship via the sharecropping system that replaced slavery. The relationship of power dynamics remained much as it had before the war.[57] The standardized land-tenure contract was structured so as to maintain the hegemony of the antebellum slave-owning aristocracy.[58] As a result of the crop lien laws passed in 1865, Black people were financially unable or not allowed to purchase land. The Black woman and her family's legal emancipation trapped them in a grossly unequal poverty cycle of debt peonage. Every year the white landowners and commissary merchants provided Black sharecroppers with high rates of interest for credit in order to purchase seed, tools, food, fuel, and other necessities. At the end of the harvest season, the sharecroppers were compelled to accept a settlement of their share of the crop minus charges according to the landlord's rendition of the farm accounts.[59]

Even with newly won civil rights, the economic opportunities for Blacks tottered between dependency and despair. A full complement of Black people soon found themselves legally bound to labor for payment on trumped-up debt-charges that accrued in excessive amounts from year to year. This type of perpetual indebtedness resulted in involuntary servitude for an overwhelming majority of Black families.

> . . . [J]udicial decisions failed to give adequate protection to Negro farmers who sought to escape the tentacles of the cruel credit system. It was too easy for landlords to secure criminal convictions of Negroes on the slightest accusation of theft. Because of this fact many Negro croppers became imprisoned by the very land they tilled.[60]

The patterns of exploitation of the Black woman as laborer and breeder were only shaken by the Civil War. By no means were they destroyed. Throughout the late nineteenth and early twentieth century, Black women were severely restricted to the most unskilled, poorly paid, menial jobs. Virtually no Black woman held a job beyond those of domestic servant or field hand. Keeping house, farming land, bearing and rearing children continued to dominate all aspects of the Black woman's life.

> Over 90 percent of all Black female workers were in agriculture or working as servants (21 percent), or laundresses (18 percent) not in laundries. Out of 2,013,981 Black female workers, the above categories accounted for 1,828,104 workers.[61]

This systematic exclusion and routinized oppression of Black females from other areas of employment served as confirmations for the continuation of the servile status of Black women.

Black Women as Farmhands

Black women sharecroppers who worked the land with or without husbands were not released from the regular household demands of cooking, cleaning, laundering and childrearing. It is estimated that three out of every four farmhands were Black females, usually put to work at a very young age, between six and eight. Black females assumed all kinds of farming responsibilities. They chopped, hoed, planted, plowed, primed and picked crops as well as completed those tasks usually defined as within the male domain such as the care and feeding of livestock. The urgency of trying to survive as sharecroppers demanded every hand—female and male—from the youngest to the oldest.

Historic practices continued to assign the Black female to an inferior status in the general society. Even though birth and death registrations of Black people were not recorded in any sufficiently reliable manner until the middle of the 1930s, it does seem reasonable to suppose that the percentage of infant mortality, congenital defects and Black women dying in childbirth were inordinately high in comparison with their white counterpart. Bertram Doyle even goes so far as to point out the requirements of interracial etiquette which made it a special taboo to interact with the Black woman in any other categories than "negress" and "wench."[62]

Black Women as Domestics

The theme of objectification inherent in the domestic servitude of the Black woman continued to permeate her life. Bereft of formal education and advanced skills, the Black woman as a domestic worker was usually at the white employer's mercy.[63] Her employment arrangements had few, if any, demands that white people were obligated to meet. In lieu of salary she was often paid with used clothing, discarded houshold items and leftover food. The low or no pay, precariousness of job security and irregular work hours and duties caused many domestic workers to situate their families in the backyards of the white household. Sexual harassment became the lineal descendant of the institutionalization of the rape of Black women under slavery. As a vestige of slavery, white male heads of households assumed the sexual accessibility of the female domestic worker.[64]

Both as a matter of principle and law, slaves were denied formal education. Hence, we find that the majority of ex-slaves in the postbellum period were not only landless and penniless but they were also illiterate.[65] Only about five percent of the Black population had been allowed the benefit of formal education in reading, writing, arithmetic, science and the classical humanities. Even during slavery, a large percentage of blacks taught each other the rudiments of reading and writing through clandestine activities.

> On a plantation in Mississippi, Milla Granson, a slave conducted a midnight school for several years. She had been taught to read and write by the children of her former master in Kentucky, an indulgent man, and in her little school hundreds of slaves benefitted from her learning. . . . School started between eleven and twelve at night and lasted until two o'clock in the morning. After laboring all day for their master, the slaves would creep stealthily to Milla's "schoolroom" (a little cabin in a back alley) carrying a bundle of pitchpine splinters for light, as the door and windows of the cabin had to be kept tightly sealed to avoid discovery. Each class was composed of twelve pupils and when Milla had brought them up to the extent of her ability, she "graduated" them and took in a dozen more. Through this means she graduated hundreds of slaves. Many whom she taught to write a legible hand wrote their own passes and set out for Canada.[66]

Next to owning land, the Black community's major aspiration was to obtain an education.

After the war, the unique alliance between the Freedman's Bureau and northern missionary and philanthropic societies afforded a few Blacks opportunities of classical education.[67] Others were privileged with liberal arts training. But the overwhelming majority of Blacks were permitted by the white landlords to attend school four months out of each year and therefore they received training in industrial education only. To accommodate the agricultural labor demands, Blacks were provided with "normal education"—training to do better what they had always done, within the framework of the racial divisions of labor that had always existed. Liberal white educators believed that Blacks could become self-supporting, industrious citizens by studying domestic science and manual art, devoid of the analytical tools to tamper with the segregated social order.

BLACK WOMEN AS EDUCATORS

Limited to special occupational pursuits by means of rigid job restrictions, the Black freedwoman understood at the "get go" the relationship between her enthusiastic desire for education and the future of the Black race in America. Black people believed that education made one less susceptible to the indignities and proscriptions of an oppressive white South. The Black female was taught that her education was meant not to "uplift" her alone but also to prepare her for a life of service in the "uplifting" of the Black community.

> From the outset, the education of the black woman differed from that of the white woman in that it was never meant to be ornamental, but was intended to fit her for a profession, a life of service, or both.[68]

Thus, teaching became the pinnacle of professional achievement for the Black woman. In this unique leadership role, the Black woman as educator attended Sunday services at local churches where she often spoke in order to cultivate interest in the Black community's overall welfare. Black women educators were crusaders in the development of various social service improvement leagues and aid societies. They sponsored fundraising fairs, concerts and all forms of social entertainment, in order to correct some of the inequities in the overcrowded and understaffed educational facilities in the Black community. These dedicated community leaders substantially reduced illiteracy among Black people.

Black women educators were also quite active in the suffrage movement in the U.S. In August 1920, when suffrage was finally ratified, Black women by the thousands went to register to vote. Within a few days, literacy tests, civil service examinations, proof of birth, and a myriad of other devices were used in devious ways to restrict the suffrage of Black women. In many instances, Black women experienced the identical obstacles that Black men had experienced in their disenfranchisement process in the 1880s.[69]

BLACK WOMEN AS VICTIMS OF RACIAL SEGREGATION, DEFAMATION AND DISCRIMINATION

Fearful of the emerging competitive race relations with Blacks, white America instituted a whole set of statutes, ordinances, policies and customs in order to maintain white supremacy and to further white privileges in the areas of education, politics and economics.[70] Whites wanted to regulate and eventually stamp out all notions of social equality between the races. Terror of Black encroachment in areas where whites claimed power and privileges even caused southern state legislatures to enact "Black Codes," similar to slave codes, designed to limit drastically the rights of ex-slaves.[71]

> Although their provisions varied among states, the Black Codes essentially prevented the freedmen from voting or holding office, made them ineligible for military service, and disbarred them from serving on juries or testifying in court against whites. Moreover, blacks were forbidden to travel from place to place without passes, were not allowed to assemble without a formal permit from authorities, and could be fined and bound out to labor contractors if they were unwilling to work.[72]

Thus, by 1890 legal authorities and public acceptability sanctioned forced racial separation as the mechanism to dilute systematically the civil liberties of Black folk. "Jim Crowism" became the calculated, invidious policy to exclude the mass of Black folk from interracial contacts in public places and on public transportation facilities. With *de jure* segregation, civil rights for Black people fell outside the realm of legal contract. Granted no protection under the law, direct steps were taken to control even the most personal spatial and social aspects of Black life.

> It became a punishable offense against the laws or the mores for whites and Negroes to travel, eat, defecate, wait, be

buried, make love, play, relax and even speak together, except in the stereotyped context of master and servant interaction.[73]

De jure segregation took a less blatantly visible form in the North, but it was only slightly less rigid.

The Supreme Court decision in the case of *Plessy vs. Ferguson* in 1896 became the legal blueprint for racial discrimination. The "separate but equal" decision meant separate and vastly unequal or nonexistent facilities for Blacks. It became the solidified doctrine for ejecting Blacks from any meaningful participation in the mainstream of the American society. This legal decision by the highest judicial tribunal in the land accelerated the drawing of territorial, cultural and economic boundaries between the races.

In much the same manner that marshalls and slave catchers pursued fugitive Blacks, the people who worked the coercive apparatuses of the State—the police, armed forces, prisons, and the criminal justice system—were given the authority and responsibility to enforce segregation. White terror organizations such as the Ku Klux Klan (organized in 1867) engaged in extra-legal violence as a way of supplementing the mechanism of "Jim Crow." Lynching, burning, castrating, beating, cross-burning, tarring and feathering, masked night rides, verbal threats, hate rallies, public humiliations and random discharging of shotguns in windows were all used by white vigilante hate groups "to shore up the color line."

> In the thirty-three year period from 1883 to 1915, the annual toll of Negroes lynched never fell below 50 but once—in 1914, when the number was 49. In nine of these years the figures rose to more than a hundred. . . . Negroes were lynched for such "crimes" as threatening to sue a white man, attempting to register to vote, enticing a white man's servant to leave his job, engaging in labor union activities, "being disrespectful to" or "disputing with" a white man, or sometimes for no discoverable reason at all. Mary Turner, Georgia, was hanged and burned when she was almost at the point of childbirth because she threatened to disclose the names of the men who killed her husband.[74]

Bettina Aptheker in *Woman's Legacy: Essays on Race, Sex, and Class in American History* summed up the extra-legal violence against Black people in this manner:

[T]he dialectics of the lynch mentality required the dehumanization of Black men (as rapists), Black women (as prostitutes), and white women (as property whose honor was to be avenged by the men who possessed them).[75]

Notes

/1/   Moses I. Finley, *Ancient Slavery & Modern Ideology* (New York: Viking Press, 1980), p. 77.
/2/   Jacqueline Jones, "My Mother Was Much of a Woman: Black Women, Work, and the Family Under Slavery," *Feminist Studies* 8 (Summer 1982): 236; Bell Hooks, *Ain't I a Woman? Black Women and Feminism* (Boston: South End Press, 1981).
/3/   Angela Y. Davis, *Women, Race & Class* (New York: Random House, 1981), p. 6.
/4/   Pierre L. van den Berghe, *Race and Racism: A Comparative Perspective* (New York: Wiley, 1967), p. 77.
/5/   James W. Blassingame, *The Slave Community: Plantation Life in the Antebellum South* (New York: Oxford University Press, 1972); Paul A. David, et al., *Reckoning with Slavery: A Critical Study in the Quantitative History of American Negro Slavery* (New York: Oxford Press, 1976); Eugene D. Genovese, *The Political Economy of Slavery* (New York: Pantheon Books, 1965); Eric Williams, *Capitalism and Slavery* (Chapel Hill, University of North Carolina Press, 1944); Harold Woodman, *Slavery and the Southern Economy* (New York: Harcourt Brace Jovanovich, 1966).
/6/   Books and anthologies on the special predicament of Black women slaves: Herbert Aptheker, *American Negro Slave Revolts* (New York: International Publishers, 1970; first edition, 1948); *To Be Free: Studies in American Negro History* (New York: International Publishers, 1969; first edition, 1948); *A Documentary History of the Negro People in the United States*, vol. 1 (New York: The Citadel Press, 1969; first edition, 1951).
/7/   The law forbade the importation of slaves into the United States after January 1, 1808, but illicit slave traffic continued until the Civil War. Richard B. Morris, ed., *Encyclopedia of American History* (New York: Harper & Brothers, 1961), p. 544.
/8/   La Frances Rodgers-Rose, ed., *The Black Woman* (Beverly Hills, Cal.: Sage Publications, 1980), p. 18.
/9/   Jones, p. 238.
/10/   Moses Grandy, in Franklin Frazier, *The Negro Family in the United States* (Chicago: University of Chicago Press, 1939), chap. IV passim.
/11/   Davis, p. 5.
/12/   Robert S. Starobin, *Industrial Slavery in the Old South* (New York: Oxford University Press, 1970), pp. 165 ff. discusses the various kinds of slave labor with emphasis on the presence of women in all areas.
/13/   Kenneth M. Stampp, *The Peculiar Institution: Slavery in the Ante-*

bellum South (New York: Vintage Books, 1956), p. 343.

/14/   Davis, p. 6.

/15/   Dorothy Burnham, "The Life of the Afro-American Woman in Slav-ery," *International Journal of Women's Studies* 1 (July/August 1978), 363–77; Angela Davis, "Reflections on the Black Woman's Role in the Community of Slaves," *Black Scholar* 3 (December 1971), 3–15; Eugene Genovese, "The Slave Family, Women—A Reassessment of Matriarchy, Emasculation, Weakness," *Southern Voices* 1 (August/September 1974), 9–16.

/16/   Barbara Christian, *Black Women Novelists: The Development of a Tradition, 1892–1976* (Westport, Conn.: Greenwood Press, 1980), pp. 12–13.

/17/   Herbert George Gutman, *The Black Family in Slavery and Freedom 1750–1925* (New York: Vintage Books, 1976); Nathan Irvin Huggins, *Black Odyssey: The Afro-American Ordeal in Slavery* (New York: Vintage Books, 1977); George P. Rawick, ed., *From Sundown to Sunup: The American Slave: A Composite Autobiography* (Westport, Conn.: Greenwood Publish-ing Co., 1972); Thomas L. Webber, *Deep Like the Rivers: Education in the Slave Quarter Community 1831–1865* (New York: W.W. Norton & Co., 1978).

/18/   Huggins, p. 123.

/19/   W. Augustus Low, ed., and Virgil A. Clift, asst. ed., *Encyclopedia of Black America* (New York: McGraw Hill Book Company, 1981), p. 862.

/20/   Winthrop Jordan, *White Over Black* (New York: Penguin Books, 1969), detailed discussion in chapter two.

/21/   Jones, pp. 237–238; Davis, p. 23; a detailed discussion in Joan Kelly-Gadol's article, "The Social Relations of the Sexes: Methodological Implica-tions of Women's History," *Signs* 1 (Summer 1976), 809–10, 819.

/22/   Charles Ball, *Slavery in the United States: A Narrative of the Life and Adventures of Charles Ball, a Black Man* (Lewiston: John W. Shugert, 1836), p. 204, quoted by Walker, p. 341.

/23/   Hooks, pp. 20–22.

/24/   Christian, p. 13.

/25/   Rodgers-Rose, p. 20. Also, Paul David, et al., "Victorians All, The Sexual Mores and Conduct of Slaves and Their Masters," in *Reckoning with Slavery*.

/26/   Frazier, Chapter IV, passim.

/27/   Bettina Aptheker, *Woman's Legacy: Essays on Race, Sex, and Class in American History* (Amherst: The University of Massachusetts Press, 1982), p. 3. Discussed in greater detail in Lerner, pp. 4–48; Eugene D. Genovese, *Roll, Jordan, Roll: The World the Slaves Made* (New York: Pantheon Books, 1974); Norman R. Yetman, *Life Under the "Peculiar Institution": Selections from the Slave Narrative Collection* (New York: Holt, Rinehart & Winston, 1970).

/28/   George Stocking, *Race, Culture and Evolution: Essays in the History of Anthropology* (New York: The Free Press, 1968), pp. 49–50; Winthrop D. Jordan, *White Over Black: American Attitudes Toward the Negro, 1550–1812* (New York: Penguin Books, 1969); George Frederickson, *The Black Image in the White Mind: The Debate on Afro-American Character, 1817–1914* (New York: Harper and Row, 1971).

/29/ Two important books that deal with the plight of white women in the antebellum South are: Anne Firor Scott, *The Southern Lady: From Pedestal to Politics, 1830–1930;* Julia Cherry Spruill, *Women's Life and Work in the Southern Colonies* (Chapel Hill: University of North Carolina Press, 1938).

/30/ Walker, p. 343.

/31/ Jones, p. 249.

/32/ Aptheker, p. 116.

/33/ Van Den Berghe, 18, 29, 77, 101. Also, Gary B. Nash, *Red, White and Black: The Peoples of Early America* (Englewood Cliffs, N.J.: Prentice-Hall, Inc., 1974).

/34/ David, p. 99. A detail discussion of the internal slave trade, Frederick Bancoft, *Slave Trading in the Old South* (New York: Ungat, 1959).

/35/ Frederick Douglass, *My Bondage and My Freedom* (New York: 1855), pp. 176–177.

/36/ A quotation by Fannie Barrier Williams in *Black Women in Nineteenth Century American Life: Their Words, Their Thoughts, Their Feelings*, eds. Bert James Loewenberg and Ruth Bogin (University Park: The Pennsylvania State University Press, 1976), p. 15. The slave narratives are of utmost value in capturing the denial of social bonds in slavery. Benjamin A. Botkin, ed., *Lay My Burden Down: A Folk History of Slavery* (Chicago: University of Chicago Press, 1945); Julius Lester, ed., *To Be a Slave* (New York: Dial Press, 1968); Charles H. Nichols, ed., *Many Thousands Gone: The Ex-Slaves' Account of Their Bondage and Freedom* (New York: E. J. Brill, 1963).

/37/ Books that discuss the way Black people were treated as subhuman species: Oliver C. Cox, *Caste, Class and Race: A Study in Social Dynamics* (New York: Doubleday & Co., Inc. 1948), pp. 353–391; Brion Davis David, *The Problem of Slavery in Western Culture* (Ithaca, N.Y.: 1966), pp. 223–288; George M. Frederickson, "Toward a Social Interpretation of the Development of American Racism" in *Key Issues in the Afro-American Slave Experience*, vol. 1, eds. Nathan Huggins, Martin Kilson, and Daniel Fox (New York, 1971); Carol George, *Segregated Sabbaths* (New York: Oxford University Press, 1973); Eli Ginzberg and Alfred S. Eichner, *The Troublesome Presence, American Democracy and the Negro* (New York: Free Press, 1964); Thomas F. Gossett, *Race, the History of an Idea in America* (Dallas: Southern Methodist University Press, 1963); Marvin Harris, *Patterns of Race in the Americas* (New York: Walker, 1964), pp. 65–94; H. Hoetnik, *Race Relations in the Americas: An Inquiry into Their Nature and Nexus* (New York: 1973), pp. 3–86; 192–209; Claude H. Nolen, *The Negro Image in the South: The Anatomy of White Supremacy* (Lexington: 1967).

/38/ Henry Allen Bullock, *A History of Negro Education in the South from 1619 to the Present* (Cambridge: Harvard University Press, 1967), pp. 155–156.

/39/ Stated by the Chief Justice in the Dred Scott case.

/40/ Cox, p. 357.

/41/ Jordan, p. 31.

/42/ Peter Camejo, *Racism, Revolution, Reaction 1861–1877: The Rise and Fall of Radical Reconstruction* (New York: Monad Press, 1976), p. 9.

/43/ "When the war came in 1861 there were approximately 4,449,830

Negroes in the United States, of whom 3,953,000 were slaves." *The Black American Reference Book*, ed. Mable M. Smythe (Englewood Cliffs, N.J.: Prentice-Hall, 1976), pp. 39–40. Invaluable to this study of the Black woman's moral situation in the U.S. from 1619 to 1982 is *The Social and Economic Status of the Black Population in the United States: An Historical Overview, 1790–1978* by U.S. Department of Commerce, Bureau of the Census, Current Population Reports, Special Studies Series P-23, No. 70, June 1979.

/44/   Albert P. Blaustein and Clarence Clyde Ferguson, *Desegregation and the Law* (New Brunswick, N.J.: Rutgers University Press, 1957); Robert J. Harris, *The Quest for Equality* (Baton Rouge: Louisiana State University Press, 1960); A. Leon Higginbotham, Jr., *In the Matter of Color: Race and the American Legal Process: The Colonial Period* (New York: Oxford University Press, 1978).

/45/   Martin L. Abbott, *The Freedmen's Bureau in South Carolina, 1865–1872* (Chapel Hill: University of North Carolina Press, 1967); George R. Bentley, *A History of the Freedmen's Bureau* (Philadelphia: University of Pennsylvania, 1955).

/46/   W. E. B. DuBois, *The Souls of Black Folk* (Chicago: 1903).

/47/   Maurine Christopher, *America's Black Congressmen* (New York: Thomas Y. Crowell Co., 1971); Samuel Denny Smith, *The Negro in Congress, 1870–1901* (Chapel Hill: University of North Carolina Press, 1940); Okon Edet Uya, *From Slavery to Public Service: Robert Smalls, 1839–1915* (London: Oxford University Press, 1971).

/48/   W. E. B. DuBois, *Black Reconstruction in America* (New York: Harcourt Brace Jovanovich, 1935); Lerone Bennett, Jr., *Black Power: The Human Side of Reconstruction* (Chicago: Johnson Publications, 1967); Robert Cruden, *The Negro in Reconstruction* (Englewood Cliffs, N.J.: Prentice-Hall, 1969).

/49/   James W. Vander Zander, "The Ideology of White Supremacy," in *White Racism: Its History, Pathology and Practice*, eds. Barry N. Schwarrz and Robert Disch (New York: Dell Publishing Co., 1970), pp. 121–139; Rayford W. Logan, *The Betrayal of the Negro* (New York: Macmillan Co., 1954), chapter 13; August Meier, *Negro Thought in America, 1880–1915: Racial Ideologies in the Age of Booker T. Washington* (Ann Arbor: University of Michigan Press, 1964); C. Vann Woodward, *Strange Career of Jim Crow*, 3rd revised ed. (New York: Oxford University Press, 1974).

/50/   Manning Marable, *Blackwater: Historical Studies in Race, Class Consciousness and Revolution* (Dayton, Oh.: Black Praxis Press, 1981).

/51/   A quotation in *The Black American Reference Book*, p. 39.

/52/   Alexis de Tocqueville, *Democracy in America*, ed. J. P. Meyer (New York: Doubleday, 1969), p. 343.

/53/   *The Black American Reference Book*, ed. Mable M. Smythe (Englewood Cliffs, N.J.: Prentice-Hall, Inc., 1976), p. 41; Camejo lists the following as additional racist publications of this era: *Lippincott's Magazine*, North American Review, Youth's Companion, Cosmopolitan, Munsey's and *McClure's*, pp. 207–211. See Gossett, chapter 11, and B. Aptheker, chapter 3.

/54/   John Hope Franklin, *Reconstruction After the Civil War* (Chicago:

The University of Chicago Press, 1961); Lewis H. Blair, *A Southern Prophecy: The Prosperity of the South Dependent Upon the Elevation of the Negro*, ed. C. Vann Woodward (Boston: Little, Brown & Co., 1964; originally published in 1889); Elizabeth Hyde Botume, *First Days Among the Contrabands* (New York: Arno Press/New York Times, 1969; originally published in 1865); Henrietta Buckmaster, *Freedom Bound* (New York: Macmillan & Co., 1965); John R. Lynch, *The Facts of Reconstruction* (New York: Arno Press, 1969; originally published in 1913); Whitelaw Reid, *After the War: A Tour of the Southern States, 1865–1866* (New York: Harper & Row, 1969; originally published in 1866); Kenneth Stampp, *The Era of Reconstruction, 1865–1877* (New York: Alfred A. Knopf, 1965); Kenneth M. Stampp and Leon F. Litwack, eds., *Reconstruction: An Anthology of Revisionist Writings* (Baton Rouge: Louisiana State University Press, 1969); Emma Lou Thronbrough, ed., *Black Reconstructionists* (Englewood Cliffs, N.J.: Prentice-Hall, 1972); Joel Williamson, *After Slavery* (Chapel Hill: University of North Carolina Press, 1965).
For a rather complete analysis of judicial attrition and the contraction of the equal protection clauses, see Robert J. Harris, *The Quest for Equality*, pp. 82–108.

/55/ Jeanne Noble, *Beautiful, Also, Are the Souls of My Sisters: A History of the Black Woman in America* (Englewood Cliffs, N.J.: Prentice-Hall, Inc., 1978), p. 63.

/56/ James McPhetson, *The Negro's Civil War* (New York: Pantheon Books, 1965); Benjamin Quarles, *The Negro in the Civil War* (Boston: Little, Brown, 1953); Dudley T. Cornish, *The Sable Arm: Negro Troops in the Union Army* (Longmans, Green, 1956); Bell Irwin Wiley, *Southern Negroes, 1861–1865*, (New Haven: Yale University Press, 1938).

/57/ Although they were only a tiny proportion of even the Southern white population (in 1860 there were 175,000 slave owners in a Southern white population of 8 million), slaveholders represented the single greatest economic interest in the nation prior to the Civil War. From the founding of the Republic to the presidential election of 1859, slaveholders were the controlling force in both major political parties, in all three branches of government and in the armed forces." B. Aptheker, p. 14.

/58/ Roger L. Ransom and Richard Sutch, *One Kind of Freedom: The Economic Consequences of Emancipation* (Cambridge: Cambridge University Press, 1977).

/59/ Ray Stannard Baker, *Following the Color Line* (New York: Doubleday, Page and Co., 1908); August Meier and Elliott Rudwick, *From Plantation to Ghetto*, 3rd ed. (New York; Hill and Wang, 1976); Joseph D. Reid, Jr., "Sharecropping as an Understandable Market Respnose," *Journal of Economic History* 33 (March 1973): 106–130; "Sharecropping in History and Theory," *Agricultural History* 49 (April 1975): 426–440; C. Vann Woodward, *Origins of the New South, 1877–1913* (Baton Rouge: Louisiana State University Press, 1951).

/60/ Gunnar Myrdal, *An American Dilemma* (New York: Harper & Brothers, 1944), pp. 247–248.

/61/ La Frances Rodgers-Rose, *The Black Woman* (Beverly Hills, Ca.: Sage Publications, 1980), p. 23.

/62/   Bertram Doyle, *The Etiquette of Race Relations in the South* (Chicago: University of Chicago Press, 1937).

/63/   G. Hayne, "Negroes in Domestic Service in the United States," *Journal of Negro History* 8 (1923): 384–442; Lillian Pettingill, *Toilers of the Home* (New York: Doubleday, 1903).

/64/   Sexual harassment and abuse of Black women by whites was a major concern of Black men during and after Reconstruction. Sharon Harley and Rosalyn Terborg-Penn, *The Afro-American Woman* cite Alexander Crummell, T. Thomas Furtune, Calvin Chase, W. E. B. DuBois, Monroe Majors as the leading Black men who spoke out and wrote about the verbal and sexual attacks of whites against women of the Black race. (Port Washington, N.Y.: Kennikat Press, 1978, chapter 3, "Black Male Perspectives on the Nineteenth Century Woman.")

/65/   In 1870, after emancipation, less than 10 percent of blacks over the age of twenty could read and write in the Five Cotton States. By contrast, over 80 percent of adult whites in those states were literate." Ransom & Sutch, p. 15.

/66/   Sylvia G. L. Dannett, *Profile in Negro Womanhood*, vol. 1 (Yonkers, N.Y.: Educational Heritage, Inc., 1964), p. 74.

/67/   Horace Mann Bond, "The Origin and Development of the Negro Church-Related College," *Journal of Negro Education* 29 (Summer 1960): 217–226; Henry Allen Bullock, *A History of Negro Education in the South from 1619 to the Present* (Cambridge: Harvard University Press, 1967); Hurley H. Doddy, "The Progress of the Negro in Higher Education," *Journal of Negro Education* 32, No. 4 (1963): chapter XV; Edgar Wallace Knight, *The Influence of Reconstruction on Education in the South* (New York: Arno Press, 1969; originally published in 1913); Rayford W. Logan, "The Evolution of Private Colleges for Negroes," *Journal of Negro Education* 17 (Summer 1958): 213–220; Carter G. Woodson, *The Education of the Negro Prior to 1861* (New York: Arno Press, 1968; originally published in 1915).

/68/   Ernestine Walker, "The Black Woman," in *The Black American Reference Book*, ed. Mable M. Smythe (Englewood Cliffs, N.J.: Prentice-Hall, 1976).

/69/   Rosalyn Terborg-Penn, "Discrimination Against Afro-American Women in the Women's Movement, 1830–1920," in Harley and Terborg-Penn, pp. 17–27.

/70/   Mary Frances Berry, *Black Resistance/White Law* (New York, 1971); Donald P. DeNevi and Doris A. Homes, eds., *Racism at the Turn of the Century: Documentary Perspectives, 1870–1910* (Leswing Press, 1973); Charles S. Johnson, *Patterns of Negro Segregation* (New York, 1943); Jack Temple Kirby, *Darkness at the Dawning: Race and Reform in the Progressive South* (Philadelphia, 1972); Howard Rabinowitz, *Race Relations in the Urban South, 1865–1890* (New York, 1978); Roger L. Rice, "Residential Segregation by Law, 1910–1917," *Journal of Southern History*, XXXIV (1968): 179–199.

/71/   Theodore B. Wilson, *The Black Codes of the South* (University of Alabama, 1965).

/72/   William J. Wilson, *Power, Racism and Privilege: Race Relations in*

Theoretical and Sociohistorical Perspectives (New York: Macmillan Company, 1973), p. 99.

/73/   Pierre L. van den Berghe, *Race and Racism: A Comparative Perspective* (New York: Wiley, 1967).

/74/   Gossett, pp. 269–270.

/75/   B. Aptheker, p. 62; Jessie Daniel Ames, *The Changing Character of Lynching* (Atlanta: 1942); J. E. Cutler, *Lynch Law* (New York: 1905); Ralph Ginzburgh, *100 Years of Lynching;* James Weldon Johnson, *Along the Way* (New York: The Viking Press, 1965); Peter Kolchin, *First Freedom: The Responses of Alabama's to Emancipation and Reconstruction* (Westport, Conn.: Greenwood Press, 1972); Arthur F. Raper, *The Tragedy of Lynching* (Chapel Hill: University of North Carolina Press, 1933); Ida B. Wells, *On Lynching* (New York: 1969).

CHAPTER II

THE BLACK WOMAN'S MORAL SITUATION IN THE TWENTIETH CENTURY

The Moral Situation of the Black Woman During the Great Migration

Even with periodic tides of rural-to-urban migration the geographical distribution of the Black population was concentrated in the rural South from 1790 to 1910. From 1860 to 1910 approximately 9,827,763 Black people, nine-tenths of the Black population in this country, lived in the southern region of the United States and worked in agricultural or personal service occupations.[1]

However, a series of floods and boll weevil infestations, diminishing returns on impoverished soil, wartime curtailment of European immigrants for industrial labor markets, and rampaging racial brutality in the South accelerated Black emigration to the North and West. This mass exodus began in 1910 and gained momentum after each of the world wars.[2]

The Black population of the urban North lived in very distinct residential districts. Their own habitations were limited and totally inadequate for the unprecedented influx of Black people from Southern states.

> Attics and cellars, store-rooms and basements, churches, sheds and warehouses had to be employed for the accommodation of these new-comers. Whenever a Negro had space which he could possibly spare, it was converted into a sleeping space; as many beds as possible were crowded into it, and the maximum number of men per bed were lodged.[3]

Contrary to the previous European immigration, Black families tended to migrate north and west without breaking family connections for considerable lapses in time.[4]

Some cities like Philadelphia, Detroit and Cleveland built special accommodations for the tens of thousands of Black farmers, unskilled laborers and domestics who left the South to fill the gap in the ranks of the depleted labor market.[5] The National League on Urban Conditions Among Negroes and The National League for the Protection of Colored Women (1906) were two organizations designed to secure adequate housing, food and clothing for the Black migrants.

Labor agents who recruited in the South had no altruistic motives. They worked on a per capita commission basis for northern industrialists, which meant they sought to recruit unskilled laborers at the lowest possible price. This network of employment agents told all kinds of glowing stories of a better life in the northern Land of Promise.

> Railroad tickets were dispensed gratis or advanced against forthcoming wages; trains backed into small towns and steamed away with most of the young and fit. . . .[6]

A few southern cities reacted in alarm and prohibited the soliciting of Black laborers from within their bounds.

This accelerated movement of Blacks out of the South impinged on the Black woman's moral situation in very definite ways. Black women migrated North in greater numbers than Black men.[7] Tens of thousands of Black women came seeking social democracy and economic opportunities. They soon found that their situation as women was much more difficult than that of migrant Black men.

Economic necessity dictated that most Black women who migrated to the northern urban centers find work immediately. In order to survive themselves and to provide for their families Black women once again found only drudge work available to them. Black men worked as porters, janitors, chauffeurs, window cleaners, elevator operators and menials in industry, but the restriction of white immigrant women during World War One relegated Black women to the domestic jobs which northern white women scorned or considered demeaning. Racist and male supremacist constraints forced Black women into a status of live-in domestic servants, wherein Black women tried to earn a living as cooks, cleaners, washerwomen and wet nurses under very hard and exhausting conditions.[8]

As a result of the widespread racial animosity of the white factory employers and their employees, Blacks found scant acceptance in northern communities. Small numbers of Black women were allowed inside the industrial manufacturing system but were confined to the most tedious, strenuous and degrading occupations.

White manufacturers alleged that undeniable hostility by white labor and the lack of separate entrances, doorways, drinking water buckets and cups, pay windows and lavatories forced them to exclude Black women from skilled jobs and craft positions.

> White women had no intentions of working alongside black women; even if some of them did speak of sexual equality, most did not favor racial equality.
> . . . Fear of competing with blacks as well as the possible loss of job status associated with working with blacks caused white workers to oppose any efforts to have blacks as fellow workers.[9]

In conjunction with the doctrine of white supremacy, northern Black women continued to experience discrimination in both the public and private sectors. As a result of the racist stereotypes of their lewdness and immorality which "emanated from sexual exploitation of slaves by white masters," Black women were subjected to discrimination and pettiness of all kinds.[10]

The interaction of race and sex in the labor market exacted a heavy toll on the Black woman, making all aspects of migration a problem of paramount ethical significance. As a wife and mother, the Black migrant woman was responsible for transmitting the culture, customs and values of the Black community to her children. At the same time that she was trying to organize family life according to her traditional roles, the male-dominated industrial society required that she serve as the catalyst in the transition process from the rural South to the urban North. Her own unfamiliarities and adaptation difficulties had to be repressed because she was responsible for making a home in crowded, sub-standard housing, finding inner-city schools that propagated literacy for her children while earning enough income to cover the most elementary needs. Many landlords refused housing to Black women with children. They preferred to provide room and board at excessive rates to single Black men who were thought to be at the height of their wealth-producing capacity.[11] During this period of migration, large scale urban riots by whites became the typical northern hate-expression of the southern, rural lynching and burning of Black people.[12]

In 1918 the Black migrant situation was summed up this way:

If the black man loafs in the South he starves. If he works in the South he is poorly paid, more or less in kind—chips and whetstones—and his wife becomes a 'pan-toter.' If he leaves his own estate in the South and goes to work in Northern industry, he is mobbed and killed.

He was brought to these shores from Africa a captive. He is held by his captors in economic bondage today—forbidden to rise above the lowest serving class. He is herded by himself in a ghetto, and if, while he is there, he reverts to the jungle type, he is burned alive. If he tries to break out of his ghetto, and, by assimilating the white man's civilization, rise, he is driven out by his white brothers.

If he goes to school, he becomes discontented and is unhappy and dissatisfied with his social status. If he does not go to school and remains ignorant, he is then only a 'coon,' whom everybody exploits, and who has to cheat and swindle in return, or go down in poverty to begging and shame. There aren't ships enough in the world to take him back to the land of his freedom; there isn't enough for him here except on the crowded bottom rung of the ladder, and there, always, the grinding heel of those climbing over him topward is mangling his black hands.

Race riots, lynching, political ostracism, social boycott, economic serfdom. No wonder he sings:

'Hard Trials—
Great tribulations,
Hard Trials
I'm gwine for to live with the Lord!'[13]

The Black woman who signed up for a "Justice Ticket" and migrated north shared the conditions suffered by all migrants in the Black community. She often found herself in a situation of

. . . misery and overcrowding, physical pain, sickness, poverty, cold, rain, wind rattling the boards, puddles seeping under the doors, fear of police, darkness, inhuman conditions, and suffering, endless suffering.[14]

The Black woman's added burden was that she was held accountable for mollifying the effects of these adverse conditions.[15]

The Moral Situation of the Black Woman Between the World Wars

World War I and II brought about the most visible changes in the Black woman's moral situation. Under coercive pressure from the Black community, the federal government was forced to take definite steps to halt racial discrimination in war industries.[16] With depleted labor reserves, large numbers of Black people were hired to manufacture ammunition, iron and steel products.[17] This employment policy was gradually repeated in other industries.

In segregated plants and factories, Black women attained semi-skilled, skilled and supervisory positions. A few even were granted limited rights in auxiliary unions. Most Black women, however, were assigned the most arduous tasks, worked in the least skilled jobs and received lower wages that their white counterparts.[18] Eugene Gordan and Cyril Briggs capsuled the plight of the Black woman during this period of history:

> In a society based on production for profit to be both a
> woman worker and a Negro is to suffer a double handicap.[19]

Nevertheless, these new economic opportunities at slightly better wages provided a positive change in the overall status of the Black woman.

The majority of Black women with any degree of formal education went into teaching.[20] A few pursued medical careers but encountered numerous obstacles when they sought internships which were the prerequisite for certification.[21] Black women also worked as administrators in the segregated hospitals which served the Black community. They contributed significantly to the development and work in the Black-run dispensaries, clinics and training schools. They rendered service throughout the Black community in hygenic care, preventive medicine and midwifery.[22] Smaller numbers of Black women penetrated the legal profession so as to distinguish themselves as laywers.[23]

The stringent application of Jim Crow laws and practices prevented Blacks from entering the 'free-enterprise world of the American marketplace.' Black women, along with Black men, operated service establishments and retail stores in all-Black communities. With limited kinds of businesses open to them, a minimal number of Black women excelled as funeral directors, seamstresses, hat makers, owners of pressing clubs and pioneers in the field of beauty culture.[24]

Underrepresented in almost all the professions, with the exception of education and social work, Black women formed their own professional associations.[25] The federations of women's clubs and sororities developed into a collective body with a very strong public influence.[26] Also, the wives of Black men in the fields of ministry, medicine and law formed auxiliaries to coordinate their pursuits against the "unbearable conditions" of segregation.

The status of Black women in the areas of music, dance, drama and film blossomed during these years. Bessie Smith, Marian Anderson, Mahalia Jackson, Katherine Dunham and Lena Horne symbolized the imaginative and creative minds that existed among some of the women in the Black community. These women expressed with intriguing styles some of the artistic talents of Black women.[27]

The Depression of the 1930s hit the Black community with great intensity.[28] Blacks, hungry and heartsick, stood in souplines, breadlines and picketlines. The Black community suffered catastrophically. The New Deal (1933–1939) administered dole and work projects to impoverished Blacks as well as the rest of the population.[29] For the first time in the history of this country a few Black women were allowed to participate freely and frequently in government decision-making. Federal programs and projects designed for Black people opened up job opportunities for Black women and men in all levels of the government.

Black women were hired to work in civil service jobs as statisticians, interviewers, office managers, case aides, clerks, stenographers, secretaries, and librarians. Thousands of young Black females worked for the Civilian Conservation Corps and the National Youth Administration. In essence, Blacks were able to make a few gains in government employment which have not been reversed.

Racism during the New Deal period was manifested in the way that local managers implemented federal policies and allocated federal funds. Far too often, white managers capitulated to the local customs and practices of racism, thus denying Black people substantial amounts of aid supposedly issued to alleviate conditions of destitution. A case in point was the New Deal's Agricultural Adjustment Act (AAA). This program attempted to raise prices by controlling production of staple crops through cash subsidies to farmers. Due to racial discrimination, the condition of millions of Black sharecroppers worsened while the situation of numerous white planters grew more favorable.

In 1940 the Young Women's Christian Association became the first predominantly white woman's organization to provide numerous opportunities for Black women. The YWCA made provisions for Black membership on its personnel, finance and program planning committees. The YWCA also offered staff positions to Black women in the national council as well as in the local offices. The "Y" wiped out all salary and wage differentials between Black and white employees. Throughout the forties and fifties other white women organizations implemented similar open door policies. White women and Black women worked together on projects and issues related to changing the status of the Black female.[30]

In the years following the world wars, white mob violence, bloody race riots and 'hate strikes' broke out in northern and southern cities alike. Innocent Blacks were beaten, dragged by vehicles and forced out of their homes. Substantial amounts of Black-owned property were destroyed. Throughout the country, extra-legal barriers resurged to prevent social equality.[31]

Black WACs and WAVEs who served the country in war returned home to suffer all the segregation, discrimination and harrassment meted out to the Black male veteran.

> While waiting in a bus station at Elizabethtown, Ky., on July 9, 1945, three Negro members of the Women's Army Corps (W.A.C.) were set upon and beaten by civilian policemen. The beating occurred when they did not move promptly enough on orders to leave the "white" waiting room where they had sat down because the "colored" room was crowded. . . . One policeman was reported to have raised his club saying: "Down here, when we tell niggers to move, they move," and brought the club down on the head of one of the two younger women. The oldest of the three tried to shield the younger ones, and was badly mauled, dragged across the street and jailed.[32]

Blacks served the war effort as soldiers and civilians. Millions fought in the wars. Thousands served overseas in noncombatant labor battalions.[33] So, when they returned home they called for the "double V"—victory abroad and victory at home. Black veterans objected to the second-class treatment traditionally accorded them.

During this postwar period, a number of civilian women became heads of households. Marital instability, low remarriage rates and an increase in out-of-wedlock births resulted in large numbers of Black women becoming dependent on the social welfare system.[34]

In the early 1960s, like the late 1950s, there was considerable segregation in public and private facilities. Major civil rights organizations—National Association for the Advancement of Colored People, Congress of Racial Equality, Southern Christian Leadership Conference and Student Nonviolent Coordinating Committee[35] designed nonviolent, direct civil rights activities so as to end Jim Crowism, to increase Black political activities and representation, and to institutionalize a series of statutory and constitutional rights for Black people in the U.S. Many Black women with outstanding abilitities and skills were active in these organizations. Ella Baker, Fannie Lou Hamer, Daisy Bates, Erika H. Huggins, Dorothy Cotton and Dora McDonald were a few Black women who occupied prominent leadership positions. These women combined their justice commitments with action strategies. Thousands upon thousands of Black women participated in the sit-in campaigns, prayer marches, freedom rides and the voter registration projects. In essence, the Black women in the sixties formed coalitions with Black men and members of the white community to eschew agitation for persuasion against calculated racist policies in education, in industry and in politics.

The Moral Situation of the Black Woman in Contemporary Society

The moral situation of the Black woman in contemporary society is still a situation of struggle, a struggle to survive collectively and individually against the continuing harsh historical realities and pervasive adversities in today's world. The determining existential circumstance in which the Black woman finds herself in the 1980s is little better than the situation in the 1880s. The Korean and Vietnam wars, Federal government programs, civil rights movements, and voter-education programs have all had a positive impact on the Black woman's moral situation, but they have not been able to offset the negative effects of the inherent inequities which are inextricably tied to the history and ideological hegemony of racism, sexism, and class privilege.[36]

The persistent obstacles of poverty, gender discrimination and racial prejudice continue to enslave the Black woman and her family to hunger, disease and the highest rate of unemployment since World War II. Education, housing, health care and other necessities which were gained during the mid- and late 1960s are deteriorating faster now than ever before. The National Urban League in its publication *The State of Black America 1978* provides the supporting data of how the significant formal institutions in American life—the government, the national economy and education—functionally blunt and divert equality for Black women in general and Black female family heads in particular.[37]

The new forms of definitions and participation that opened up the barriers that systematically deprived Black women of equal opportunities emerged concomittantly with a depressed economy, limited resources and the increased demand for representation and benefits by students, prisoners, white women, undocumented workers, the elderly, the handicapped, homosexuals, white ethnics, as well as the diverse rights of the most recent immigrants from Cuba, Poland, Haiti and Southeast Asia.[38] Black women find that their moral situation over the past one hundred years has had constructive changes only for a few but has worsened for the many.

In dispelling some of the myths about the benefits the Black woman has reaped from the new economic and political order of American society, Sylvia Parker, in her article "Negro Women's Progress," says the following:

> Statistics on pay and job level always can be tailored to mislead, if not to lie. That's one of the first lessons a serious reporter of economics-like-it-is must learn. I've just relearned it in a new Census Bureau study tracing the progress of Negro women since 1960.
>
> The figures seem to show that the Negro woman, for decades at the very bottom of the U.S. economic ladder, is finally moving rapidly ahead and that she is even pulling ahead of the Negro man.

She concludes: "In sum, from next to nothing to a little may be a giant statistical step. But in real life, it's a baby's crawl."[39] According to the various sex and race groups, Black women still earn the least.

Abbey Lincoln demythologizes the Black woman's social progress in her cryptic depiction of the contemporary Black woman.

> Her head is more regularly beaten than any other woman's, and by her own man; she's the scapegoat for Mr. Charlie; she is forced to stark realism and chided if caught dreaming; her aspirations for her and hers are, for sanity's sake, stunted; her physical image has been criminally maligned, assaulted, and negated; she is the first to be called ugly, and never yet beautiful. . . .[40]

Both in the informal day-to-day life and in the formal organizations and institutions in society Black women are still the victims of
the aggravated inequities of the tridimensional phenomenon of race/
class/gender oppression.[41] This is the backdrop of the ethical context
of Black women. The context by which the Black woman's moral
situation is understood and assessed consists of

> . . . all those women who toiled under the lash for their
> masters, worked for and protected their families, fought against
> slavery, and who were beaten and raped but never subdued. It
> was those women who passed on to their nominally free female
> descendants a legacy of hard work, perserverance and self-
> reliance, a legacy of tenacity, resistance and insistence in sexual
> equality—in short, a legacy spelling out standards for a new
> womanhood.[42]

/1/   Valuable sources of statistical information have been assembled by the
Bureau of Census, *Negro Population in the United States, 1790–1915* and
Negroes in the United States, 1920–1932.
/2/   George Groh, *The Black Migration* (New York: Weybright and Talley,
1972); Hollis R. Lynch, *The Black Urban Condition: A Documentary History, 1866–1971* (New York: Thomas Y. Crowell Company, 1973); Emmett J.
Scott, *Negro Migration During the War* (first published in 1920; reprinted
in New York: Arno Press, 1969); T. F. Woofter, *Negro Problems in Cities*
(first published in 1928, reprinted in New York: Harper & Row, 1969).
/3/   Abraham Epstein, *The Negro Migrant in Pittsburgh* (New York: Arno
Press and the New York Times, 1969; originally published as a pamphlet in
1918 under the supervision of the School of Economics, University of
Pittsburgh).
/4/   Arna Bontemps and Jack Conroy, *Any Place But Here* (New York: Hill
& Wang, 1966).
/5/   Karl E. Taeuber and Alma F. Taeuber, *Negroes in Cities* (Chicago:
Aldine Publishing Company, 1965).
/6/   David L. Lewis, *When Harlem Was in Vogue* (New York: Alfred A.
Knopf, 1981).
/7/   According to *Negro Population in the United States 1790–1915*, five
women for every four Black men migrated out of the South.
/8/   D. Chaplin, "Domestic Service and the Negro," in A. Shostak and W.
Gamberg (eds.), *Blue Collar World* (Englewood Cliffs, N.J.: Prentice Hall,
1964); Alice Childress, *Like One of the Family: Conversations from a
Domestic Life* (Brooklyn: Independence Publishers, 1955); Robert Ham-
burger, *A Stranger in the House* (New York: Collier Books, a division of
MacMillan Publishing Company, Inc., 1978); G. Haynes, "Negroes in Domestic Service in the United States," *Journal of Negro History* 8 (1923):

384–442; David M. Katzman, *Seven Days a Week: Women and Domestic Service in Industrializing America* (New York: Oxford University Press, 1978); Lillian Pettengill, *Toilers of the Home* (New York: Doubleday, 1903). /9/ Sharon Harley and Rosalyn Tarborg-Penn (eds.), *The Afro-American Woman, Struggles and Images* (Port Washington, N.Y.: Kennikat Press, 1978), p. 8.
/10/ Sarah M. Grimke, *Letters on the Equality of the Sexes and the Conditions of Women* (Boston: Issac Knapp, 1838), p. 53. See also Saundra Towns, "The Black Woman as Whore: Genesis of the Myth," in *The Black Position*, no. 3, ed. by Gwendolyn Brooks (Detroit: Broadside Press, 1974).
/11/ D. Schultz, *Coming Up Black: Patterns of Ghetto Socialization* (Englewood Cliffs, N.J.: Prentice-Hall, 1969); Robert C. Weaver, *The Negro Ghetto* (first published in 1948, reprinted in New York: Russell and Russell, 1967).
/12/ Elliot M. Rudwick, *Race Riot at East St. Louis, July 2, 1917* (Southern Illinois University Press, 1964); Arthur Waskow, *From Race Riot to Sit-in: 1919 and the 1960s* (New York: Doubleday, 1966); and portions of Walter White, *Rope and Faggot, a Biography of Judge Lynch* (New York: Alfred A. Knopf, 1929).
/13/ A statement by William Allen White in the *Emporia Gazette*, 1918; quoted in Abraham Epstein's *The Negro Migrant in Pittsburgh* (New York: Arno Press, 1969), p. 45.
/14/ Coll. Folio, Denoel, texte integral No. 300 (Paris, 1975), pp. 213–14; quoted in *Migrant Women Speak*, Jean Guyot et al. (Geneva, Switzerland: Church Committee on Migrant Workers by World Council of Churches, 1978).
/15/ Ira De A. Reid, *The Negro Immigrant, His Background, Characteristics, and Social Adjustment, 1899–1937* (New York: Columbia University Press, 1949); also Florette Henri, *Black Migration: Movement North, 1900–1920* (Garden City, N.Y.: Doubleday, 1976); Louise V. Kennedy, *The Negro Peasant Turns Cityward* (New York: HMS Press, 1968; orig. pub. 1930).
/16/ Discussed in great detail by Jervis Anderson, *A. Philip Randolph: A Biographical Portrait* (New YorK: Harcourt Brace Jovanovich, 1972); for background, Charles S. Johnson, *Shadow of the Plantation* (Chicago: University of Chicago Press, 1934); Lorenzo Greene and Carter G. Woodson, *The Negro Wage Earner* (Washington, D.C.: Association for the Study of Negro Life and History, 1930); Sterling D. Spero and Abram L. Harris, *The Black Worker* (New York: Columbia University Press, 1931).
/17/ Kathryn Blod, *Negro Women War Workers* (Women's Bureau, U.S. Department of Labor, Washington, D.C.); Jean Brown, *The Negro Woman Worker* (Washington, D.C.: U.S. Government Printing Office, 1938); "Negro Women in Industry," *Opportunity* XII (September 1935).
/18/ Sadie T. M. Alexander, "Negro Women in Our Economic Life," *Opportunity: Journal of Negro Life* VIII (June 1930); Elizabeth Almquist, *Minorites, Gender and Work* (Lexington, Mass.: D.C. Heath and Company, 1979); Lorenzo Greene and Carter G. Woodson, *The Negro Wage Earner* (Washington, D.C.: Association for the Study of Negro Life and History, 1930); Sterling D. Spiro and Abram L. Harris, *The Black Worker* (New

York: Columbia University Press, 1931); U.S. Department of Labor, Women's Bureau, *Minority Women Workers: Statistical Overview* (Washington, D.C.: Government Printing Office, 1977); Phyllis A. Wallace, *Black Women in the Labor Force* (Boston: The Massachusetts Institute of Technology, 1980).

/19/   Eugene Gordan and Cyril Briggs, *The Position of Negro Women* (New York: Workers Library Publishers, 1935).

/20/   Jeanne Noble, *The Negro College Woman Graduate* (New York: Columbia University Press, 1954); Lance G.E. Jones, *The Jeanes Teacher in the United States, 1908–1933* (Chapel Hill: University of North Carolina Press, 1935); Edward T. James and Janet Wilson James, eds., *Notable American Women, 1607–1950: A Biographical Dictionary* (Cambridge: Harvard University Press, 1973).

/21/   There is only a brief and fragmented mention of Black women in Herbert Morais, *The History of the Negro in Medicine* (New York: Publishers Co., 1967); see James L. Curtis, M.D., *Blacks, Medical Schools, and Society* (Ann Arbor: University of Michigan Press, 1971), esp. the chapter on "Historical Perspectives"; Mary Roth Walsh, *"Doctors Wanted: No Women Need Apply": Sexual Barriers in the Medical Profession, 1835–1975* (New Haven: Yale University Press, 1977).

/22/   Mabel Keaton Staupers, "The Negro Nurse in America," *Opportunity* 15 (November 1937):339; see also "Educational Facilities for Colored Nurses and Their Employment," *Public Health Nursing* 17 (April 1925):203–04; Elizabeth Jones, "The Negro Woman in the Nursing Profession," *Messenger* 7 (July 1923):765.

/23/   Bettine Aptheker, *Woman's Legacy: Essays on Race, Sex, and Class in American History* (Amherst: The University of Massachusetts Press, 1982), esp. Chapter Five, "Quest for Dignity: Black Women in the Professions, 1865–1900."

/24/   I am grateful to Dr. Thelma Adair for this information (Conversations with Dr. Adair in July 1982 and April 1983).

/25/   W. Montague Cobb, "Not to the Swift: Progress and Prospects of the Negro in Science and the Professions," *Journal of Negro Education* 27 (Spring 1958):120–26; Jacquelyne Johnson, "Black Women in a Racist Society," in *Racism and Mental Health*, ed. Charles V. Willie et al. (Pittsburgh: University of Pittsburgh Press, 1973).

/26/   Sadie Gola Daniel, *Women Builders* (Washington, D.C.: Associated Publishers, 1931); Elizabeth Davis, *Lifting as They Climb: The National Association of Colored Women* (Washington, D.C.: National Association of Colored Women, 1903); Gerda Lerner, "Letters from Negro Women, 1827–1950," *Masses and Mainstream*, February 1951, pp. 24–33; Claudia Jones, *An End to the Neglect of the Problems of the Negro Women* (National Women's Commission, 1930); June Sochen, *The Unbridgeable Gap: Blacks and Their Quest for the American Dream, 1900–1930* (Chicago: Rand McNally Publishing company, 1972); *Mary Church Terrell, A Colored Woman in a White World* (Washington, 1940; reprinted 1968).

/27/   Chris Albertson, *Bessie Smith: Empress of the Blues* (New York: Schirmer Books, 1975); Marian Anderson, *My Lord, What a Morning* (New York: Viking, 1956); Mahalia Jackson, *Movin' Up* (New York: Avon, 1969);

Katherine Dunham, *Touch of Innocence* (New York: Cassell, 1960); Lena
Horne, *Lena* (New York: Doubleday, 19650: Jeanne Noble, "When Malindy
Sings," in *Beautiful, Also, Are The Souls of My Black Sisters: A History of
the Black Woman in America* (Englewood Cliffs, N.J.: Prentice-Hall, Inc.,
1978), pp. 209–87.

/28/   Bernard Sternsher, ed., *The Negro in the Depression and War: Pre-
lude to Revolution, 1930–1945* (Chicago: Quadrangle Books, 1961); Raymond Wolters, *Negroes and the Great Depression: The Problem of Economic Recovery* (Westport, Conn.: Greenwood Press, 1970); James Weldon
Johnson, *Negro Americans, What Now?* (New York: Viking Press, 1935).

/29/   Jerre Mangione, *The Dream and the Deal: The Federal Writers Project, 1935–1943* (New York: Avon Books, 1972); Leslie Fishel, "The Negro in
the New Deal Era," in *The Negro in the Depression and War.*

/30/   Additional information from conversations with Dr. Thelma Adair.

/31/   Arthur Waskow, *From Race Riot to Sit-In: 1919 and the 1960s* (New
York: Doubleday, 1966); there is much information about Blacks during this
period in Gunnar Myrdal, *An American Dilemma*, 2 vols. (New York:
Harper, 1944).

/32/   Cited in Herbert Aptheker, ed., *A Documentary History of the Negro
People in the United States, 1933–1945* (Secaucus, N.J.: The Citadel Press),
pp. 538–39.

/33/   Richard M. Dalfiume, *Desegregation of the U.S. Armed Forces:
Fighting on Two Fronts, 1939–1953* (Missouri: University of Missouri Press,
1969); Thomas W. Higginson, *Army Life in a Black Regiment* (New York:
Collier Books, 1962); Lee Nichols, *Breakthrough on the Color Front* (New
York: Random House, 1954); Richard Stillman II, *The Integration of the
Negro in the U.S. Armed Forces* (New York: Frederick A. Praeger, Pub-
lisher, 1968).

/34/   Andrew Billingsley, *Black Families in White America* (Englewood
Cliffs, N.J.: Prentice-Hall, inc., 1968); J. Miller and L. Ferman, *Welfare
Careers and Low Wage Employment* (Institute of Labor and Industrial
Relations, University of Michigan, December 1972); Heather I. Ross and
Isabel V. Sawhill, *Time of Transition: The Growth of Families Headed by
Women* (Washington, D.C.: Urban Institute, 1975); Phyllis A. Wallace,
Black Women in the Labor Force (Cambridge: The MIT Press, 1980).

/35/   James Farmer, *Freedom-When?* (New York: Random House, 1966);
Leon Friedman (ed.), *The Civil Rights Reader* (New York: Walker, 1967);
Langston Hughes, *Fight for Freedom: The Story of the NAACP* (New York:
Norton, 1962); C. F. Kellog, *The History of the National Association for the
Advancement of Colored People, Vol. 1, 1909–1920* (Baltimore: Johns
Hopkins Press, 1967); Martin Luther King, Jr., *Stride Toward Freedom:
The Montgomery Story* (New York: Harper & Row, 1958); James Peck,
Freedom Ride (New York: Simon and Schuster, 1962); Howard Zinn, *SNCC:
The New Abolitionists* (Boston: Beacon Press, 1964).

/36/   Gwendolyn Cherry et al., *Portraits in Color: The Lives of Colorful
Negro Women* (Paterson, N.J.: Pageant Books, 1962); H. H. Clarke, "The
Black Woman: A Figure in World History," *Essence*, June 1971, pp. 36–44;
Marianna W. Davis, *Contributions of Black Women to America* (New York:
Urban League, 1982); Mabel E. Deutrich and Virginia C. Purdy (eds.),

CLIO Was a Woman: Studies in the History of American Women (Washington, D.C.: Howard University Press, 1980); Nathan Hare and Julia Hare, "Black Woman 1970," *Transaction*, December 1970, pp. 65–68, 90; Gloria T. Hull, Patrica Bell Scott, and Barbara Smith, *All the Women are White, All the Blacks are Men, But Some of Us are Brave* (Old Westbury, N.Y.: Feminist Press, 1982); Jacquelyne Jackson, "A Critique of Lerner's Work of Black Women," *Journal of Social and Behavioral Sciences* 21 (1975): 63–89; Joyce Ladner, *Tomorrow's Tomorrow, the Black Woman* (Garden City, N.Y.: Doubleday & Company, 1971); Gerda Lerner (ed.), *Black Women in White America: A Documentary History* (New York: Random House, 1972); Inez Reid, *"Together" Black Women* (New York: Emerson Hall, 1971); La Frances Rodgers-Rose (ed.), *The Black Woman* (Beverly Hills, Ca.: Sage Publications, 1980); C. Stack, *All Our Kin: Strategies for Survival in a Black Community* (New York: Harper & Row, 1974); Robert Staples, *The Black Woman in America: Sex, Marriage and the Family* (Chicago: Nelson-Hall Publishers, 1973); Filomina Chioma Steady, *The Black Woman Cross-Culturally* (Boston: Schenkman Publishing Company, 1981); *The State of Civil Rights: 1977* (Washington, D.C.: U.S. Comission on Civil Rights, Government Printing Office, 1977).

/37/   The National Urban League, *The State of Black America 1978* (New York: National Urban League, 1978).

/38/   Joyce A. Ladner and Walter W. Stafford, "Defusing Race: Developments Since the Kerner Report," in *Impacts of Racism on White Americans*, ed. Benjamin P. Bowser and Raymond G. Hunt (Beverly Hills, Ca.: Sage Publications, 1981), pp. 51–69. Also, Marian Wright Edelman, *Portrait of Inequality: Black and White Children in America* (Washington, D.C.: Children's Defense Fund, 1980).

/39/   Quoted by Nathan Wright in "Black Power vs. Black Genocide," *The Black Scholar* 1, no. 2 (December 1969): 50. See also: Janice Gump, "Reality and Myth: Employment and Sex Role Ideology in Black Women," in *Psychology of Women: New Directions for Research*, ed. Julia Sherman and Florence Denmark (New York: Psychological Dimensions, 1979); Patricia Gurin and Anne Pruitt, "Counseling Implications of Black Women's Market Position, Aspirations and Expectancies," presented this paper at the meeting of the National Institute of Education's Conference in Washington, D.C., December 1975; Randall Puryear's article, "The Black Woman: Liberated or Oppressed?," in *Comparative Perspectives of Third World Women: The Impact of Race, Sex and Class*, ed. Beverly Lindsay (New York: Praeger Publishers, 1980), pp. 251–75; Deloris Aldridge, "Black Women in the Economic Market: A Battle Unfinished," *Journal of Social and Behavioral Sciences* 21 (1975).

/40/   Abbey Lincoln, "Who Will Revere the Black Woman?," *Negro Digest*, September 1966, p. 18. This reality is spelled out in explicit detail in Gloria Joseph's sections of *Common Differences: Conflicts in Black and White Feminist Perspectives*, ed. Gloria I. Joseph and Jill Lewis, Garden City, N.Y.: Anchor Press/Doubleday, 1981; C. Clark, "Black Studies or the Study of Black People," in *Black Psychology*, ed. St. Jones (New York: Harper & Row, 1972).

/41/   Herbert Aptheker, "The Negro Woman," *Masses and Mainstream*,

February 1949, pp. 10–17; J. Beckett, "Working Wives: A Racial Comparison," *Social Work*, November 1976; Felice George, "Black Woman, Black Man," *Harvard Journal of Afro-American Affairs* 2 (1971): 1–17; Nancy Hoffman, "White Woman, Black Woman: Inventing an Adequate Pedagogy," *Women's Studies Newsletter* 5 (Winter/Spring 1977): 21–24; Fletcher Knebel, "Identity, the Black Woman's Burden," *Look*, September 23, 1969; Joyce Ladner, "Women in Poverty—Its Roots and Effects," in *What's Happening to American Women* (Southern Newspaper Publishers, 1970); Sonia Pressman, "Job Discrimination and the Black Woman," The Crisis, March 1970; Michele Wallace, *Black Macho and the Myth of the Super-Woman* (New York: Warner Books, Inc., 1980).

/42/   Angela Y. Davis, *Women, Race & Class* (New York: Random House, 1981).

CHAPTER III

THE BLACK WOMAN'S LITERARY TRADITION AS A SOURCE FOR ETHICS

The combined force of the inherited tradition of race, sex and economic discrimination imposes on the vast majority of Black women a severely disadvantaged status. Black women in their development, analysis and appraisal of various coping mechanisms against the white-oriented, male structured society do not appeal to fixed rules or absolute principles of what is right or wrong and good or bad, but instead they embrace values related to the causal conditions of their cultural circumstances. The cherished assumptions of dominant ethical systems predicated upon both the existence of freedom and a wide range of choices have proven to be false in the real-lived texture of Black life. Thus, Black women have created and cultivated a set of ethical values that allow them to prevail against the odds, with moral integrity, in their ongoing participation in the white-male-capitalist value system. The best available literary repository for this underground treasury of values is the Black woman's literary tradition.

The story of the Afro-American has been told quite coherently and has repeatedly left the Black woman out of it in significant ways.[1] Seldom in history has a group of women been so directly responsible for exerting indispensable efforts to insure the well-being of both the Black family and the white. At the same time the Black woman is placed in such a sharp disadvantaged position as to accept obligingly the recording of her own story by the very ones who systematically leave her out.[2] Hence, the specificity of the Afro-American female experience is cryptically described by Black women in the Black woman's literary tradition.

Despite their tragic omission by the literary establishment, Black women have been expressing ideas, feelings and interpreta-

tions about the Black experience since the early days of the eigh-
teenth century.[3]

> Denied education and the opportunity to become liter-
> ate, slaves turned their verbal skills to oral storytelling, ser-
> mons, proverbs, boasts, elaborate courtship rituals, toasts and
> spirituals.[4]

Throughout the various periods of their history in the United States,
Black women have used their creativity to carve out "living space"
within the intricate web of multilayered oppression. From the beginning, they had to contend with the ethical ambiguity of racism,
sexism and other sources of fragmentation in this acclaimed land of
freedom, justice and equality. The Black woman's literary tradition
delineates the many ways that ordinary Black women have fashioned
value patterns and ethical procedures in their own terms, as well as
mastering, transcending, radicalizing and sometimes destroying
pervasive, negative orientations imposed by the mores of the larger
society.[5]

For instance, Black women and men, as early as the 1600s,
refused to obey the moral precepts held up to them by white
Christian slaveholders. They resented the white man's message of
docility which acted to render them defenseless in the face of white
violence. Living under a system of cheating, lying and stealing,
enslaved Blacks learned to consider these vices as virtues in their
dealings with whites.[6] The bittersweet irony of Afro-American experience forces Black people to examine critically the conventional,
often pretentious, morality of middle-class American ideals.[7]

Black writers in particular have had to deal with the par-
ochialism of white culture which projects racist images upon the
whole extent of the universe, giving Blacks a zero image of themselves. Sterling A. Brown summarized these zero-image stereotypes
in his 1933 article entitled "Negro Characters as Seen by White
Authors."

> The Negro has met with as great injustice in American
> literature as he has in American life. The majority of books
> about Negroes merely stereotype negro character. It is the
> purpose of this paper to point out the prevalence and history of
> these stereotypes. Those considered important enough for sep-
> arate classification, although overlappings do occur, are seven
> in number: (1) The Contented Slave, (2) The Wretched Free-

man, (3) The Comic Negro, (4) The Brute Negro, (5) The Tragic Mulatto, (6) The Local Color Negro, (7) The Exotic Primitive.[8]

Over against these stereotypes, the Black woman's literary tradition provides a rich resource and a cohesive commentary that brings into sharp focus the Black community's central values, which in turn frees Black folk from the often deadly grasp of these parochial stereotypes. The observations, descriptions and interpretations in Black literature are largely reflective of cultural experiences. They identify the frame of social contradiction in which Black people live, move and have their being. The derogatory caricatures and stereotypes ascribed to Black people are explicitly rejected. Instead, writings by Blacks capture the magnitude of the Black personality. Spanning from the antebellum period to today's complex technological society, Black women writers authenticate, in an economy of expressions, how Black people creatively strain against the external limits in their lives, how they affirm their humanity by inverting assumptions, and how they balance the continual struggle and interplay of paradoxes. Blacks win by losing, retain their blessings by giving them away.

The Black Woman's Literary Tradition Parallels Black History

The Black woman's literary tradition is a source in the study of ethics relative to the Black community, because the development of the Black woman's historical and literary legacy is tied up with the origin of Black people in America. Most of the writing by Black women captures the values of the Black community within a specific location, time and historical context.[9] The literary tradition is not centered automatically upon the will and whims of what an individual writer thinks is right or obligatory, nor even upon whatever she personally believes to be true for her own localized consciousness. The majority of Black women who engage in literary compositions hold themselves accountable to the collective values that underlie Black history and culture. Dexter Fisher makes the point this way:

> . . . to be totally centered on the self would be to forget one's history, the kinship of a shared community of experience,

the crucial continuity between past and present that must be
maintained in order to insure the future.[10]

From the early times to now, Black women's writings have
paralleled Black history. As creators of literature these women are
not formally historians, sociologists, nor theologians, but the patterns and themes in their writings are reflective of historical facts,
sociological realities and religious convictions that lie behind the
ethos and ethics of the Black community. As recorders of the Black
experience, Black women writers convey the Black community's
consciousness of values which enable them to find meaning, in spite
of social degradation, economic exploitation and political oppression. They record what is valued or regarded as good in the Black
community. Seldom, if ever, is their work art-for-art's-sake. "Whatever else may be said of it, Black American writing in the United
States has been first and last, as Saunders Redding once observed, a
'literature of necessity'."[11]

> The appeal of a basically utilitarian literature written to
> meet the exigencies of a specific historical occasion usually
> declines after the occasion has passed. That this is much less
> true of Black literature is due to the constant factors in Afro-
> American history—the Black presence and white racism.[12]

BLACK WOMEN WRITERS BEFORE 1800

The Black women who published before 1800 were slaves.
Lucy Terry (1730–1821), who commemorated an Indian raid on the
town of Deerfield, Massachusetts ("Bars Fight, August 28, 1746"),
was the first Black poet to be recognized in America.[13] In 1773,
Phillis Wheatley (1753[?]–1784) was the first Afro-American
woman[14] and the second American woman[15] to publish a book of
poetry. It was entitled *Poems on Various Subjects, Religious and
Moral*.[16] Wheatley was trained in the classical disciplines and mastered both the English and Latin languages in exquisite form. With
no Black audience, she omitted any reference to her Blackness,
femaleness, or the conditions of her most intimate experiences.[17]
Instead, Wheatley imitated the felicity of thought and the literary
style of the patron slaveowners. The themes of her elegies, com-
memorations and devotional poems can be exclusively classified as
Christian apologies for slavery.

> 'Twas mercy brought me from my Pagan land,
> Taught my benighted soul to understand
> That there's a God, that there's a Saviour too:
> Once I redemption neither sought nor knew.
> Some view our sable race with scornful eye;
> "Their colour is a diabolic dye."
> Remember, Christians, Negroes, black as Cain,
> May be refined, and join the angelic train.
>
>   Phillis Wheatley,
>   "On Being Brought from Africa to America"[18]

Both Wheatley and Terry overcame the obstacles to literacy but found their status as slaves directly controlling what they said and how they said it.

BLACK WOMEN WRITERS OF THE NINETEENTH CENTURY

By the mid-nineteenth century, the enslavement of human beings was ruled illegal in the new state constitutions and in various legislatures. The country was grappling with industrial labor, abolition of slavery and women suffrage. And, once again, we find the literary themes of Black women writers intimately related to the varieties of coercion, repression and discrimination inflicted on the Black community.[19]

A surprising number of slave narratives, autobiographies and biographies has survived to attest to Black women's experience during this era. This literature captures the abominable daily practices of injustice that Blacks suffered under slavery. It also records the Black woman's participation in the searing conflicts for freedom.

Many northern abolitionists used the *Narrative of Sojourner Truth, A Bondswoman of Olden Time, Emancipated by the New York Legislature in the Early Part of the Present Century; with a History of Her Labors and Correspondence Drawn from Her "Book of Life"* and other chronicles by former slaves to buttress their arguments for a radical reconstruction after the Civil War. Also, during the nineteenth century, nine Black women published their autobiographies. Their life stories offer penetrating and unusual insight into the experiences of Black women:

Memoirs of Elizabeth Eldridge (1846)
Louisa Picquet, the Octoroom; or, The Inside Views of Southern Domestic Life (1861)

Behind the Scenes by Elizabeth Keckley, Formerly a Slave, but
   More Recently Modiste and Friend to Mrs. Abraham Lin-
   coln; or, Thirty Years a slave and Four Years in the White
   House (1868)
Meditations from the Pen of Mrs. Maria W. Stewart (1879)
Sylvia Dubois (now 116 year old) a biografy of the slav who
   whipt her mistress and gand her freedom (1883)
Aunt Lindy: A Story Founded on Real Life (1893)
Kate Dormigold's *A Slave Girl's Story* (1889)
Susie King Taylor's *Reminiscences of My Life in Camp with the
   33rd United States Colored Troops, late 1st S.C. Volunteers*
   (1902)
Annie I. Campbell Burton's *Memories of Childhood Slavery
   Days* (1909)

Three Black women published biographies which touch on every
aspect of Black life:

Josephine Brown's *Biography of an American Bondsman* (1855)
Sarah Bradford's *Scenes in the Life of Harriet Tubman* (1869)
Helen Pitts Douglass' *In Memorium: Frederick Douglass*
   (1897)

Incidents in the Life of a Slave Girl (1861) is Harriet Brent Jacob's
"told to" account written by Lydia Maria Child. This book effectively charts the daily existence of the Black female slave. Designated as sub-human personal-property, the Black woman slave was
used and disposed of in whatever way slaveowners wished. Martha
Griffith Brown's *Autobiography of a Female Slave* (1857) and Emily
Pierson's *The Fugitive* (n.d.) are classified as fictionized truth. The
two novels depict the trials and tribulations that come with being
Black and female in a society that despises both.

In 1859, Frances Ellen Watkins Harper (1825–1911), the best
known antislavery poet, published the first short story by a Black
American, entitled "The Two Offers." It is a story about a white
woman committed to the abolition of slavery. As an active member
of abolitionist and suffragist groups, Harper's choice of subject matter, in this story, as well as in most of her writings, was clearly
selected to expose the inhumanity of the twin evils—racism and
sexism. Harper, nevertheless, was caught in the dilemma of most
Black women as pioneer writers.[20] She wanted to present wholistic
images of Black life without exclusively limiting herself to racial
themes. In a letter she wrote to Thomas Hamilton, editor of the

Anglo-African in 1861, Harper summed up the dilemma in this manner:

> If our talents are to be recognized we must write less of
> issues that are particular and more of feelings that are general.
> We are blessed with hearts and brains that compass more than
> ourselves in our present plight. . . . We must look to the future
> which , God willing, will be better than the present or the past,
> and delve into the heart of the world. [21]

Charlotte L. Forten (Grimke) (1837–1914), a member of Phila-delphia's most prestigious Black family, was the first Black woman to publish a personal journal detailing her day-to-day activities, her involvement in the Salem Female Anti-Slavery Society and her work with the Port Royal Experiment (the transition experiment of ex-slaves into free citizens in Port Royal, South Carolina) from 1854 to 1864. [22]

Between 1890 and 1920, nearly thirty novels by Black authors were published in the United States (as opposed to only three known novels before 1890). [23] The two earliest novels by Black women were *Clarence and Chlorine; or, In God's Way* (1891) by Amelia E. Johnson, and *Iola Leroy; or, Shadows Uplifted* (1892) by Frances E. W. Harper. [24] These books capture the mood of cultural dualism, the destiny of newly freed Blacks and the quest for equality which were the paramount concerns of Black writers during the post-Reconstruction years.

BLACK WOMEN WRITERS OF THE EARLY TWENTIETH CENTURY

The beginning of the twentieth century found the events in Black history and the themes in Black literature inextricably bound as one. The years from 1877 to 1920 were a period of virtually complete disenfranchisement of Black people from the national mainstream in America. Segregation was legally maintained in al-most every area of social contact, the horrors of lynching became an acceptable reality and the blackface minstrel-burlesque shows were used to reinforce the stereotype of Blacks as inferior.

The few Black women who were published during the early years of the twentieth century were women of the caliber of Anna Julia Haywood Cooper (1858–1964), [25] Hallie Quinn Brown (1845[?]–1949), [26] and Ida B. Wells Barnett (1862–1931). [27] These women as crusaders for justice acquired a prophetic quality in their writing. Employing subjects, language, attitudes and scenes from the Black folk culture, they recorded the grimness of struggle among the least visible people in this society. Given the hostile environment, deteriorating conditions, along with the enduring humiliation of social ostracism of the prewar years, it is easily understood how and why these writers produced a literature of protest, critical essays, and social polemics about the most pressing problems of their race.[28] Their speeches, pamphlets, articles and letters are an intrinsic part of the Black literary experience. In both their lives and their work, the Black women writers of this period maintained that one of the most serious and unyielding problems of the twentieth century is the question of color—the single most determining factor of Black existence in America.[29]

BLACK WOMEN WRITERS OF THE RENAISSANCE PERIOD

In their cry against the ideological supremacy of racist practices and values, Black artists, writers, and scholars won prominence in a wide variety of fields during the 1920s. Their music, dance, art and literature became saleable items. White people in the U.S. as well as from Europe flocked to Harlem to experience the wealth and variety of Black talent.

The three most important Black women writers who participated in the unprecedented literary upsurge of the Negro Renaissance (often referred to as the Harlem Renaissance)[30] in the decades following World War I are Jessie Redmond Fauset, Nella Larsen and Zora Neale Hurston.[31] Their writings provide prophetic insights as to the sociocultural impulses and political beliefs affecting the turn of events in the Black community from 1923 to 1933. Drawing from their own backgrounds, observations and experiences, these women crystallize in words the complexity of Black life during the years in question.

Jessie Redmond Fauset (1882–1961), a Phi Beta Kappa graduate of Cornell University, used her poetry, short stories, essays and four novels to depict honestly and accurately her combined experiences of racism and sexism. Fauset's heroines assert the narrow-minded, the caste-ridden, the colorlessness of the middle strata of Black life.[32]

Nella Larsen's (1893–1960) two novels, *Quicksand* (1928) and *Passing* (1929), explore the themes of cultural dualism and the superficiality of color differences within the Black community.

Larsen's depiction of the unpleasant consequences of Blackness in the larger society and the pressures of racism on the Black personality encompasses everything—life, death and hope.[33]

Zora Neale Hurston (1903[?]–1960), the only Renaissance female writer from a Southern background (whose life and literature will be elaborated in explicit detail in chapters IV and V), realized the richness and wholeness of Black culture and built her writings on it.

BLACK WOMEN WRITERS SINCE WORLD WAR II

Even though Black women writers have continued from the period of urbanization of World War II to the present to record multifarious experiences that affirm the values by which Black people live, they have been allowed to occupy only an obscure niche within the overall literary tradition of this country.[34] The paucity of publications is a result of the predominantly white, patriarchal control of the literary canon. Examining only genres developed in the European literary lineage, the conventional corpus of the national literature has become severely restricted.[35] Anthologies, bibliographical essays, biographical sketches of writers' lives, critical/historical/analytical studies, and other literary texts either exclude Black women or include their tradition as a token, minor afterthought.[36] This type of disenfranchisement reflects the racial prejudices of the dominant group in society, thus, ignoring the diverse, eclectic and multi-cultural traditions that exist within the literary life of America. In *The Forgotten Pages of American Literature*, Gerald W. Haslam identifies this dynamic:

> American literary scholarship has traditionally tended to reflect the social and racial prejudices of the nation's dominant white majority and, in so doing, has denied the efficacy of values reflected in the forgotten pages of our national literature: what have the members of America's ethnic minorities been saying, and how have they said it?[37]

From 1773, when the first book by a Black woman was published, until the present, we find only a tidy, nonsprawling collection of Black women's literature. All too frequently, writings by Black women that eventually get published are isolated in small press publications that are inaccessible or published by regional press; and when their work is requested it is often out of print. Mary Helen Washington, in her essay "These Self-Invented Women: A

Theoretical Framework for a Literary History of Black Women,"
sums up this literary injustice in this manner:

> In the Afro-American literary tradition the power to
> select and influence and thus become a model, precursor, a
> literary foreparent is a power that has been almost exclusively
> in the hands of men—both white and black.[38]

So, in a world that is both racist and male centered, the
opportunities for Black women to display initiative and enterprise
have been severely restricted and limited. Black women writers
have been recognized and published in large numbers only during
the final quarter of the twentieth century. Since the sixties, Black
women writers have been acclaimed by some of the literary critics as
the eloquent "prophets for a new day."[39] Their writing continues to
parallel Black history, and to arouse feelings not previously experienced.

> These new feelings, in turn call our attention to still
> more facts not previously noticed. Both the new feelings and
> the new facts, therefore, upset our intentional orientations, so
> that our blindness is little more removed.[40]

The Black Woman's Literary Tradition
Uses the Oral Narrative Devices
of the Black Community

The irresistible power in the Black woman's literary tradition is
its power to convey the assumed values of the Black community's
oral tradition in its grasp for meaning. The suppression of book
learning and the mental anguish of intellectual deprivation obliged
Black literature to be expressed mainly in oral form.[41] What is
critical for my purpose is that these women reveal in their novels,
short stories, love lyrics, folktales, fables, drama and nonfiction, a
psychic connection with the cultural tradition transmitted by the
oral mode from one generation to the next. As serious writers who
have mastered in varying degrees the technique of their craft, Black
women find themselves causally dependent on the ethos and ethics
of the Black masses. Black women writers draw heavily upon the
Black oral culture.[42]

Folk tales, songs (especially the blues), sermons, the dozens, and the rap[43] are all expressions of creativity which provide Black writers wtih the figurative language and connotations of dim hallways and dank smells, caged birds and flowers that won't sprout, curdled milk and rusty razors, of general stores and beauty parlors, nappy edges and sheened legs. The social and cultural forces within the Black oral tradition form the milieu out of which Black writers create.

Black women writers document the attitudes and morality of women, men, girls and boys who chafe at and defy the restrictions imposed by the dominant white-capitalist value system. They delineate in varying artistic terms the folk treasury of the Black community, in terms of how Black people deal with poverty and the ramifications of power, sex as an act of love and terror, the depersonalization that accompanies violence, the acquisition of property, the drudgery of a workday, the inconsistencies of chameleon-like racism, teenage mothers, charlatan sorcerers, swinging churches, stoic endurance and stifled creativity. Out of this storehouse of Black experiences comes a "vitally rich, ancient continuum" of Black wisdom.[44]

As Black female artists, they creatively identify the implicit, positive metaphors of interrelated symbols used in the community's effort to assert its ingenuity and self-sufficiency. For instance, Ann Petry's *The Street* (1946) depicts the inevitability of crime for Black mothers who provide for their families against all odds in hostile urban environments. Gwendolyn Brooks' novel *Maud Martha* (1953) focuses on the coming of age for the Black woman-child who has dark complexion and untameable hair and must learn how to ward off assaults to her human dignity. Margaret Walker's *Jubilee* (1966) captures the richness of Black folk culture: the songs, sayings, customs, food, medicinal remedies and the language. This historical novel is the character Vyry's mosaic movement from slavery to freedom.

This capacity to catch the oral tradition also means an ability to portray the sense of community. Barbara Christian in *Black Women Novelists: The Development of a Tradition, 1892–1976* recognizes this unique characteristic common to Black women's literature as the "literary counterpart of their communities' oral tradition."

> The history of these communities, seldom related in textbooks, are incorporated into the tales that emphasize the marvelous, sometimes the outrageous, as a means of teaching a

lesson. In concert with their African ancestors, these story-
tellers, both oral and literary, transform gossip, happenings,
into composites of factual events, images, fantasies and fables.[45]

This important characteristic of Black women's writing is in-
creasingly recognized by literary interpreters. Jeanne Noble says,
"We would be scripted in history with little true human understanding without the black writer telling it like it is." Mary Helen
Washington says that this deeper-than-surface knowledge of and
fondness for the verbal tradition is a truth that is shared by the
majority of Black women writers.

> This remembrance of things past is not simply self-in-
> dulgent nostalgia. It is essential to her vision to establish
> connections with the values that nourish and strengthen her.[46]

Verta Mae Grosvenor captures the essence of the oral tradition at
the very outset of her book, *Vibration Cooking:*

> Dedicated to my mama and my grandmothers and my
> sisters in appreciation of the years that they have worked in
> miss ann's kitchen and then came home to TCB in spite of
> slavery and moynihan report.[47]

Marcia Gillespie, in the 1975 May editorial of *Essence*, concludes
that Black women are always releasing the memories of their mamas
and grandmamas.

> . . . the race memory of our women who, though bur-
> dened, neither broke nor faltered in their faith in a better
> world for us all.[48]

Gail Jones maintains that in all of her novels, *Corregidora*,
Eva's Man, and *Palmares*, and short stories, *White Rat: A Collection*,
she draws on the storehouse of folklore which expresses the morality
of the Black community. All of her characters utilize the original
language of the people. They talk convincingly and naturally, without diluting the frankness of the documented experiences being
transmitted in the oral tradition. Alice Walker's novels, *Meridian*,
The Third Life of Grange Copeland and *The Color Purple*; volumes
of poetry, *Revolutionary Petunias and Other Poems, Once, Good-
night, Willie Lee, I'll see you in the morning*; collections of short

stories, *In Love and Trouble* and *You Can't Keep a Good Woman Down*, emerge from a profound respect for oral histories. Walker provides realistic appraisals of given situations. Her own summation is that one's personal identity depends on the continuity from past to present.

Black women's combination of the Western literate form with their unique sensibility to the oral narrative devices expresses with authority, power and eloquence the insidious effects of racism, sexism and economic exploitation on members of their communities. By not abandoning the deeply ingrained traditions of the Black community, these writers are then able to utilize common sources which illustrate common values that exist within the collective vision of Black life in America.[49]

The Black Woman's Literary Tradition Capsulizes the Insularity of the Black Community

Black female writers, as participant-observers, capsulize on a myriad of levels, the insularity of their home communities. Due to systemic, institutionalized manifestations of racism in America, the Black community tends to be situated as marginated islands within the larger society. The perpetual powers of white supremacy continue to drop down on the inhabitants of the Black community like a belljar—surrounding the whole, yet separating the Black community's customs, mores, opinions and system of values from those in other communities. Black female authors emphasize life within the community, not the conflict with outside forces. In order to give faithful pictures of important and comprehensive segments of Black life, these writers tie their character's stories to the aesthetic, emotional and intellectual values of the Black community.

> Stories do occur in places, but what the women writers emphasize is the importance of place and community as a character. By confining their landscapes of action to the community and examining the routines of daily life and feelings under a magnifying glass, black women writers accomplish two things: they highlight the art of daily living and give back to the community a mirror of itself; and in that mirror, they can correct the stereotypes about black life that seem to proliferate so irresponsibly in our society.[50]

Black women writers find value consciousness in their home communities which serve as the orthodox framework for their circular literary structure. As insiders they venture into all strata of Black life. Black women writers transform the passions and sympathies, the desires and hurts, the joys and defeats, the praises and pressures, the richness and diversity of real-lived communities into the stuff for art through the medium of literature.

> . . . Zora Neale Hurston's Janie (in *Their Eyes Were Watching God*) gives the meaning of her story back to the community, Seline (in Paule Marshall's *Browngirl, Brownstone*) gives her mother and the Barbadian community its due, Grange Copeland (in Alice Walker's *Third Life of Grange Copeland*) gives Ruth the sum of his people's wisdom so she might continue on, and Claudia (in Toni Morrison's *The Bluest Eye*) tells us that the cause of Pecola's tragedy is the land of her town.[51]

Mary Helen Washington, in her excellent essay "In Pursuit of Our Own History," lifts up the community-based female characters as representing the distinct and unique patterns of the heroic image found in Black women's literature. These heroines are not superficial characters. Instead, they are ordinary women who embrace the great wealth of knowledge amassed by the Black female community over many years.

> These are women who struggle to forge an identity larger than the one society would force upon them. They are aware and conscious, and that very consciousness is potent. In searching out their own truths, they are rebellious and risk-taking, and they are not defined by men.[52]

The protagonist in the Black man's literary tradition moves quite differently. Christian contends that Black men are less circular in movement. The movement for the Black male writer is outward and downward. The prominent Black male writers develop storylines that move horizontally within the community with the major development occurring once the characters have moved away from their natal roots.[53] In their classics, *Invisible Man*,[54] *Native Son*, *Black Boy*,[55] *Another Country*,[56] to mention some of the best known, the male protagonists step "beyond their communities in an attempt to exert some control over their lives," find themselves in a

hole, and move downward as the heroes acknowledge their predicament.

> It is through their confrontation, buttressed by their own
> often imperfect understanding of their own communities, that
> they seek their identity. These male protagonists discover their
> identity as racial beings, their experience as members of a
> particular community, or of a particular family, is not as crit-
> ical.[57]

Male writers tend to focus their literature on the confrontation
between the white and Black worlds.[58] Black women writers concentrate more intensely on the Black community and the human
relationships within that community.

Using the subject matter close to the heart of Black America,
the Black woman's literary tradition shows how the results of slavery
and their consequences forced the Black woman into a position of
cultural custodian.[59] Black female protagonists are women with
hard-boiled honesty, a malaise of dual-allegiance, down-to-earth
thinking, the ones who are forced to see through shallowness,
hypocrisy and phoniness in their continual struggle for survival.
Alice Childress paints the picture of the cultural custodian in this
manner:

> The emancipated Negro woman of America did the only
> thing she could do. She earned a pittance by washing, ironing,
> cooking, cleaning, and picking cotton. She helped her man,
> and if she often stood in the front line, it was to shield him from
> a mob of men organized and dedicated to bring about his
> destruction.
> The Negro mother has had the bitter job of teaching her
> children the difference between the White and the Colored
> signs before they are old enough to attend school. She had to
> train her sons and daughters to say "sir" and "Ma'am" to those
> who were their sworn enemies.
> She couldn't tell her husband "a white man whistled at
> me," not unless she wanted him to lay down his life before
> organized killers who strike only in anonymous numbers. Or
> worse, perhaps to see him helpless and ashamed before her.
> Because he could offer no protection or security, the
> Negro woman has worked with and for her family. She built
> churches, schools, homes, temples and college educations out
> of soapsuds and muscles.[60]

Conclusion

The work of Black women writers can be trusted as seriously mirroring Black reality. Their writings are important chronicles of Black survival. In their plots, actions, and depictions of characters, Black women writers flesh out the positive attributes of Black folks who are "hidden beneath the ordinariness of everyday life." They also plumb their own imaginations in order to crack the invidiousness of the worn-out stereotypes. Their ideas, themes and situations provide truthful interpretations of every possible shade and nuance of Black life.

Black women writers partially, and often deliberately, embrace the moral actions, religious values and rules of conduct handed down by word of mouth in the folk culture. They then proceed in accord with their tradition to transform the cultural limitations and unnatural restrictions in the community's move toward self-authenticity. Francis S. Foster concludes:

> Black art is not a luxury to be isolated and viewed by a select group of persons. It is an attempt to communicate realities. It is an attempt to meet the needs and desires of all Black people. It strives to inform them of their past and its implications, to identify their enemies, and thus to give them the strength and vision to bring about the necessary changes in their existence.[61]

The special distinctiveness of most Black women writers is the knack to keep their work intriguing and refreshing amidst its instructiveness. They know how to lift the imagination as they inform, how to touch the emotions as they record, how to delineate specifics so that they are applicable to oppressed humanity everywhere.[62] In essence, there is no better source for comprehending the "real-lived" texture of Black experience and the meaning of the moral life in the Black context than the Black woman's literary tradition. Black women's literature offers the sharpest available view of the Black community's soul.

/1/   The leading sources are Lerone Bennett, Jr., *Before the Mayflower: A History of the Negro in America 1619–1964* (New York: Penguin, 1966); John Hope Franklin, *From Slavery to Freedom: A History of American*

Negroes, 5th ed. (New York: Knopf, 1980); E. Franklin Frazier, *The Negro in the United States* (New York: Macmillan Co., 1949); August Meier and Elliott P. Rudwick, eds., *Making of Black America*, 2 vols. (New York: Atheneum, 1969). The most underrepresented area in Black history concerns Black women. These sources pay little (almost no) attention to the Black woman's role in the making of America.

/2/   For example, William Chafe, *The American Woman: Her Changing Social, Economic and Political Roles, 1920–1970* (New York: Oxford University Press, 1972) mentions "Negro" women twice.

/3/   Richard K. Barksdale and Kenneth Kinnamon, eds., *Black Writers in America: A Comprehensive Anthology* (New York: Macmillan Co., 1972); Robert Bone, *Down Home: A History of Afro-American Short Fiction from its Beginnings to the End of the Harlem Renaissance* (New York: G. P. Putnam's Sons, 1975); Arna Bontemps, "The Black Contribution to American Letters: Part I," in *The Black American Reference Book*, ed. Mable M. Smythe (Englewood Cliffs, N.J.: Prentice-Hall, Inc., 1976); Arthur P. Davis and Saunders Redding, eds., *Cavalcade: Negro American Writing from 1760 to the Present* (Boston: Houghton Mifflin, 1971); Vernon Loggins, *The Negro Author, His Development in America, from 1760 to 1900* (New York: Columbia University Press, 1931; reprint ed., Port Washington, N.Y.: Kennikat Press, 1964); Kenny Jackson Williams, *They Also Spoke: An Essay on Negro Literature in America, 1787–1930* (Nashville, Tenn.: Townsend Press, 1970).

/4/   Dexter Fisher, ed., *The Third Woman: Minority Women Writers of the United States* (Boston: Houghton Mifflin Co., 1980), p. 139.

/5/   Jervis Anderson, "Black Writing: The Other Side," *Dissent* 15 (May–June 1968): 233–242; Rebecca C. Barton, *Race Consciouness and American Negro Literature* (Copenhagen: Arnold Busck, 1934); John Henrik Clarke, "The Origin and Growth of Afro-American Literature," *Journal of Human Relations* 16 (Third Quarter 1968): 368–384; "The Negro Woman in American Literature," *Freedomways* 6 (Winter 1966); 8–25 (remarks by the panel members at a conference on "The Negro Writer's Vision of America," Sarah Wright, Abbey Lincoln, Alice Childress, and Paule Marshall).

/6/   Albert J. Raboteau, *Slave Religion: The "Invisible Insitution" in the Antebellum South* (New York: Oxford University Press, 1978), passim.

/7/   Sterling Brown, *The American Negro: His History and His Literature* (New York: Arno, 1969); Johnetta B. Cole, "Culture: Negro, Black and Nigger," *Black Scholar* 1 (June 1972): 40–46; Cole maintains that the "new Black aesthetic" begins with the understanding that the Black experience in the United States is complex, for it involves three components—"those drawn from mainstream America, those which are shared in varying proportions with all oppressed peoples, and those which appear to be peculiar to Blacks." S. P. Fullwinder, *The Mind and Mood of Black America: Twentieth Century Thought* (Homewood, Ill.: Dorsey, 1969); Carolyn F. Gerald, "The Black Writer and His Role," in *The Black Aesthetic*, ed. Addison Gayle, Jr. (Garden City, N.Y.: Doubleday & Co., 1972); Herbert Hill, ed., *Anger, and Beyond: The Negro Writer in the United States* (New York: Harper & Row, 1966); Rod W. Horton and Herbert Edwards, eds., *Backgrounds of American Literary Thought*, 3rd ed. (Englewood Cliffs, N.J.: Prentice-Hall, Inc.,

1974), especially the chapter, "Black Writers: Soul and Solidarity."; Margaret Walker, "Some Aspects of the Black Aesthetic," *Freedomways* 16 (Second Quarter 1976): 95–103.

/8/   Sterling A. Brown, "Negro Characters as Seen by White Authors," *The Journal of Negro Education,* vol. II (April 1933); see also the article by Zora Neale Hurston, "What White Publishers Won't Print," *Negro Digest* (April 1950): 85–89.

/9/   Houston A. Baker, Jr., *Long Black Song: Essays in Black American Literature and Culture* (Charlottesville: The University of Virginia Press, 1972); Bernard W. Bell, "Literary Sources of the Early Afro American Novel," *CLA Journal* 18 (September 1974): 29–43; Rita Dandridge, "On Novels by Black American Women: A Bibliographic Essay," *Women's Studies Newsletter* 6 (Summer 1978): 28–30; *Negro American Literature Forum* (Fall 1975): entire issue devoted to Black women writers; Roger Whitlow, *Black American Literature: A Critical History* (Totowa, N.J.: Littlefield, Adams, & Co., 1974).

/10/   Fisher, p. 148

/11/   Quoted in Arna Bontemps article, "The Black Contribution to American Letters: Part I,", p. 752.

/12/   Barksdale and Kinnamon, p. 59.

/13/   Joan R. Sherman, *Invisible Poets: Afro-Americans of the Nineteenth Century* (Urbana: University of Illinois Press, 1974); Erlene Stetson, ed., *Black Sister: Poetry by Black American Women, 1746–1980* (Bloomington: Indiana University Press, 1981).

/14/   Angelene Jamison, "Analysis of Selected Poetry of Phillis Wheatley," *Journal of Negro Education* 43 (Summer 1974): 408–416; W. H. Robinson, *Phillis Wheatley in the Black American Beginnings* (Detroit: Broadside Press, 1975); *The Poems of Phillis Wheatley,* ed., Julian D. Mason, Jr. (Chapel Hill: University of North Carolina Press, 1966), includes a reprint of 1786 American edition.

/15/   Anne (Dudley) Bradstreet (1612–1672) claimed to be the first woman author whose poems were printed in a volume, entitled *The Tenth Muse Sprung Up in America; or, Several Poems.* It was published in England in 1650. Sara Wentworth Apthorp Morton (1759–1846) and William Mill Brown are attributed with publishing the first novel in the U.S. in 1789, *The Power of Sympathy; or, The Triumph of Nature Founded in Truth.* Jupiter Briton Hammon (1718[?]–1806[?]) was the first Black person to publish some half dozen works, poems and essays, in 1760. The first novel by an Afro-American appeared in London in 1853, *Clotelle; or, The President's Daughter* by Wiliam Wells Brown. The Boston edition was published more than a decade later (1867) with a new subtitle: *A Tale of the Southern States.* It consisted of 104 pages and sold for ten cents.

/16/   Phillis Wheatley, *Poems on Various Subjects, Religious and Moral, by Phillis Wheatley, Negro Servant to Mr. John Wheatley, of Boston, in New England* (London: printed for A. Bell, bookseller, Aldgate, and sold by Messrs. Cox and Berry, King Street, Boston, 1773); G. Herbert Renfro, ed., *Life and Works of Phillis Wheatley* (Freeport, N.Y.: Books for Libraries Press, 1970); Charles F. Heartman, *Phillis Wheatley (Phillis Peters): A Critical Attempt and a Bibliography of Her Writings* (New York: C. F.

Heartman, 1915); Merle Richmond, *Bid the Vassal Soar; Interpretive Essays on the Life and Poetry of Phillis Wheatley and George Moses Horton* (Washington: Howard University Press, 1974); Benjamin B. Thatcher, *Memoir of Phillis Wheatley, A Native African and a Slave* (Boston: G. W. Light; New York: Moore and Payne, 1834).

/17/   R. Lynn Malson, "Phillis Wheatley—Soul Sister?", *Phylon* 23 (Fall 1972): 222–230.

/18/   Printed in Roger Whitlow, *Black American Literature: A Critical History* (Totowa, N.J.: Littlefield, Adams & Co., 1974), p. 23.

/19/   Russell L. Adams, ed., *Great Negroes Past and Present* (Chicago: Afro-American, 1969); Margaret Just Butcher, *The Negro in American Culture* (New York: Mentor, 1971); Janheinz Jahn, *Neo-African Literature: A History of Black Writing*, trans. Oliver Coburn and Ursula Lehrburger (New York: Grove Press, 1969); George Kent, *Blackness and the Adventure of Western Culture* (Chicago: Third World Press, 1972).

/20/   M. G. Cooke, ed., *Black American Novelists: A Collection of Critical Essays* (Englewood Cliffs, N.J.: Prentice-Hall, Inc., 1971); Robert A. Corrigan, "Afro-American Fiction: A Checklist, 1853–1970," *Midcontinent American Studies Journal* (Fall 1970): 114–135; Lina Mainiero, ed., *American Women Writers: A Critical Reference Guide from Colonial Times to the Present in Four Volumes* (New York: Frederick Ungar Publishing Co., 1979); Theressa Gunnels Rush, Carol Fairbanks Myers, and Esther Spring Arata, eds., *Black American Writers Past and Present: A Biographical and Bibliographical Dictionary* (Metuchen, N.J.: Scarecrow Press, Inc. 1975); Maxwell Whiteman, *A Century of Fiction by American Negroes, 1853–1952* (Philadelphia: Jacobs, 1955); *Women and Literature: An Annotated Bibliography of Women* Writers (Cambridge, Mass.: Sense and Sensibility Collective, 1971).

/21/   Bontemps, p. 745.

/22/   W. L. Katz, ed., *Two Black Teachers During the Civil War* (1969); Willie Lee Rose, *Rehearsal for Reconstruction: The Port Royal Experiment* (1964).

/23/   Benjamin Brawley, *the Negro in Literature and Art*, 3rd ed. (New York: Dodd, Mead, 1929); Sterling Brown, Arthur P. Davis, and Ulysses Lee, eds., *The Negro Caravan* (New York: Dryden, 1941; reprint ed., New York: Arno, 1969); Otelia Cromwell, Dow Turner Lorenzo, and Eva B. Dykes, eds., *Readings from Negro Authors* (New York: Harcourt, Brace, 1931); Herman Dreer, ed., *American Literature by Negro Authors* (New York: Macmillan, 1950); Langston Hughes, ed., *The Best Short Stories by Negro Writers: An Anthology from 1899 to the Present* (Boston: Little, Brown & Company, 1967); David Littlejohn, *Black on White: A Critical Survey of Writing by American Negroes* (New York: Grossman, 1966); Mary Mace Spalding, *In Black and White: Afro-Americans in Print; a Guide to Afro-Americans Who Have Made Contributions to the United States of America from 1619 to 1969* (Kalamazoo, Mich.: Kalamazoo Library System, 1971).

/24/   Henry Louis Gates, a scholar at Yale University, is currently engaged in literary detective work in order to prove that the first novel by a Black woman was published in Boston in 1859 by Harriet E. Wilson, entitled *Our*

Nig; or Sketches from the Life of a Free Black, in a Two-Story White House, North. Showing That Slavery's Shadows Fall Even There.
/25/ *A Voice from the South by a Black Woman of the South* (1892); *L'Attitude de La France a L'Egard de L'Esclavage Pendant La Revolution* (1925); *Le Pelerinage de Charlemagne: Voyage a Jerusalem et a Constantinople* (1925); *Legislative Measures Concerning Slavery in the United States* (1942); *Equality of Races and the Democratic Movement* (1945); *The Life and Writings of the Grimke Family* (1951); *The Third Step* (n.d.).
/26/ *Bits and Odds: A Choice Selection of Recitations* (1880); *First Lessons in Public Speaking* (1920); *Our Women: Past, Present and Future* (1925); *Tales My Father Told and Other Stories* (1925); *Homespun Heroines and Other Women of Distinction* (1926); *Pen Pictures of Pioneers of Wilberforce* (1937).
/27/ *Southern Horrors: Lynch Law in All Its Phases* (1892); *The Reason Why the Colored American Is Not in the World's Columbian Exposition— The Afro-American's Contribution to Columbian Literature* (1893); *A Red Record: Tabulated Statistics and Alleged Causes of Lynchings in the United States, 1892-1893-1894* (1895); *Mob Rule in New Orleans: Robert Charles and His Fight to the Death* (1900); *On Lynchings; Southern Horrors; A Red Record; Mob Rule in New Orleans* (1969); *Crusader for Justice: The Autobiography of Ida B. Wells*, ed. A. M. Duster (1970).
/28/ Other Black women who were published during this period: Charlotte Hawkins Brown (1882–   ), *"Mammy" An Appeal to the Heart of the South* (1919); Christina Moody Briggs, *The Story of the East St. Louis Riot* (1917); Sarah D. Brown, *Launching Beyond the Color Line* (1905); Andasia Kimbrough Bruce, *Uncle Tom's Cabin of Today* (1906); Selena S. Butler, *The Chain-Gang System* (1897); Arabella Virginia Chase, *A Peculiar People* (1905); Maggie Shaw Fullilove, *Who Was Responsible?* (1919); Emma Azalia Smith Hackley, *The colored girl is beautiful* (1916); Maud Cuney Hare, *Morris Wright Cuney: A Tribune of the Black People* (1913); Pauline Elizabeth Hopkins, *Contending Forces: A Romance Illustrative of Negro Life, North and South* (1900); *A Primer of Facts Pertaining to the Early Greatness of the African Race and Possibility of Restoration by Its Descendants—with Epilogue* (1905); Gertrude E. H. Bustill Mossell, *The Work of the Afro-American Woman* (1894); Susal L. Shorter, *Heroines of African Methodism* (1891).
/29/ Sylvia G. Dannett, *Profiles in Negro Womanhood* (Yonkers, N.Y.: Educational Heritage, Inc., 1964); Lenwood G. Davis, *The Black Woman in American Society: A Selected, Annotated Bibliography* (Boston: G. K. Hall, 1975); Jacqueline Jackson, "A Partial Bibliography on or Related to Black Women," *Journal of Behavioral Sciences* 21 (Winter 1975): 90–135; Willa D. Johnson and Thomas Green, eds., *Perspectives on Afro-American Women* (Washington: Ecca Publications, 1975); Janet L. Sims, *The Progress of Afro-American Women: A Selected Bibliography and Resource Guide*, with a foreword by Bettye Thomas (Westport, Conn.: Greenwood Press, 1980); Dorothy Sterling, *Black Foremothers: Three Lives* (Old Westbury, N.Y.: The Feminist Press, 1979); Ora Williams, *American Black Women in the Arts and Social Sciences: A Bibliographic Survey* (Methuchen, N.J.: Scarecrow Press, 1973); James O. Young, *Black Writers of the Thirties* (Baton Rouge: Louisiana State University Press, 1973).

/30/ Jervis Anderson, *This Was Harlem: 1900–1950* (New York: Farrar Straus Giroux, 1982); Charles S. Johnson, ed., *Ebony and Topaz* (New York: Urban League, 1927); James Weldon Johnson, *Black Manhattan* (New York: Alfred A. Knopf, 1930); David L. Lewis, *When Harlem Was in Vogue* (New York: Alfred A. Knopf, 1981); Claude McKay, *Harlem: Negro Metropolis* (New York: Dutton, 1940). For a discussion of the literature during this period: Arna Bontemps, ed., *The Harlem Renaissance Remembered* (New York: Dodd, Mead, 1972); Abraham Chapman, "The Harlem Renaissance in Literary History, *CLA Journal* 11 (September 1967): 38–58; Hoyt W. Fuller, ed., *Black World* (November 1970), special issue devoted to the Harlem Renaissance; Nathan I. Huggins, *Harlem Renaissance* (New York: Oxford University Press, 1971); John Oliver Killens, "Another Time When Black Was Beautiful," *Black World* 20 (November 1970): 20–36; Alain Locke, "A Retrospective Review (and Biography) of the Literature of the Negro: 1937," *Opportunity* (January 1938); Martin A. Olsson, *A Selected Bibliography of Black Literature: The Harlem Renaissance* (Exeter, England: University of Exeter, 1973); Margaret Perry, *Silence to the Drum: A Survey of the Literature of the Harlem Renaissance* (Westport, Conn.: Greenwood Press, 1976); Amritjit Singh, *The Novels of the Harlem Renaissance: Twelve Black Writers 1923–1933* (University Park: Pennsylvania State University Press, 1976).

/31/ Gwendolyn Cherry, Ruby Thomas, and Pauline Willis, *Portraits in Color: The Lives of Colorful Negro Women* (New York: Pageant, 1967); Wilhelmina S. Robinson, *Historical Negro Biographies*, 2nd rev. ed. (New York: Publishers, Inc. 1969); Hugh Gloster, *Negro Voices in American Fiction* (Chapel Hill: University of North Carolina Press, 1948; reissued, New York: Russell & Russell, 1965). There is a good discussion of Pauline Hopkins, Frances Harper, Sarah Fleming, Jessie Fauset, Nella Larsen and Zora Hurston in Robert Bone, *The Negro Novel in America* (New Haven: Yale University Press, 1959; revised ed., 1965); Arthur P. Davis, *From the Dark Tower: Afro-American Writers, 1900–1960* (Washington: Howard University Press, 1974).

/32/ *There Is Confusion* (New York: Boni and Liveright, 1924); *Plum Bun, A Novel Without a Moral* (London: Matthews and Marrot, 1928; New York: Stokes, 1929); *The Chinaberry Tree: A Novel of American Life* (New York: Stokes, 1931; New York: AMS Press, 1969; New York: Negro Universities Press, 1969; College Park, Md.,: McGrath, 1969); *Comedy American Style* (New York: Stokes, 1933; New York: AMS Press, 1969; College Park, Md.: McGrath, 1969; New York: Negro Universities Press, 1969).

/33/ *Quicksand* (New York and London: Knopf, 1928; Negro Universities Press, 1969); *Passing* (New York and London: Knopf, 1929; New York: Arno, 1969; New York: Negro Universities Press, 1969; New York: Collier Books, 1971).

/34/ Juliet Bowles, ed., *In the Memory and Spirit of Frances, Zora and Lorraine: Essays and Interviews Relating to Black Women and Writing* (Washington: Institute for the Arts and Humanities, 1979); Mari Evans, ed., *Black Women Writers, 1950–Present* (New York: Doubleday & Co., 1981); Addison Gayle, Jr., *The Way of the New World: The Black Novel in America* (Garden City, N.Y.: Doubleday & Co., 1975); Chester Higgins, *Black Women* (New York: McCall Publishing Co., 1970); Clarence Major, *The*

Dark and Feeling: Black Americans Writers and Their Works (New York: The Third Press, 1974).

/35/ Consult the "authorities" on American literature and notice how many Black perspectives, especially how many Black women writers, are included in the texts: Robert Spiller, *Literary History of the United States;* Arthur Quinn, *The Literature of the American People;* and Vernon Parrington, *Main Currents in American Thought.* See also Ernest Kaiser, "Black Images in the Mass Media: A Bibliography," *Freedomways* 14 (Third Quarter 1974): 274–287.

/36/ Elizabeth Catlett, "The Role of the Black Artist," *Black Scholar, Arts and Literature* 6 (June 1975); Richard Gilman, "White Standards and Negro Writing," *New Republic,* March 9, 1968, pp. 25–30; Richard Gilman, "More on Negro Writing," *New Republic,* April 13, 1968, pp. 25–28; Langston Hughes, "The Negro Artist and the Racial Mountain," *The Nation,* June 23, 1926, pp. 692–694; Saunders Redding, "The Negro Writer: The Road Where," *Boston University Journal* 17 (Winter 1969): 6–10; "The Problem of the Negro Writer," *Massachusetts Review* 6 (Autumn-Winter 1964–65): 57–70; Joseph F. Trimmer, *Black American Literature: Notes on the Problem of Definition* (Muncie, Ind.: Ball State University Press, 1971); John A. Williams, "The Crisis in American Letters," *Black Scholar* (June 1975):

/37/ Gerald W. Haslan, *Forgotten Pages of American Literature* (Boston: Houghton Mifflin Co., 1970), p. 1.

/38/ Mary Helen Washington, "These Self-Invented Women: A Theoretical Framework for a Literary History of Black Women," *The Radical Teacher* (November 1980): 3. See also Seymour L. Gross, "Stereotype to Archetype: The Negro in American Literary Criticism," in *Images of the Negro in American Literature,* ed. Seymout L. Gross and John Edward Hardy (Chicago, 1966).

/39/ Mari Evans, "Contemporary Black Literature," *Black World* 19 (June 1970); Carolyn Gerald, "Symposium: The Measure and Meaning of the Sixties: What Lies Ahead for Black Americans," *Negro Digest* (November 1969); The Negro in Literature: The Current Scene," *Phylon* 11 (Winter 1950): 297–394, especially Margaret Walker's article; Barbara Smith, "The Souls of Black Women," *Ms.,* February 1974, pp. 42–43, 78; Mel Watkins, "The Black Revolution in Books," *New York Times Book Review,* 10 August 1969, p. 8.

/40/ Samuel I. Hayakawa, *Language in Thought and Action,* in Consultation with Leo Hamilton and Geoffrey Wagner, 2nd ed. (New York: Harcourt, Brace, Jovanovich, 1964), p. 326.

/41/ Ruth Miller, ed., *Backgrounds to Black American Literature* (New York: Chandler Publishing Co., 1971); Carolyn Rodger, "The Literature of Black," *Black World* 19 (June 1970): 5–13; John Wideman, "Defining the Black Voice in Fiction," *Black American Literature Forum* 10 (Winter 1976):

/42/ Wade Baskin and Richard Runes, *Dictionary of Black Culture* (New York: Philosophical Library, 1973); Robert Hemenway, ed., *The Black Novelist* (Columbus, Oh.: Charles E. Merrill, 1970).

/43/ Gene Bluestein, "Blues as a Literary Theme," *Massachusetts Review* 8 (Autumn 1967): 593–617; Clyde Taylor, "Black Folk Spirit and the Shape of Black Literature," *Black World* 21 (August 1972): 31–40; Barbara T.

Christian, *Black Women Novelists: The Development of a Tradition, 1892–1976* (Westport, Conn.: Greenwood Press, 1980).

/44/   Mary Helen Washington, "Black Women Image Makers," *Black World* (August 1974): 10–18; See also Walter I. Daykin, "Social Thought in Negro Novels," *Sociology and Social Research* 19 (1935): 247–252; Edward Margolies, *Native Sons: A Critical Study of Twentieth-Century Negro-American Authors* (Philadelphia: Lippincott, 1969); Noel Schraufnagel, *From Apology to Protest: The Black American Novel* (Deland, Fla.: Everett/Edwards, 1973).

/45/   Christian, p. 239.

/46/   Mary Helen Washington, *Midnight Birds: Stories of Contemporary Black Women Writers* (Garden City, N.Y.: Doubleday & Co., 1979), pp. 95–96.

/47/   Verta Mae Grosvenor, *Vibration Cooking* (New York: Doubleday, 1970)

/48/   Marcia Gillispie, Editorial, *Essence Magazine*, May 1975, p. 39.

/49/   Frances S. Foster, "Changing Concepts of the Black Woman," *Journal of Black Studies* 3 (June 1973): 433–454; Toni Morrison, "Behind the Making of *The Black Book*," *Black World* 23 (February 1974): 86–90

/50/   Barbara Christian, *Black Women Novelists: The Development of a Tradition, 1892–1976* (Westport, Conn.: Greenwood Press, 1980), p. 144.

/51/   Christian, p. 241.

/52/   Mary Helen Washington, *Midnight Birds: Stories of Contemporary Black Women Writers* (Garden City, N.Y.: Doubleday & Co., 1979), p. xv.

/53/   Steven Marcus, "The American Negro in Search of Identity," *Commentary*, November 1953, pp. 456–463, a comparative study of Wright's *The Outsider*, Ellison's *Invisible Man*, and Baldwin's *Go Tell It on the Mountain;* Harold Isaac, "Five Writers and Their African Ancestors," *Phylon* 21 (Fall 1960): 245–265; also, *Phylon* 21 (Winter 1960): 317–336, reflections on the works of Langston Hughes, Richard Wright, Ralph Ellison, James Baldwin and Lorraine Hansberry.

/54/   Stewart Lilliard, "Ellison's Ambitious Scope in *Invisible Man*," *English Journal* 58 (September 1969): 833–839; Therman B. O'Daniel, "The Image of Man as Portrayed by Ralph Ellison," *CLA Journal* (June 1967): 277–284; Richard Kostelanetz, "Politics of Ellison's Booker: Invisible Man as Symbolic History," *Chicago Review* 19, no. 2 (1967): 5–26; William J. Schafer, "Ralph Ellison and the Birth of the Anti-Hero," *Critique* 10, no. 2 (1968): 81–93; Raymond M. Olderman, "Ralph Ellison's Blues and Invisible Man," *Wisconsin Studies in Contemporary Literature* 7 (Summer 1966): 142–159.

/55/   Edward Margolies, *The Art of Richard Wright* (Carbondale: Southern Illinois University Press, 1969); Constance Webb, *Richard Wright* (New York: Putnam, 1968); Irving Howe, "Black Boys and Native Sons," *Dissent* 10 (Fall 1963): 353–368.

/56/   Colin MacInnes, "Dark Angel: The Writings of James Baldwin," *Encounter* 21 (August 1963): 22–33; a careful study of all of Baldwin's writings to date is Therman B. O'Daniel, ed., *James Baldwin: A Critical Evaluation* (Washington: Howard University Press, 1981).

/57/   Christian, p. 241.

/58/   Mary Helen Washington also points out, "In the writing of Black
men, women are almost always subordinate to men. They are often relegated to domestic roles, while the men are involved in the 'larger' issues of
life. The quest of the Black man to achieve manhood has always inspired the
highest respect, but the equivalent struggle of the Black woman has hardly
been acknowledged—except by Black women writers" (p. xv). For further
discussion, Mary Louise Anderson, "Black Matriarchy: Portrayal of Women
in Three Plays," *Negro American Literature Forum* 10 (Fall 1976): 93–95;
Rita B. Dandridge, "The Black Woman as a Freedom Fighter in Langston
Hughes' 'Simple's Uncle Sam'," *CLA Journal* 18 (December 1974): 273–283;
Patricia Kane and Doris Wilkerson, "Survival Strategies: Black Women in
Ollie Miss and *Cottom Comes to Harlem*," *Critique: Studies in Modern
Fiction* 16 (1974): 101–109; Velma P. Potter, "New Politics, New Mothers,"
CLA Journal 16 (December 1972): 247–255, discussion of Black women in
drama.
/59/   Fletcher Knebel, "The Black Woman's Burden," *Look*, September
23, 1969, pp. 77–79; Barbara Molette, "They Speak: Who Listens? Black
Women Playwrights," *Black World* 25 (April 1976): 28–34; Carol Fairbanks
Myers, *Women in Literature: Criticism of the Seventies* (Metuchen, N.J.:
Scarecrow Press, 1976).
/60/   Alice Childress, "The Negro Woman in American Literature," in
Keeping the Faith: Writings by Contemporary Black Women, ed. Pat
Crutchfield Exum (Greenwich, Conn.: Fawcett Publications, 1974), p. 32.
/61/   Francis S. Foster, "Changing Concepts of the Black Woman," *Journal
of Black Studies* 3 (June 1973): 446.
/62/   Roseann P. Bell, Bettye J. Parker, and Beverly Sheftall, eds., *Sturdy
Black Bridges: Visions of Black Women in Literature* (New York: Doubleday
& Co., 1979); Josephine Carson, ed., *The Southern Negro Woman Today*
(New York: Delacorte Press, 1969); Toni Cade, ed., *The Black Woman: An
Anthology* (New York: New American Library, 1970); D. W. Culp, ed.,
Twentieth Century Negro Literature (Naperville, Ill.: n.d., 1902); also the
following articles and essays: Paula Giddings, "A Special Vision, A Common
Goal," *Encore* 12 (June 23–July 4, 1975): 44–48; Gloria T. Hull, "Re-Writing
Afro-American Literature: A Case for Black Women Writers," *The Radical
Teacher* 6 (December 1979): 10–13; Barbara Smith, "Toward a Black Femi-
nist Criticism," *Conditions: Two* 1 (October 1977): 25–44; Sonia Sanchez,
"Uh, Huh; But How It Free Us?" in *The New Lafayette Theatre Presents:
Plays with Aesthetic Comments by Six Black Playwrights*, ed. Ed Bullins
(New York: Anchor Press, 1975); Alice Walker, "In Search of Our Mothers'
Gardens: The Creativity of Black Women in the South," *Ms.*, May 1974, pp.
64–70, 105; "The Unglamourous but Worthwhile Duties of the Black Revo-
lutionary Artist or of the Black Writer Who Simply Works and Writes," *The
Black Collegian* 1 (October 1971).

CHAPTER IV

RESOURCES FOR A CONSTRUCTIVE
ETHIC IN
THE LIFE OF ZORA NEALE HURSTON

Zora Neale Hurston's life, like that of the women she wrote about, exemplifies the Black woman's loss of innocence at an early age. Her life conveys the way the Black woman embraces, out of this loss of innocence, an invisible dignity in the self-celebration of her survival against great odds.

Because she was a Black female, Hurston's parents schooled her in how to live with the tension of the irrational facticity of life. Even though Hurston was born and grew up in the first incorporated all-Black town in the United States (Eatonville, Florida in 1865), where her father served three terms as mayor, Hurston's parents still made her aware of evil systems and social institutions that existed outside of her supportive, nourishing environment. During her pre-puberty years, Hurston's parents tried to teach her how to deal with insults and humiliations of the larger society so that she would not make the wrong step or wrong response that could literally jeopardize her life.

Hurston's mother was Lucy Ann Potts (1865–1904), a former schoolteacher. She exhorted Zora to "jump at de sun" so that Zora would not "turn out to be a mealy-mouthed rag doll" with a squinched spirit by the time she was grown.

"We might not land on the sun, but at least we would get off the ground. . . ."[1] In other words, Lucy Potts encouraged Hurston to strive continually for individuality and self-expression. She did not want Hurston to feel hampered and held down by the heinous pressures of racist reality.

At the same time, Hurston's father tried to induce a spirit of docile compliancy. He warned that it did not do for Blacks to have too much spirit because white folks would not tolerate it. In her autobiography, Hurston recorded her father's speech to her:

> He predicted dire things for me. The white folks were
> not going to stand for it. I was going to be hung before I was
> grown. Somebody was going to blow me down for my sassy
> tongue. Mama was going to suck sorrow for not beating my
> temper out of me before it was too late. Posses with ropes and
> guns were going to drag me out sooner or later on account of
> that stiff neck I toted. I was going to tote a hungry belly by
> reason of my forward ways.[2]

Her father, John Hurston (1861–1917) was a carpenter, a Baptist
preacher and the moderator of the South Florida Baptist Association. He wanted Hurston to be aware of the burgeoning complexities imposed by discrimination. He attempted to inculcate her with
the awareness that whites and males support racial imperialism in a
patriarchal social order.

Living on her memories, Zora Hurston's maternal grandmother—Grandma Potts—offered moral counsel in light of events
and their possible consequences. She tried to warn Hurston of how
her actions would offset the prospects of her survival.

> Git down offa dat gatepost! You li'l sow, you! Git down!
> Setting up dere looking dem white folks right in de face! They's
> gwine to lynch you, yet.[3]

Like the vast majority of Black children, Hurston by the age of nine
had learned how life goes awry. With the death of her mother,
Hurston moved swiftly from the tranquility of childhood to early
womanhood.

> Mama died at sundown and changed a world. That is the
> world which had been built out of her body and heart. Even
> the physical aspects fell apart with a suddenness that was
> startling. . . . I was deprived of the loving pine, the lakes, the
> wild violets in the woods and the animals I used to know. No
> more holding down first base on the team with my brothers and
> their friends. Just a jagged hole where my home used to be.[4]

The counsel of her dying mother helped Hurston to leave
behind the carefree days of childhood. The 37-year-old woman's
deathbed speech, captured in the fictional character of Lucy in
Jonah's Gourd Vine, is a series of proverbial sayings that were a sort
of ethical treatise to help Hurston consider more deeply the worth
and meaning of her life.

> Stop cryin', Isie, you can't hear whut Ahm sayin', 'member tuh git all de education you kin. Dat's de onliest way you kin keep out from under people's feet. You always strain tuh be de bell cow, never be de tail uh nothin'. Do de best you kin, honey, 'cause neither yo' paw or dese older chillun is goin' tuh be bothered too much wid youh, but you goin' tuh git 'long. Mark mah words. You got spunk, but mah po' lil'l sandy-haired child goin' suffer uh lot 'fo' she git tuh de place she can 'fend fuh herself. And Isie, honey, stop cryin' and lissen tuh me. Don't you love nobody bettern'n you do yo'self. Do, you'll be killed 'thout being struck uh blow. Some uh dese things Ahm tellin' yuh, you won't understand 'em fuh years tuh come, but de time will come when you'll know . . .[5]

Her mother's instruction was concerned not so much with the ascertainment of fact or elaboration of theories as with the means and ends of practical life. Hurston's mother pointed to the people, attitudes and structures that were inimical to Hurston's ongoing survival. She spelled out those things that Hurston needed to do in order to protect the quality and continuity of her life. Hurston need not be a muzzled, mutilated individual but must continue to grow as a woman-child with a vibrant, creative spirit. This moral wisdom, handed down from mother to daughter as the crystallized result of experience aimed to teach Hurston not only how to survive but also how to prevail with integrity against the cruel systems of triple oppression.

At age nine, Hurston was sent away from home to live with older siblings who attended a boarding school in Jacksonville, Florida. Hurston was the seventh of eight children, and the younger of two daughters.[6] Financial straits forced her to leave school and to be passed back and forth from relatives and friends.

> Papa's children were in his way, because they were too much trouble for his wife. Ragged, dirty clothes and hit-and-miss meals. The four older children were definitely gone for good. One by one, we four younger ones were shifted to the homes of Mama's friends.[7]

By the age of fourteen, due to deteriorating relationships with her father and stepmother, Hurston was completely on her own. At age fifteen, after a little schooling and many domestic jobs, she left Florida. Before her teen years were fully lived, Hurston had worked as a receptionist in a doctor's office, as a wardrobe girl for the traveling Gilbert and Sullivan repertory company, as a manicurist in a barbershop, as a waitress in a nightclub, and as a servant and live-in nursemaid in the homes of bourgeois Blacks and wealthy whites in Washington, D.C.[8] Hurston never held a job for very long. Her refusal to accept the assigned shuffling, subservient role of the Black domestic worker and her assertive defense against the advances of her male employers, combined with her passionate love for reading, resulted in numerous walkouts and terminations.[9]

In 1917, owning only one dress, a change of underwear and a pair of tan oxfords, Hurston enrolled in evening classes at Morgan Academy in Baltimore, Maryland. Her successful completion of competency examinations allowed her to advance two grades in one year. In 1918 Hurston enrolled in the Howard Preparatory School. Out of necessity she continued to work several part-time jobs. After studying philosophy, art and drama with renowned scholars such as Georgia Douglas Johnson, Alain Locke and Montgomery Gregory, Hurston received an Associate Arts degree from Howard Academy in 1920.

In 1921 she published her first short story, "John Redding Goes to Sea," in the Howard Literary Club magazine, *Stylus*. Three years later Alain Locke, Hurston's mentor, recommended Hurston's "Drenched in Light," "Spunk" and "Color Struck" to Charles Spurgeon Johnson, the founding editor of the Urban League's magazine, *Opportunity: A Journal of Negro Life*. In recognition of her talents, Hurston won two prizes and was invited to the League's first award dinner where she and her work were introduced to the public.[10]

Hemenway captured the meaning of Hurston's early transformation of lost innocence into invisible dignity:

> In the first week of January 1925, Zora Neale Hurston arrived in New York City with one dollar and fifty cents in her purse, no job, no friends, but filled with "a lot of hope." . . . She carried most of her belongings in her bag, including a number of manuscripts that she hoped would impress. Even if they did not, she was confident in her ability to survive in the big city; she had been on her own since the age of fourteen.[11]

Hurston's ability to masterfully frame the necessary perceptive system of intuitive behavior, in terms of cognitive apprehensions of her immediate reality, resulted from the moral sensibility of her family within the wider context of her natal community. Hurston knew how to fight back and salvage her selfhood amid the odds. June Jordan contends that Hurston's membership in a leading Black family, in a proud and independent self-governing, all-Black town sensitized her to understand the existential circumstances in which she could relax from the hunted/warrior posture and revel in the natural, person-posture within Black life.[12]

During her middle years (1925–1948), Zora Neale Hurston continued to incarnate the counsel she learned from her mother and from her community. Hurston's arrival in New York City came at a most opportune time. The Harlem Renaissance was flourishing. At the 1925 Urban League award dinner, Hurston met one of the contest judges, novelist Fannie Hurst. This initial meeting resulted in Hurston working for Hurst as live-in secretary, chauffeur and confidante for several years. At the award dinner, Hurston also met Annie Nathan Meyer, a novelist and one of the founders of Barnard College. Meyer was so keenly impressed with Hurston that she arranged for Hurston to enroll at Barnard on scholarship the following semester. While completing the requirements for the B.A. degree (1925–1928), Hurston studied with Gladys Reichard, an anthropology professor at Bárnard who was so excited by the quality of Hurston's work that she introduced Hurston to Columbia's famed anthropology professor, Franz Boas. The result was an opportunity for Hurston to work as an anthropological apprentice with Boas.[13]

Early on, Hurston discovered that her love for writing was quite compatible with this new vocational interest in anthropology. She recorded this inherent kinship in *Mules and Men:*

> From the earliest rocking of my cradle, I have known about the capers Brer Rabbit is apt to cut and what the Squinch Owl says from the house top. But it was fitting me like a tight chemise. I couldn't see it for wearing it. It was only when I was off in college, away from my native surroundings, that I could see myself like somebody else and stand off and look at my garment. Then I had to have the spy-glass of Anthropology to look at that.[14]

In *The Big Sea*, Langston Hughes depicted in graphic fashion how Hurston's flamboyant personality, combined with her newly acquired skills, assisted her in gathering the data needed either to support or to refute a scientific concept related to race and culture.

> Almost nobody else could stop the average Harlemite on
> Lenox Avenue and measure his head with a strange-looking

anthropological device and not get bawled out for the attempt,
except Zora, who used to stop anyone whose head looked
interesting and measure it.[15]

Two weeks before Hurston graduated from Barnard, she received a fellowship from Carter G. Woodson's Association for the
Study of Negro Life and History. Hurston's assignment was to travel
South to collect folklore. She failed miserably in her first attempt to
gather data outside of Harlem. In her autobiography she compared
the miniscule amount of material collected during this first visit with
"not being enough to make a flea a waltzing jacket."

> When I went about asking, in carefully-accented Barnar-
> dese, "Pardon me, do you know any folk-tales or folk-songs?"
> the men and women who had whole treasuries of material
> seeping through their pores looked at me and shook their
> heads. No, they had never heard of anything like that around
> there. Maybe it was over in the next county. Why didn't I try
> over there? I did, and got the self-same answer.[16]

Combining the moral counsel which she learned from her
family (especially from her mother) with the folk wisdom accentu-
ated in the Black community, Zora Neale Hurston came to appreciate that surviving the continual struggle and the interplay of contradictory opposites was genuine virtue.[17] Hurston knew that there
could be no "perfectionism" in the face of the structures of oppression she experienced as a Black-woman-artist. For her, the moral
quality of life was expressed not as an ideal but was to be fulfilled as a
balance of complexities in such a way that suffering did not over-
whelm, and endurance with integrity was possible.

Hurston, like Black people generally, understood suffering not
as a moral norm nor as a desirable ethical quality, but rather as the
typical state of affairs. Virtue is not the experiencing of suffering, nor
in the survival techniques for enduring. Rather, the quality of moral
good is that which allows Black people to maintain a feistiness about
life that nobody can wipe out, no matter how hard they try.

Some of Hurston's critics charged her with writing shallow,
romantic, naive counter-revolutionary literature[18] because she portrayed a sense of psychic and physical pleasure amidst desperation
and tragedy. She portrayed the humor and good times among people who lived, day in and day out, with pathetic and inarticulate

needs. Hurston reminded individuals that they were a part of the communal kinship within the Black cultural heritage.

The result of this type of moral agency in Hurston is culminated in a quality that Alice Walker identifies as "unctuousness."[19] On her own from an early age, and a runaway since the age of fourteen, Hurston repeatedly found herself in situations wherein her head was in the lion's mouth and she was being forced to treat the lion very gently.[20] Zora Hurston often had to act sincere in the most insincere situations. Confrontation with ignominious circumstances caused her to be like the earth, "soaking up urine and perfume with the same indifference."[21]

As an unctuous moral agent, Hurston learned to look at the world with her own eyes, form her own judgments and demythologize whole bodies of so-called social legitimacy. Hurston balanced forethought with discerning deliberation so as to act from a perspective that was right for her. In essence, being unctuous helped Zora Neale Hurston decipher the various sounds in the larger world, to resist the demands for capitulation to the status quo, to affirm her worth without scampering around for male validation, to find meaning in the most despotic circumstances and to create possibilities where none existed before.

Thus, I maintain that this quality of unctuous moral agency, in a situation of triple oppression was directly responsible for Zora Neale Hurston's brief periods of professional notoriety and also for her professional demise.

"Invisible Dignity" as It Relates to Moral Agency and Racism in Hurston's Life

After her brief research fellowship expired, Zora Neale Hurston returned to New York City with a little bit of folklore, no money and no job. She was able to continue her data-gathering for several more years under the auspices of Charlotte Osgood Mason, a white Park Avenue dowager of enormous wealth and influence.[22] Some of Hurston's critics mercilessly discredited her as a respectable artist because she "got money from white folks."[23] More often than not, these same critics, who caricatured Hurston as a charming, manipulative minion, "who lived up to the whites' notion of what a 'darky' should be," were financially backed by the same white patrons.[24]

Hurston acted with unctuousness in racist situations. Implicit in her contract, as in all of Mason's contracts with Black artists— Alain Locke, Langston Hughes, Richard Wright, Miguel Covarrubias, Aaron Douglas, Raymond Barthè and Louise Thompson— was a votive understanding that their work reflect unalloyed primitivism.[25] Mason wanted her protegees to "slough off white culture— using it only to clarify the thoughts that surge in your being."[26] Mason also insisted that her Harlem beneficiaries never mention her name to others. They were only to refer to her as "Godmother."[27] Hurston knew that she needed Mason's financial sponsorship in order to preserve the Black cultural heritage, and at the same time, she was aware of the razor-blade tension between obsequious accommodation to "Godmother" and fidelity to her own values.

As a Black-woman-writer who was never able to make a living from her craft, Hurston experienced this situation as a moral dilemma and as a yoke around her neck. On the one hand, she knew the value of the rich reservoir of materials passed along in the oral tradition of her parents, neighbors and of common, everyday people. And, on the other hand, Hurston had to assess the almost universal misunderstanding outside of the context of Black culture of Black folkways as inferior, comic, and primitive.

Langston Hughes described Hurston as a very "spirited and lively girl" and reported that her financial backers "felt that she should be very quiet and studious while preparing her manuscripts."[28] Hughes noted that these restrictions made Hurston restless and moody and caused her to work in a very nervous manner.

Drawing on the detailed correspondence between Zora Neal Hurston and Charlotte O. Mason in the Alain Locke Collection at Howard University, Lillie P. Howard underscored Hurston's anxiety-ridden attempts to live up to the expectations and terms of her contract with "Godmother." Mason had strict control over all of Hurston's work. She forbade Hurston to display in revues or publish any of the information, data, or music transcripts she gathered without her permission.[29]

During this period, Zora Neale Hurston coined the term "Negrotarian" for whites such as Charlotte Mason, Carl Van Vechten, Fannie Hurst, Florenz Ziegfeld, Clarence Darrow, Pearl Buck, Amy and Joe Springarn, all of whom specialized in "uplifting" all areas of Negro life.[30] Negrotarians not only patronized Blacks and socialized with them, but sometimes used their white privileges to lionize Black artists in the most elite social circles. They would feature Black writing in leading national magazines, invite Blacks to participate in lecture series at Ivy League institutions, and publish Black manuscripts through the most notable publishing houses.[31]

Karla Holloway described this type of WASP and Jewish philanthropy as New York's own form of the "peculiar institution."[32] Holloway contends that the criteria for defining Black art, literature and music as "truly Black" were determined by the economic imbalance between the relatively wealthy white patrons and the poverty of the struggling Black artists.[33] Thus, Black culture was commercialized and perverted. David L. Lewis, who described and analyzed the Negrotarians in significant detail in *When Harlem Was in Vogue,* said that the premise for the uplift mentality among whites was a combination of "inherited abolitionism, Christian charity and guilt, social manipulation, political eccentricity and a certain amount of persiflage."[34] Jeanne Noble, commenting on this "peculiar institution" within the Harlem Renaissance, observes that even though Black writers were inspired by the Black experience, they were almost completely dependent on whites for public exposure and financial help. This dependency sucked the vitality and creativity from Black artists.[35] Whites either co-opted Black writers' ideas and style, in an attempt to transfuse new and vigorous creativity into their own culture, or they repressed the literary movement when awareness struck that what Black writers were communicating was not all fun and games.[36] Harold Cruse insists that the Black intellectual "must deal intimately with the white power structure and America's cultural institutions while dealing as spokesperson for the inner realities of the black world at one and the same time."[37]

Hurston had to deal intimately with the white power structure while dealing with the inner realities of the Black world. She was caught between the rock and the hard place. She accepted financial assistance from wherever it was offered so that Black Culture would survive. Hurston had to consider the implications of accepting the financial backing of Negrotarians. She concluded that it was more important to uncover Black folk culture in all its rare beauty. Hurston understood the rich resources in the Black cultural heritage for her ongoing process of determining who she was and who she would become.[38]

"Invisible Dignity" as It Relates to Moral Agency and Gender Discrimination in Hurston's Life

Gender discrimination as a complex social force had a profound negative impact on Zora Neal Hurston's career. Black men, such as Alain Locke, the leader and chief interpreter of the cultural revitalization in Harlem during the 1920s, believed that by virtue of their gender they were in charge of the infrastructures in the Black community.[39] As the prime movers of the Harlem Renaissance, Claude McKay,[40] Countee Cullen,[41] Jean Toomer,[42] Langston Hughes,[43] Arna Bontemps,[44] Sterling Brown,[45] Wallace Thurman,[46] James Weldon Johnson,[47] and W. E. B. DuBois[48] used their privileged positions and monopoly of power to identify, nurture and promote the artists who best represented their interests. As "godfathers" of the Black Art Movement, these men used their eminence to give a rubber stamp to some and to filter out other young artists. As males, subtly socialized to perpetuate superiority over females, most of these men were unaware of the pervasive ideologies they harbored which subordinated, distorted and devalued Black women. Hence, Zora Neale Hurston, both in the life she lived and in the writings she produced, challenged the assumptions of the men. Hurston tapped her inner strength and pushed against the structural limits which did not adhere to her own standard of self-fulfillment. Hurston's modus operandi of unctuousness was a genuine threat to her male colleagues.

Hurston was twice stigmatized—once for race and once for gender. Yet, Hurston refused to fit into a male mold. She would not succumb to the subtle, debilitating pressures to comform to the norms and values of the Black male literary tradition.[49] While some of Hurston's contemporaries were busily proving that well-bred, intelligent Blacks could mimic the attitudes, behavior and standards dictated by well-bred, intelligent whites,[50] Hurston invested her energies into entertaining whites, and all who would listen, with vivid, metaphorical stories of the Black oral tradition.[51] While Hurston's other colleagues were expropriating white antagonism as the cause for the poverty of the masses who supposedly languished in despair, anger and defeatism,[52] Hurston was trekking through the South collecting the Black classics in music, art, dance and literature with hopes of eventually correcting dominant misconceptions about the quality of life in the Black context.[53]

Mary Helen Washington affirmed Zora Hurston's Black frame of reference in this way:

> What is significant about the all-Black setting is that it enables the novel to escape one of the plagues of Black literature—the handicap of having the most passionate feelings directed at "The Man." The Black writer sometimes get their eyes so fixed on the white world and its ways of acting towards us that his vision becomes constricted. He reflects, if he is not careful, but one aspect of his people's experiences: suffering, humiliation, degradation. And he may fail to show that Black people are more than simply reactors, that among ourselves, we have laughter, tears, and loving that are far removed from the white horror out there.[54]

The folk wisdom that Hurston received from her all-Black southern context encouraged her to "jump at de sun," not to bend to the demeaning will of her critics, most of whom were members of a self-selected male sanctioning body. Thus, Hurston's behavior was seen as an "unnatural" anomaly. The more successful she became as a writer, researcher and critic, the more her motives were subjected to misinterpretations. The men in the literary guild had difficulty accepting the seriousness Hurston brought to her work.[55] She made it clear to everyone that her writings were an integral part of her life. She was unwilling to be defined by others or limited in exchange for male endorsement and support. Hurston fought hard. She faced rigorous demands and obstacles. Her professional aspirations posed such a threat that, in a review, she was attacked by a male writer for "shuttling between the sexes, the professions and the races as if she were a man and a woman, scientist and creative writer, white and colored."[56] Hurston's "unctuousness" trespassed on something that her male critics felt was exclusively theirs. The Black male literary guild picked apart Hurston's person and viciously satirized her work.[57] Both Robert Hemenway and Lillie P. Howard provide cogent evidence as to how Hurston, the most prolific Black woman writer in the U.S., was "lauded by the white world, but suspiciously regarded and often lampooned by the black."[58]

When Zora Hurston wrapped her hair in beautiful cloth turbans, her critics charged that she was trying to pass for an African queen.[59] When she dared to divorce, not one, but two husbands, with rumor alluding to the possibility of a third marriage, her critics portrayed her as indecent.[60] However, Hurston refused to take a defensive posture for acting in ways which were not acceptable for women until decades later.[61] In 1938, while working with the Florida Federal Writers Project, Hurston was described as "flighty" because she loved to show off, refused to cooperate with her co-workers, and hated to stay inside at her desk.

On the other hand, Carl Van Vechten, a white critic and one of her closest friends, assessed Hurston not as "flighty" but as a woman with a "magnetic" personality.[62]

> What it comes down to is the fact that Zora was put together entirely different from the rest of mankind. Her reactions were always original because they were always her own. When she breezed into a room (she never merely entered), tossed a huge straw hat (as big as a cart wheel) on the floor and yelled "I am the queen of the "niggerati," you knew you were in the presence of an individual of the greatest magnitude.[63]

One of the most damning and damaging charges against Hurston focused upon her fight against integration. When most Black leaders were organizing around integration as a goal, Zora Hurston was a lonely frontrunner who saw the implementation of integration as an affront and threat to the Black community. Hurston believed that the integration of schools was needed only if "some residual, some inherent and unchangeable quality in white schools were impossible to duplicate anywhere else."[64]

> The Supreme Court would have pleased [her] more if they had concerned themselves about enforcing the compulsory education provisions for Negroes in the South as is done for white children.[65]

Hurston, busy affirming Black values and Black life, saw no benefit in forsaking the Black reality under the pretense of being bleached into acceptance in a so-called superior white world. Hurston wrote:

> The whole matter revolves around the self-respect of my people. How much satisfaction can I get from a court order for somebody to associate with me who does not wish me near them. . . . It is a contradiction in terms to scream race pride and equality while at the same time spurning Negro teachers and self-associations.[66]

Hurston personally believed in the principle of an integrated society, but she did not support the invidious comparisons that inhered Black people as divergent deviants from the "norm."[67] She did not believe that Black people were a negligible factor in the thought of the world. Instead, her life was committed to redressing ignorance about Black culture. Her work was an affirmation of the Black race as one of the great human races, inferior to none in its accomplishments and in its ability.[68]

Hurston's emphasis on "the Negro farthest down" brought criticism from many quarters. Richard Wright condemned Hurston for being unconcerned with racism, class struggle and the revolutionary tradition of Black people.[69] Roy Wilkins, after reading Hurston's article on Jim Crow, went so far as to say:

> Now is no time for tongue-wagging by Negroes for the sake of publicity. The race is fighting a battle that may determine its status for fifty years. Those who are not for us, are against us.[70]

Lester B. Granger of the *California Eagle* responded to some of Hurston's articles in this manner:

> Miss Hurston has written seldom in recent years and so far as her public is concerned, when she has come out with a production it has been readily evident that she "shoulda stayed in bed."[71]

In 1932, Wallace Thurman wrote an elaborate satire on himself and his colleagues of the Harlem Renaissance entitled *Infants of the Spring*. Unfortunately his "bas-relief" caricature of Zora Hurston as Sweetie May Carr, "a short story writer, more noted for her ribald wit and effervescence than any actual literary work," [72] has haunted the authentic Hurston up to the present time. As recently as 1971, Black men like Darwin Turner still depicted Zora Neal Hurston as

> superficial and shallow in her artistic and social judgments. . . . Always, she remained a wandering minstrel. It was eccentric but perhaps appropriate for her to return to Florida to take a job as a cook and maid for a white family and to die in poverty. She had not ended her days as she once had hoped—a farmer among growing things she loved. Instead she had returned to the level of life which she proposed for her people.[73]

Hurston's social contacts put her in close contact to her male colleagues. Often she was in the limelight of the "Niggerati" gather-

ings.[74] Her apartment was always open, with a communal pot on the
stove. Hurston entertained entire parties with stories, group sing-
ing, and stand-up comedy routines mimicking snobbish Park Avenue whites who she called "Astorperious."[75] Hurston discovered
that there was to be no support when these peers put their critic
hats on to review her work. Hurston's refusal to behave in ways that
conformed to the status quo hampered her popularity in the Black
community.

While the *Saturday Review* was praising Hurston's autobiography as a significant contribution to the field of race relations, Arna
Bontemps denounced her life story.

> Miss Hurston deals very simply with the more serious
> aspects of Negro life in America—she ignores them. She has
> done well for herself in the kind of world she found.[76]

Harold Preece, writing for the *Crisis*, dismissed Hurston's autobiography as no more than

> the tragedy of a gifted, sensitive mind, eaten up by an ego-
> centrism fed on the patronizing admiration of the dominant
> white world.[77]

Hurston's scientific study of folklore in novelistic form, *Mules
and Men*, was of such quality that it resulted in invitations for her to
become a member of three prestigious organizations: American
Folklore Society, the American Ethnological Society and the American Anthropological Society. By direct contrast, Sterling Brown's
review of this work found the characters "naive, quaint, complacent
and bad enough to kill each other in looks, but meek otherwise, and
socially unconscious."[78] There were other critics who lauded
Hurston's third novel: "If Hurston had written nothing else she
would deserve recognition for *Moses, Man of the Mountain*."[79] But
Alain Locke called it "a caricature instead of portraiture."[80] Ralph
Ellison claimed that "for Negro fiction, it did nothing."[81] Robert
Bone, the white critic of Black literature, heralded Hurston's *Their
Eyes Were Watching God* as "a classic of Black literature, one of the
finest novels of the period,"[82] while Richard Wright reviewed this
work and found it to be a "shallow romance, lacking in protest
value."[83]

Poor reviews also shut down in fast order the song-dance

revues, *Fast and Furious, Jungle Scandals,* and *Spunk,* which Hurston had arranged from her exclusive collection of folklore material. Hall Johnson, of *Run Little Chillun* fame, summed up the popular sentiments of Hurston's colorful revues among the Renaissance artists.

> The world was not ready for Negro music unless it was highly arranged. The barbaric melodies and harmonies were simply not fit for musical ears.[84]

George Antheil, a U.S. composer known internationally for his ultramodern music, attended one of the revues Hurston had arranged, *The Great Day,* when it was performed at the New School for Social Research in 1932. Antheil's assessment of Hurston's musical contribution was quite opposite from Hall Johnson's. Antheil insisted that the quality of Hurston's revue was so superb that she would be the most plagiarized Black person in the world for at least a decade.

> This sort of thievery is unavoidable. Unpleasant, of course but at the bottom a tribute to one's originality.[85]

In 1948, Zora Neale Hurston was falsely charged with sexually molesting a ten-year-old boy.[86] Hurston was able to prove that she was not in the country when the alleged crimes were supposed to have happened.[87] The charges were dropped but not before the Black press in Baltimore, Chicago and New York had exploited the scandal to the hilt. This was the straw that broke Hurston's back. In a letter to Carl Van Vechten dated October 30, Hurston described the devastating catastrophe in this manner:

> The thing is too fantastic, too evil, too far from reality for me to conceive of it. . . . One inconceivable horror after another swept over me. I went out of myself, I am sure, though no one seemed to notice. It seemed that every hour some other terror assailed me, the last being the Afro-American filth. I care nothing for anything anymore. My country has failed me utterly. My race has seen fit to destroy me without reason, and with the vilest tools conceived of by men so far. A society, eminently Christian, and supposedly devoted to super-democracy has gone so far from its announced purpose, not to *protect* children, but to exploit the gruesome fancies of a pathological case and do this thing to human decency. Please do not forget

that this thing was not done in the South, but in the so-called liberal North. Where shall I look in the country for justice?

This has happened to me, who has always believed in the essential and eventual rightness of my country. I have been on my own since I was fourteen, scuffling my way through high school and college, and as you know, I have never lived an easy life, but struggled on and on to achieve my ideals. I have believed in America; I have fought the good fight; I have kept the faith. . . .

All that I have ever tried to do has proved useless. All that I have believed in has failed me. I have resolved to die. It will take a few days for me to set my affairs in order, and then I will go . . . no acquital will persuade some people that I am innocent. I feel hurled down a filthy privy hole.[88]

"Invisible Dignity" as It Relates to Moral Agency and Poverty in Hurston's Life

The idyllic comforts of Hurston's childhood—an eight-room house with a five-acre garden and numerous fruit trees—all passed away when her mother died. No such security was ever fully known by Hurston again. During the creation of most of her work, Hurston had no way to generate income. She was constantly saddled with financial burdens She began her professional career in New York City with "$1.50, no job, no friends, and a lot of hope."[89]

At the 1925 award dinner, Fannie Hurst was so impressed with Hurston that she offered her a job right on the spot to work as her live-in secretary. Hurston, in dire need of income, accepted the job but was soon fired. Hurst gave the following reasons for Hurston's dismissal:

> Her shorthand was short on legibility, her typing hit or miss, mostly the latter, her filing, a game of find-the-thimble. Her mind ran ahead of my thoughts and she would interject with an impatient suggestion or clarification of what I wanted to say. If dictation bored her she would interrupt, stretch wide her arms and yawn: "Let's get out the car, I'll drive you up to Harlem bad-lands or down to the wharves where men go down to the sea in ships.[90]

Even though Hurston was a high energy person capable of intense work for long stretches of time, she was constantly haunted by financial worries which hampered her creative productivity. In

1931, Hurston wrote a letter to Charlotte Osgood Mason, the "God-mother," proposing the opening of "an exclusive mouth-to-mouth chicken specialist service . . . very fine chicken bouillon, chicken salad, chicken a la king, and hot fried chicken."[91]

> I firmly believe that I shall succeed as a writer, but the time element is important. I know that you worry about my future. Therefore if I had a paying business—which after all could not take up a great deal of my time, I'd cease to be a problem.[92]

Another indication of Hurston's poverty was manifested in her music-dance revue, *The Great Day*, in 1932. Disgruntled but not discouraged, Hurston recruited adept performers and borrowed $250 from "Godmother" for costumes, publicity and photography, producing her revue at the John Golden Theater. The show received good reviews.[93]

> She [Hurston] had already sold her car to put up deposit for theatre and had pawned her radio for $16 to pay carfares for her group of fifty-two people. . . . When it was over, however, Zora again had to borrow money from Mason, this time to pay the cast. The show had not generated enough money. . . .[94]

While writing her first novel in 1934,

> She lived in a one-room house in Sanford renting for $1.50 per week. She composed on a flimsy card table and survived on the fifty cents for groceries her cousin lent her each Friday. By the time the manuscript was completed, she owed eighteen dollars in rent, and on the morning of October 16 the landlord evicted her, despite the fact that she was to earn her first money in three months by booking some folksingers for a city festival.[95]

Zora Neale Hurston's final years dramatized the poverty which haunted her most of her life. In 1948, she returned to Florida. She continued to write, to garden and to tend her dogs. She lived in house trailers, houseboats, and small single-family dwellings. With a career going nowhere and with a dire need for money, Hurston agreed to write political essays for conservative magazines, such as *The American Legion*. She also worked as a domestic, a cook, a librarian and a substitute teacher. In 1952, Hurston became a reporter on the Ruby McCollum case and published more than twenty stories for the *Pittsburgh Courier*.[96]

Weary from the numerous rejection letters concerning her new works of fiction, Hurston wrote to her literary agent, Jean Parker Waterbury, and described her penniless status in this manner:

> Just inching along like a stepped-on worm from day to day. Borrowing a little here and there. . . . The humiliation is getting too much for my self-respect, speaking from inside my soul. I have tried to keep it to myself and just wait. To look and look at the magnificent sweep of the Everglade, birds included, and keep a smile on my face.[97]

In early 1959, Hurston suffered a severe stroke. In October she entered the Saint Lucie County Welfare Home. Three months later, on January 28, 1960, Hurston died of "hypertensive heart disease." At the funeral C. E. Bolen said:

> Zora Neale Hurston went about and didn't care too much how she looked. Or what she said. Maybe people didn't think so much of that. But Zora Neale, every time she went about, had something to offer. She didn't come to you empty.[98]

Alice Walker concludes that one of the clearest lessons of Zora Neale Hurston's life is that there is no such thing as independence in a capitalist society without money of one's own.

> Without money, an illness, even a simple one, can undermine the will. Without money, getting into a hospital is problematic, and getting out without money to pay for the treatment is nearly impossible. Without money, one becomes dependent on other people who are likely to be—even in their kindness—erratic in their support and despotic in their expectations of return. Zora was forced to rely . . . "on the kindness of strangers." Can anything be more dangerous, if the strangers are forever in control?[99]

/1/ Zora Neale Hurston, *Dust Tracks on a Road* (Philadelphia: J. B. Lippincott Co., 1942; reprint ed. 1971), p. 21.
/2/ Ibid.
/3/ Hurston, *Dust Tracks on a Road,* p. 46.

/4/   Ibid., p. 89.

/5/   Zora Neale Hurston, *Jonah's Gourd Vine* (Philadelphia: J. B. Lippincott Co., 1934; reprint ed., 1971), p.

/6/   Robert Hemenway, *Zora Neale Hurston: A Literary Biography* (Urbana: Universtiy of Illinois Press, 1977), p. 32 n. 8, reports, "Hurston's deception about her birth date was consistent through her lifetime. On her second marriage license she claimed to be born in 1901. Her brother, Everette Hurston, Sr., who has prepared a family genealogy, thinks that she was born in 1891. At various times she claimed to be either nine or thirteen at the time of her mother's death; most family members think that the mother died in 1904. . . . I do not have a great deal of confidence in the 1901 date, although it does make the most sense in the context of the verifiable dates pertaining to her life, and it seems to be the date she used most often (with 1903 coming in a close second)." Lillie P. Howard, *Zora Neale Hurston* (Boston: Twayne Publishers, 1980), p. 13, says that based on conversations with Zora Neale Hurston's brother Everette, Zora was not the seventh of eight children but the sixth child with two brothers coming after her.

/7/   Hurston, *Dust Tracks on a Road*, p. 113.

/8/   Hurston, *Dust Tracks on a Road*, especially chapters 8 and 9; see also B. Alsterlund, "Zora Neale Hurston, A Biographical Sketch," *Wilson Bulletin for Libraries* 13 (May 1939); Florence Edwards Borders, "Zora Neale Hurston: Hidden Woman," *Callaloo: A Black Southern Journal of Arts and Letters* 2, ii (1979): 89–92; Larry Neale, Introduction to Zora Neale Hurston, *Dust Tracks on a Road* (reprint ed., New York: J. B. Lippincott Co., 1971), pp. vii–xxiii; Darwin Turner, Introduction to Zora Neale Hurston, *Dust Tracks on a Road* (reprint ed., New York: Arno and *New York Times*, 1969).

/9/   Hemenway, *Zora Neale Hurston*, p. 17.

/10/   Hemenway, *Zora Neale Hurston*, pp. 9–10; see also Patrick Gilpin, "Charles S. Johnson: Entrepreneur of the Harlem Renaissance," in *The Harlem Renaissance Remembered*, ed. Arna Bontemps (New York: Dodd, Mead, 1972), pp. 215–146; "The *Opportunity* Dinner: An Impression," *Opportunity* 5 (July 1927): 208–209; Charles S. Johnson, ed., *Ebony and Topaz: A Collectanea* (New York: National Urban League, 1927).

/11/   Hemenway, *Zora Neale Hurston*, p. 9.

/12/   June Jordan, "On Richard Wright and Zora Neale Hurston," *Black World* 23 (August 1974): 6.

/13/   Hurston, *Dust Tracks on a Road*, pp. 174–205; Hemenway, *Zora Neale Hurston*, pp. 20–21, 62, 63, 81, 88–101 passim, 106, 206–214 passim, discusses in significant detail Hurston's relationship with Fannie Hurst, Annie Meyer and Franz Boas; see also Zora Neale Hurston, "Fannie Hurst," *Saturday Review*, October 9, 1937, pp. 15–16; Robert L. Taylor, "The Doctor, the Lady and Columbia University" [a profile of Annie Nathan Meyer], *New Yorker*, October 23, 1943, pp. 27–32 and October 30, 1943, pp. 28–37.

/14/   Zora Neale Hurston, *Mules and Men* (Philadelphia: J. B. Lippencott Co., 1935; reprint ed., New York: Collier, 197), p. 17; further reading in Marian Murray, *Jump at the Sun: The Story of Zora Neale Hurston* (Chi-

cago: The Third World Press, 1975); Thelma Berlack-Boozer, "Zora Neale
Hurston Success as Author and Scientist," *New York Amsterdam News*, 6
April 1935; Larry Neale, "Eatonville's Zora Neale Huston: A Profile," *Black
Review*, no. 2 (1975), ed. Mel Watkins.

/15/   Langston Hughes, *The Big Sea* (New York: Hill and Wang, 1940).

/16/   Hurston, *Dust Tracks on a Road*, pp. 182–183.

/17/   See Fannie Hurst, "Zora Hurston: A Personality Sketch," *Yale University Library Gazette* XXXV (1961): 17–22; Theodore Pratt, "A Memoir:
Zora Neale Hurston, Florida's First Distinguished Author," *Negro Digest*
11 (February 1962): 52–56; Alice Walker, "In Search of Zora Neale
Hurston," *Ms. Magazine*, March 1975, pp. 74–79, 85–89; Mary Helen
Washington, "The Black Woman's Search for Identity: Zora Neale Hurston's
Work," *Black World* (August 1972): 68–75.

/18/   Hemenway, *Zora Neale Hurston*, pp. 199–201.

/19/   Alice Walker, Foreward to Robert Hemenway, *Zora Neale Hurston*,
p. xvii.

/20/   This is a common folk expression that I learned from my mother.

/21/   Zora Neale Hurston, *Their Eyes Were Watching God* (Philadelphia: J.
B. Lippincott Co., 1938; reprint ed., Urbana: University of Illinois Press,
1978), p. 119.

/22/   I am indebted to Robert Hemenway for his detailed discussion of the
mysterious character, Charlotte van der Veer Quick Mason, in *Zora Neale
Hurston*, pp. 104–117 passim, 124, 127–133 passim, 138–147 passim, 159,
160, 175–185 passim, 203, 207, 282, 341.

/23/   Walker, Foreword to Hemenway, *Zora Neale Hurston*, p. xvi.

/24/   David Levering Lewis, *When Harlem Was in Vogue* (New York::
Alfred A. Knopf, 1981), pp. 151–155 passim, 256–259, 261, 303.

/25/   Langston Hughes, *The Big Sea*, p. 316: "Concerning Negroes, she
(Charlotte Osgood Mason) felt that they were America's great link with the
primitive, and that they had something very precious to give to the Western
world. She felt that there was a mystery and mysticism and spontaneous
harmony in their souls, but that many of them had let the white world
pollute and contaminate that mystery and harmony, and make it something
cheap and ugly, commercial and 'white'."

/26/   Cited by Lewis in *When Harlem Was in Vogue*, p. 154.

/27/   Howard, *Zora Neale Hurston*, pp. 22–25, says that Hurston referred
to Charlotte Mason as "Dearest Godmother," "little mother of the primitive
world," "the immaculate conception," and "a glimpse of the holy grail."

/28/   Hughes, *The Big Sea*, pp. 311–334.

/29/   The contract between Mrs. R. Osgood Mason and Zora Neale
Hurston is part of the Alain Locke Papers, Moorland-Springarn Research
Center, Howard University, Washington, D.C.

/30/   Lewis, *When Harlem Was in Vogue*, pp. 98–103; Jervis Anderson,
This Was Harlem: A Cultural Portrait, 1900–1950 (New York: Farrar, Straus
& Giroux, 1981), especially Part Four: "Life and letters"; Steven Bloom,
"Interaction Between Blacks and Jews in New York City, 1900–1930, As
Reflected in the Black Press" (Ph.D. dissertation, New York University,
1973); Bruce Kellner, *Carl Van Vechten and the Irreverent Decades* (Norman: University of Oklahoma Press, 1968); Edward Luedens, *Carl Van*

Vechten and the Twenties (Albuquerque: University of New Mexico Press, 1955); Alan Schoener, ed., *Harlem on My Mind: Cultural Capital of Black America, 1900–1968* (New York: Random House, 1968).

/31/ Digby Baltzell, *The Protestant Establishment: Aristocracy and Caste in America* (New York: Random House, 1964); John Chamberlain, "When Spring Comes to Harlem," *New York Times*, 11 March 1928; Allen Churchill, *The Literary Decade* (Englewood Cliffs, N.J.: Prentice-Hall, 1971); Rudolph Fisher, "The Caucasian Storms Harlem," *American Mercury*, May 1927; Nathan Huggins, *The Harlem Renaissance* (New York: Oxford University Press, 1971); Wallace Thurman, "Negro Artists and the Negro," *New Republic*, August 31, 1927, pp. 36–39; Carl Van Vechten, *Nigger Heaven* (New York: Grosset & Dunlap/Alfred A. Knopf, 1926).

/32/ Karla F. C. Holloway, "Critical Investigation of Literary and Linguistic Structures in the Fiction of Zora Neale Hurston" (Ph.D. dissertation, Michigan State University, 1978).

/33/ W. E. B. DuBois, "Criteria of Negro Art," *The Crisis* 32 (October 1926): 290–297; Arna Bontemps, "The Two Harlems," *American Scholar* (Spring 1945); Langston Hughes, "The Negro Artist and the Racial Mountain," *The Nation*, June 23, 1925; James Weldon Johnson, "Race Prejudice and the Negro Artist," *Harpers*, November 1928, pp. 769–776; C. V. Calverton, "The Negro's New Belligerent Attitude," *Current History* (September 1929), and "The Negro and American Culture," *Saturday Review*, September 21, 1940; George Schuyler, "The Negro Art Hokum," *The Nation*, June 16, 1926, pp. 662–663; Carl Van Vechten, *"Keep A-Inchin' Along": Selected Writing About Black Arts and Letters*, ed. Bruce Kellner (Westport, Conn.: Greenwood Press, 1979).

/34/ Lewis, *When Harlem Was in Vogue*, p. 99.

/35/ Jeanne Noble, *Beautiful, Also, Are the Souls of My Black Sisters: A History of the Black Woman in America* (Englewood Cliffs, N.J.: Prentice-Hall, 1978), p. 148.

/36/ Noble, ibid., p. 147.

/37/ Harold Cruse, *The Crisis of the Negro Intellectual* (New York: William Morrow & Co., 1967), pp. 9–10, 451–475.

/38/ Mary Helen Washington, "Zora Neale Hurston: A Woman Half in Shadow," Introduction to *I Love Myself When I Am Laughing . . . A Zora Neale Hurston Reader*, ed. Alice Walker (Old Westbury, N.Y.: The Feminist Press, 1979), pp. 7–25.

/39/ Alain Locke, *The New Negro: An Interpretation* (New York: Albert and Charles Boni, 1925; reprint ed., New York: Atheneum, 1970); Alain Locke and W. E. B. DuBois, "The Younger Literary Movement," *Crisis* 27 (1924); Alain Locke, "The Ethics of Culture," *Special Articles: Howard University Records* 17 (February 1923): 178–185.

/40/ Claude McKay, *Harlem: Negro Metropolis* (New York: E. P. Dutton & Co., 1940); *A Long Way from Home* (New York: Arno Press, 1969); Alan L. McLeod, ed., *The Negroes in America*, trans. from the Russian by Robert J. Winter (Port Washington, N.Y: Kennikat Press, 1979); Addison Gayle, *Claude McKay: The Black Poet at War* (Detroit: Broadside Press, 1972).

/41/ Countee Cullen, *On These I Stand* (New York: Harper & Bros., 1947); Stephen H. Bronz, *Roots of Negro Racial Conscious, the 1920s: Three*

Harlem Renaissance Authors (New York: Libra, 1964); Blanche Ferguson, *Countee Cullen and the Negro Renaissance* (New York: Dood, Mead, 1966); Margaret Perry, *A Bio-bibliography of Countee P. Cullen, 1903–1966*, with a Foreword by Don M. Wolfe (Westport Conn.: Greenwood Press, 1971).

/42/ Jean Toomer, *The Wayward and the Seeking: A Collection of Writings by Jean Toomer*, ed. and with an Introduction by Darwin T. Turner (Washington, D.C.: Howard University Press, 1980).

/43/ Langston Hughes, *The Langston Hughes Reader* (New York: G. Braziller, 1958); *I Wonder as I Wander, An Autobiography* (New York: Hill and Wang, 1964); *Good Morning, Revolution, Uncollected Social Protest Writings*, ed. Faith Berry, with a Foreword by Saunders Redding (New York: L. Hill, 1973); Donald C. Dickinson, *A Bio-bibliography of Langston Hughes, 1902–1967*, revised 2nd ed., with a Preface by Arna Bontemps (Hamden, Conn: Archon Books, 1972); Therman B. O'Daniel, ed., *Langston Hughes: Black Genius, A Critical Evaluation* (New York: Morrow, 1971).

/44/ Arna Bontemps, *The Harlem Renaissance Remembered: Essays Edited with a Memoir* (New York: Dodd, Mead, 1972); Charles H. Nichols, ed., *Arna Bontemps-Langston Hughes Letters, 1925–1967* (New York: Dodd, Mead, 1980).

/45/ Sterling A. Brown, *The Negro in American Fiction* (Port Washington, N.Y.: Kennikat Press, 1937; reprint ed.: 1968).

/46/ Mae Gwendolyn Henderson, "Portrait of Wallace Thurman," in *The Harlem Renaissance Remembered*, ed. Arna Bontemps (New York: Dodd, Mead, 1972); Theophilus Lewis, "Wallace Thurman Is Model Harlemite, *New York Amsterdam News*, 4 March 1931.

/47/ James Weldon Johnson, *Along the Way: The Autobiography of James Weldon Johnson* (New York: Viking, 1961; originally published 1933).

/48/ W. E. B. DuBois, *The Gift of Black Folk: The Negro in the Making of America* (Boston: The Stratford Co., 1924); Arnold Rampersad, *The Art and Imagination of W. E. B. DuBois* (Cambridge: Harvard University Press, 1976).

/49/ Jeanne Noble, *Beautiful, Also, Are the Souls*, p. 164, identifies Zora Neale Hurston as the first Black female scholar and writer who cut loose from the typical bourgeoisie pattern of living and writing which characterized the writers before her. Noble goes on to say, "Zora Neale Hurston, anthropologist and writer, not only broke the bonds of bourgeoisie respectability, but defied the rigid expectations of educated, gifted black females and strutted across the pages of the black Renaissance as its Amazon!"

/50/ "A Stern Discipline," interview with Ralph Ellison, *Harper's*, March 1967, pp. 76–95; Darwin Turner, "W. E. B. DuBois and the Theory of a Black Esthetic," *Studies in the Literary Imagination* 7 (Fall 1974): 1–23.

/51/ Gloria Joyce Johnson, "Hurston's Folk: The Critical Significance of Afro-American Folk Tradition in Three Novels and the Autobiography" (Ph.D. dissertation, University of California at Irvine, 1977); Lloyd W. Brown, "Zora Neale Hurston and the Nature of Female Perception," *Obsidian* 4, iii (1978); 39–45; Theresa R. Love, "Zora Neale Hurston's America," *Papers on Language and Literature: a Journal for Scholars and Critics of Language and Literature* 12 (1976): 423–437.

/52/ Stanley J. Kunitz and Howard Haycraft, *Twentieth Century Authors*

(New York: Wilson, 1942); Alain Locke, "A Retrospective Review (and Biography) of the Literature of the Negro," *Opportunity* (January 1938); James O. Young, *Black Writers of the Thirties* (Baton Rouge: Louisiana State University Press, 1973).

/53/ Emma Blake, "Zora Neale Hurston: Author and Folklorist," *Negro History Bulletin* 29 (April 1966): 149–150, 164; James Byrd, "Zora Neale Hurston: A Negro Folklorist," *Tennessee Folklore Society Bulletin* 21 (1955): 37–41; Hugh Gloster, Zora Neale Hurston, Novelist and Folklorist," *Phylon* 3 (Second Quarter 1943): 153–156; Robert Hemenway, "Folklore Field Notes from Zora Neale Hurston," *Black Scholar* 7 (April 1976): 39–46.

/54/ Mary Helen Washington, "The Black Woman's Search for Identity, Zora Neale Hurston's Work," *Black World* (August 1972): 68–75.

/55/ Mary Helen Washington, *A Zora Neale Hurston Reader*, p. 11, suggests that the "intellectual lynching of Zora Neale Hurston" may have resulted from Hurston being a Black woman "whose entire career output was subjected to the judgments of critics, both white and black, who were all men."

/56/ See Holloway, "Critical Investigation," p. 36.

/57/ Mary Helen Washington, *A Zora Neale Hurston Reader*, p. 8: "To a large extent, the attention focused on Zora Hurston's controversial personality and lifestyle have inhibited any objective critical analysis of her work. Few male critics have been able to resist sly innuendos and outright attacks on Hurston's personal life, even when the work in question was not affected by her disposition or her private affairs. But these controversies have loomed so large in the reviews of her work that once again the task of confronting them must precede any reappraisal or reevaluation of her highly neglected work."

/58/ Hemenway, *Zora Neale Hurston*, pp. 218–220, 241–242, 333–334; Howard, *Zora Neale Hurston*, pp. 170–175.

/59/ Walker, Foreword to Hemenway, *Zora Neale Hurston*, p. xv.

/60/ Hemenway, *Zora Neale Hurston*, pp. 93–94, 308, 314 (first marriage to Herbert Sheen); pp. 273–274, 314 (second marriage to Albert Price III).

/61/ Alice Walker, Foreword to Hemenway, *Zora Neale Hurston*, p. xv., writes, "They [Hurston's critics] disliked her apparent sensuality: the way she tended to marry or not marry men, but enjoyed them anyway, while never missing a beat in her work. They hinted slyly that Zora was gay, or at least bi-sexual—how else could they account for her drive?—though there is not a shred of evidence that this is true. The accusation becomes humorous—and, of course, at all time irrelevant—when one considers that what she *did* write was some of the most healthily rendered heterosexual loving in our literature."

/62/ Carl Van Vechten to Fannie Hurst, 5 July 1960, Johnson Collection, Yale University Library, New Haven.

/63/ Ibid.

/64/ Zora Neale Hurston to the *Orlando Sentinel*, 11 August 1955, in response to the Supreme Court desegregation decision in 1954.

/65/ Ibid.

/66/ Ibid.

/67/ Hemenway, *Zora Neale Hurston*, p. 338, points out that Zora Hurston objected to the implied pathological stereotype in the desegregation decision wherein it was thought that Black students could learn only if they were in close proximity with whites. Black students would be "uplifted" to white standards and a white way of life. "The Supreme Court ruling," she said, "implied that just like mules being led by a white mare, black students had to be led by white pupils and white teachers."

/68/ Several of Hurston's essays and articles addressed specifically this viewpoint: "Cujo's Own Story of the Last American Slaver," *Journal of Negro History* 12 (October 1927): 648–663; "Race Cannot Become Great Until It Recognizes Its Talent," *Washington Tribune*, 29 December 1934; "Negroes Without Self-Pity," *American Mercury*, November 1943, pp. 601–603; "Crazy for This Democracy," *Negro Digest* 4 (December 1945): 45–48.

/69/ Richard Wright, "Between Laughter and Tears," *New Masses*, October 5, 1937; "Blueprint for Negro Writing," *New Challenges* 2 (Fall 1937): 53–65.

/70/ Roy Wilkins, "The Watchtower," *New York Amsterdam News*, 27 February 1943.

/71/ Lester Granger, *California Eagle*, 20 December 1951.

/72/ Wallace Thurman, *Infants of the Spring* (New York: Macaulay, 1932), pp. 229–230.

/73/ Darwin Turner, *In a Minor Chord* (Carbondale: Southern Illinois University Press, 1971), p. 120.

/74/ "Niggerati" was a term Hurston coined to identify the pomp and circumstance that existed among the Renaissance literati.

/75/ Hurston coined this term, "Astorperious," to capture her many experiences of whites on Park Avenue while visiting Mrs. Mason.

/76/ Arna Bontemps, "From Eatonville, Fla. to Harlem," review of *Dust Tracks on a Road*, by Zora Neale Hurston, *New York Herald Tribune*, 23 November 1942.

/77/ Harold Preece, "The Negro Folk Cult," review of *Dust Tracks on a Road*, by Zora Neale Hurston, *Crisis* 43 (1936): 364, 374.

/78/ Sterling Brown, "Old Time Tales," review of *Mules and Men* (1936), a clipping in the James Weldon Johnson Collection, Yale University Library, New Haven.

/79/ Turner, *In a Minor Chord*; see also Blyden Jackson, "Some Negroes in the Land of Goshen," *Tennessee Folklore Society Bulletin* 19 (December 1953): 103–107.

/80/ Alain Locke, "Dry Fields and Green Pastures," review of *Moses, Man of the Mountain*, by Zora Neale Hurston, *Opportunity* 18 (January 1940): 7.

/81/ Ralph Ellison, "Recent Negro Fiction," review of *Moses, Man of the Mountain*, by Zora Neale Hurston, *New Masses*, August 5, 1941, p. 211.

/82/ Robert Bone, *The Negro Novel in America* (New Haven: Yale University Press, 1965), p. 41; see also reviews in *New York Herald Tribune Books*, 26 November 1939; *Boston Transcript*, 18 November 1939; *New York Times*, November 1939, p. 21; *New Yorker*, November 11, 1939, p. 75; *Saturday Review*, November 11, 1939, p. 11; *New York Post*, 9 November 1939.

/83/ Hemenway, *Zora Neale Hurston*, pp. 241–242, 333–335.

/84/ Zora Neale Hurston's manuscript chapter, "Concert," *Dust Tracks on a Road,* James Weldon Johnson Collection, Yale University Library, New Haven.

/85/   Zora Neale Hurston to Charlotte Osgood Mason, 25 September 1931 and 15 October 1931, Locke Collection, Howard University.

/86/   Hemenway says that he pieced together the story of the Hurston morals charge from a number of sources: interviews in New York City with Burroughs Mitchell of Scribner's, with her lawyer, Louis Waldman, and with her agent, Jean Parker Waterbury. My understanding of the episode is based on Hemenway, *Zora Neale Hurston,* pp. 319–324.

/87/   *Baltimore Afro American,* National Ed., 16, 23 October, 6 November 1948; *New York Age,* 16 October 1948.

/88/   Zora Neale Hurston to Carl Van Vechten, 30 October 1948, James Weldon Johnson Collection, Yale University Library, New Haven.

/89/   For a detailed discussion of Hurston and her economic situation, see Hemenway, *Zora Neale Hurston,* p. 9; also, Howard, pp. 13–31.

/90/   Fannie Hurst, "Zora Hurston: A Personality Sketch," *Yale University Library Gazette* 35 (1961): 17.

/91/   Zora Neale Hurston to Charlotte Osgood Mason, 25 September 1931, Alain Locke Collection, Howard University.

/92/   Ibid.

/93/   Review of *The Great Day, New York Herald Tribune,* 17 January, 1932.

/94/   Howard, *Zora Neale Hurston,* p. 26.

/95/   Cited in Hemenway, *Zora Neale Hurston,* p. 189, based on Hurston, *Dust Tracks on a Road,* chapter 11, "Books and Things."

/96/   William Bradford Huie, *Ruby McCollum: Woman in the Suwannee Jail* (New York: Dutton, 1956), especially Hurston's writings, pp. 89–101.

/97/   Quoted in Hemenway, *Zora Neale Hurston,* p. 338.

/98/   Ibid.

/99/   Walker, foreword to Hemenway, *Zora Neale Hurston,* p. xvi.

CHAPTER V

RESOURCES FOR A CONSTRUCTIVE ETHIC IN THE WORK OF ZORA NEALE HURSTON

Resources in the Fiction of Zora Neale Hurston

In Zora Neale Hurston's fiction there is evidence of a second characteristic of moral agency which is expressed in the "never practiced delicacy" which Black women oftentimes convert into quiet grace. The quality of being dainty, luxurious and feeble in constitution, characterized by modesty with an extreme respect for protocol, was not a part of the moral counsel of Zora Neale Hurston, nor a part of the ethical behavior of the female characters in her writings.[1]

Hurston and her literary counterparts acknowledge the raw coarseness of life. They face life squarely, front and center, without reverence or protection by the dominant powers in society. The white, elitist attributes of passive gentleness and an enervative delicacy, considered particularly appropriate to womanhood,[2] proved to be non-functional in the pragmatic survival lifestyle of Black women. Cultivating conventional amenities has not been a luxury afforded to Black women.[3]

"Quiet" is the qualifying word describing grace as a virtue in the moral agency of Black women. "Quiet" acknowledges the invisibility of their moral character. Black women have never been granted the protective privileges that allow one to become immobilized by fear and rage.[4] The Black woman's very life depends upon her being able to decipher the various sounds in the larger world, to hold in check the nightmare figures of terror, to fight for basic freedoms against the sadistic law enforcement agencies in her community, to resist the temptation to capitulate to the demands of the status quo, to find meaning in the most despotic circumstances and to create something where nothing was before.[5] Most of the time this is done without the mumble of a single word, without an eruptive cry to the hierarchical systems that oppress her.

Hurston, a novelist, an anthropologist and a critic, never presented a coherent ethical system which the reader could apply to her work. Instead, Hurston's work implies the values that evolve from the moral wisdom of the Black community.[6] The contrapuntal movement of "never practiced delicacy" and "quiet grace" is at the heart of her writings. A clue to her aims and techniques, particularly in the development of the plots, focuses on the special ethical quality by which Hurston's characters evoke, sustain and augment their actions in order to avert capricious and uncalculating perils. The presupposition behind her cryptic statements and dramatic utterances is that the Black community is called forth to fashion a set of values in their own terms as well as mastering, radicalizing and sometimes destroying pervasive, negative orientations. For Hurston, this is the essence of quiet grace.

Even though Zora Neale Hurston's work is not an ethical treatise, her fiction does give indication of the values the Black community embraces in order to continue living despite abusive and dehumanizing restrictions imposed by the larger society.[7] Hurston's characters provide elucidation as to the symmetrical and transitive moral values which have evolved from shared common experiences. Hurston's view is formulated on the premise that the ethical quality of quiet grace is derived from living in close association with others. Through her literature, Zora Neale Hurston provided vicarious experiences of grace wherein this particular virtue serves as the motivation for channeling the power for change along definite lines and toward definite ends.

Zora Neale Hurston's method of characterization involved both ethos and pathos. She provided representative experience from the lives of Black folks as moral agents. Her fiction bears a plausible stamp of veracity. Hurston created literary types that are both historically true and morally instructive. Her she/roes and he/roes learn to glean directives for living in the here-and-now.[8]

Of particular importance in understanding Hurston's handling of the moral agency of the characters in her fiction is that the protagonists are always connected with the general history of the race in the context of community. Hurston identified significant incidents in ordinary life and the moral wisdom that evolves.[9] Selecting those aspects of experience that show how each generation is dependent upon the last for its understanding of moral wisdom and in turn, each new generation creates it for the next, Hurston developed characters who possess this quality of quiet grace. They are women and men who refuse to become inwardly brutalized. Hurston's moral agents are neither strictly allegorical nor simply naturalistic. They are living human beings who "overturn the normative moral structure of the oppressing society."[10]

In assessing the work of Hurston, it can be said that her characters are not crippled by oppression. Since the plots are not contrived, Hurston's fiction provides incident after incident of Black people facing ignominious circumstances. With a quality of irresistible efficacy, they adopt and accept their lot in life, while simultaneously embracing the external energy of replenishing help, which makes easier the realization of limits imposed on them. Hurston's characters are not dominated by the exigencies of plot but are involved in a continuous search for equilibrium between irreconcilable opposites. The community's values come through clearly in the critical speeches in her novels.[11]

The agony and urgency just beneath the surface of the Black existential reality lend little time for wound licking frailty.[12] Hurston introduces characters who take risks.[13] As real-life prototypes they do not become dysfunctional by magnifying the nightmare of terror. Instead, they function with prudence. Like Janie (nee Crawford) Killick Stark Woods, in *Their Eyes Were Watching God*, the Black community sees life as a great tree in leaf, "with things suffered, things enjoyed, things done and undone. Dawn and doom was in the branches."[14]

QUIET GRACE AS TRUTH

Zora Neale Hurston's basic assumption in all of her fiction was that quiet grace is manifested in the search for truth. Both in tone and language, Hurston's characters look at the world with their own eyes, form their own judgments and demythologize whole bodies of so-called social legitimacy. Encouraged by the oral-aural wisdom of the community, these women and men consider the inferences they receive from implicit data within the folk culture and then try to recover the deeper meaning of life by reflecting on their own experiences. Karla Holloway contends, "Each of Hurston's novels, in different fashion, enjoins a search for truth. Usually the search ends in some internal recognition of sin or weakness. The search can end in a fulfillment after rectifying this weakness."[15]

The themes and language in all of Hurston's fiction embrace a moral wisdom wherein grace and truth constitute each other. They are not fixed, eternal structures but dynamic and evolving qualities that force consideration of new possibilities. In other words, grace as the search for truth is not understood as the element that rescues Black people from the bewildering pressures and perplexities of institutionalized social evils, but rather, it serves to designate images of options that are possible, to illuminate choices in human interaction.

Satisfying not only aesthetic demands with her folkloric fiction, Zora Neale Hurston introduced characters who knew how to reduce the enigmas and elusive mysteries of social structures. And, even when they are forced to participate in the pervasiveness of racist/patriarchal values, they eventually come to understand where they have been and why they have been there. Hurston's characters emerge full scale with a complex and dynamic communal structure, interpreting tradition and perceptions, in light of the relativity of truth, or else, their destruction becomes both necessary and inevitable in the context of the community.[16]

Hurston saw herself in her fiction and in the occasional articles she wrote, especially on racial matters and the experience of the American Black, as someone particularly qualified to see the truth— "to hit a straight lick with a crooked stick."[17] A just appraisal of moral agency within the Black community is one of the attributes of Hurston's work. This is precisely one of the positions that I believe Hurston was working from.

QUIET GRACE AS TRUTH IN JONAH'S GOURD VINE

Zora Neale Hurston's first novel, *Jonah's Gourd Vine* (1934), was published before, but written after, her first folklore collection, *Mules and Men* (1935). Using material from her own family history, Hurston sketches in broad outline grace as a search for truth in the life of a man who is at war with the world of the flesh and the world of the spirit.[18] She exposed the paradoxical sensibilities of being a southern Black man, living under a superimposed Jewish-Christian culture. In the introduction to *Jonah's Gourd Vine* Larry Neale says that there are two distinctly different cultural attitudes towards the concept of spirituality in this early twentieth-century Black community. "The one springs from a formerly enslaved communal society, non-Christian in background where there is really no clean-

cut dichotomy between the world of spirit and the world of flesh.
The other attitude is clearly more rigid, being a blend of Puritan
concepts and the fire-and-brimstone imagery of the white evan-
gelical tradition."[19]

In a letter Zora Neale Hurston wrote to James Weldon Johnson
in April 1934, she summarized the depth and subtlety of the plot: "I
have tried to present a Negro preacher who is neither funny nor an
imitation Puritan ram-rod in pants. Just the human being and poet
that he must be to succeed in a Negro pulpit. . . ."[20]

The Reverend John Buddy Pearson's chief failing is his insatia-
ble desire for women. He is portrayed as a man who has an unusual
susceptibility to female charm. He ventures from one affair to
another. As the pastor, John justifies his mercurial but uncontrolled
behavior to his congregation in this manner—"Ah just uhnother one
uh God's crumblin' clods. . . . Ahm uh natchel man but look lak
some uh y'all is dumb tuh de fack."[21] Thus, the ethical understanding of quiet grace as the search for truth becomes John's battle to
find out if fleshly cravings obviate one's ministry. The denouement of
the novel gives an affirmative answer to this question.

John Buddy Pearson is also a dramatic example of the biblical
Jonah in that he is in constant escape from responsibility. In the
early part of this novel, Pearson's stepfather advises him to "Stop
running away. Face things out."[22] But John Pearson chooses a life of
flight. He runs away from any person, place or thing that demands
more of him than he is willing to give. In the first chapter John has a
serious quarrel with his stepfather so he runs away to pursue life
"over de creek." He says, "Ahm goin' tuh zar, and dat's on de other
side of far."[23] John's attempt to go to "zar" is an escape from an old
world in favor of a new world. "He finds the ways of the new world
baffling, finds acculturation next to impossible and is only meta-
morphosed externally. Internally he still clings to the old ways; he
can not forsake them, partly because he is unaware that he should,
and partly because they are part of his blood. . . ."[24]

Soon after John crosses "over de creek" he gets into a fight and
takes to the road. As the story unfolds, John returns and marries, but
runs back and forth between Lucy, his wife, and a number of other
women. John's call to the ministry underscores, once again, his
Jonah symdrome. As he tells the congregation, God "called me long
uhgo, but Ah wouldn't heed tu de voice, but brothers and sisters,
God done whipped me tuh it."[25] Even when John's baby daughter

becomes deathly ill, John runs away: "Ah can't stand 'round and see
mah baby girl die. Lucy! Lucy! God don't love me. Ah got tuh go
'way 'til it's all over. Ah jus' can't stay."[26]

For a brief time John Buddy Pearson experienced a glimmer of
quiet grace in his life. John stops running away from life and becomes willing to face the truth for a short while. "He was going
about learning old truths for himself as all men must and the
knowledge he got burnt his inside like acid."[27] In the end, John is
killed in flight from his last affair with a young prostitute. He "drove
on but half-seeing the railroad from looking inward."[28]

Grace as the search for truth can be summarized in *Jonah's
Gourd Vine* in this manner:

> This novel is about John Buddy Pearson, a likeable,
> exasperating, bewildering character who at times resembles
> the Biblical Jonah, Samson, and sometimes even Christ him-
> self. Like Jonah, John Buddy runs away from life, responsibility
> and God; like Samson, his weakness is women and it is because
> of them that he loses his strength and position of power; like
> Christ, he "wore the cloak of a cloud about his shoulders . . ."
> As a Christ figure, he is also something of a Jonah's gourd vine
> who provides at least spiritual comfort to his parishioners; like
> Christ's detractors, John's "friends" who variously refer to him
> as a Jonah's gourd vine, believe that he must be destroyed for
> the welfare of the community.[29]

To create her most evocative effect, Hurston introduced Lucy
Ann Potts as the leading woman in this novel. Lucy symbolizes the
ephemeral gourd vine in her husband's life and ministry. Over and
over again, she provides the shade for her sun-stricken preacher-
husband. Like her husband, Lucy does not search for truth. Instead, she spends most of her life rescuing and protecting John from
the harsh consequences of his promiscuity. Lucy even teaches John
how to dispel the church members' discontent with his behavior.

> You preach uh sermon on yo'self, and you call tuh they
> remembrance some uh de good things you done, so they kin
> put it long side de other and when you lookin' at two things at
> de same time neither one of 'em don't look so big, but don't tell
> uh lie, John. If youse guilty you don't need tuh git up dere and
> put yo' own name on de sign post uh scorn, but don't say you
> didn't do it neither. Whut you say, let it be de truth. Dat what
> comes from de heart will sho reach de heart again.[30]

Sitting unprotected under the sun, John would have suffered severely but Lucy saved him from such discomfort.

Lucy is the strongest character in the novel, "serving as both a mainstay for John, a cohesive force for her family, all but wills him the backbone necessary to rise in the world."[31]

Before Lucy's death, at age thirty-seven, she confides to a friend about the manifestation of quiet grace in her life (despite her continual experiences of sorrow and agony). "Ah done been in sorrow's kitchen and Ah done licked out all the pots. Ah done died in grief and been buried in de bitter waters, and Ah done rose agin from de dead lak Lazarus. Nothin' kin touch mah soul no mo'."[32]

A crucial scene in this novel is when Lucy, lying sick on her deathbed, makes reference to John's philandering. John tells her to "shut up! Ahm sick and tired uh yo' yawin' and jawin'. 'Taint nothin ah hate lak gittin sin throwed in mah face dat done got cold. A do ez Ah please. You jus' uh hold back tuh me nohow . . . uh man can't utilize hisself."[33] Lucy retorts, "Big talk ain't changin' what you doin'. You can't clean yo self wid yo tongue lak uh cat."[34] In an act of malice John slaps Lucy for the first and only time of their marriage. "Ah don't need you no mo' nor nothin you got tuh say, Ahm uh man grown. Don't need no guardzeen atall."[35] John's insistence upon "escape" dooms him to extinction. Lucy's obsession to shield John from the brunt of the world means she negates her own life. While the Black man struggles with God, the Black woman struggles with the man.[36]

Both the aesthetic richness and the ethical understanding in this novel can be summarized in the following way:

> *Jonah's Gourd Vine* captures the culture of black men and women as they love and hate, dream and die in a culture-denying society . . . The ebb and flow of life presented in the novel belongs to every person who will not or cannot reconcile himself to life.[37]

QUIET GRACE AS TRUTH IN "THEIR EYES WERE WATCHING GOD"

Their Eyes Were Watching God (1937) is Zora Neale Hurston's second and most popular novel. For thirty years Janie Crawford, the protagonist, engages in her search for self-fulfillment. The drama is based on the values of the community and the tension that arises

when the community advises Black women on what they ought to do
and what, in fact, is done.[38] "Janie is not afraid to balk at the
conventions of culture and upbringing to follow what she feels is the
best course for her life."[39] "This is the first novel of a Black woman
who has her eyes on the horizon, searching for joy, love, happiness,
searching for people, rather than things."[40]

One of Hurston's characteristic techniques is her use of dramatic irony. Janie returns home after a two-year absence to tell her
best friend, Phoeby Watson, the story of her struggle for full humanity. Janie repeats her journey accurately without romantic illusions.
Her gratuitous retelling of her past, her stratagems and her linguistic idioms all correspond to the existential reality of the Black
community. Janie's pattern of grace is visible only in retrospect. The
way she is transformed in the search for truth is explicit.

The high point of this novel occurs when Janie comes to the
end of her search. After thirty years of looking, Janie finally finds a
spiritual freedom and a physically satisfying love in Vergible (Tea
Cake) Woods. The tragedy is that Janie has to kill him to save her
own life. However, Janie accepts this loss and all other losses as part
of the quiet grace that brings one to self-authenticity. In sum, in
Their Eyes Were Watching God, Hurston developed a new character
type, who embodies in creative ways radical aspects of the Black
community. Janie surmises, "If you kin see de light at daybreak, you
don't keer if you die at dusk. It's so many people never seen de light
at all. Ah wuz fumblin' round and God opened de door."[41] Hurston's
characters whose self-esteem and identity are based on illusion and
false values are alienated from the Black folk community. Those, like
Janie herself, who struggle against self-alienating values toward a
deeper sense of community, experience wholeness.[42]

It is important to see how Zora Neale Hurston prepared her
heroine, Janie, for newly found identity and freedom. Janie's re-
counting of her experiences begins with her being weighed down
with false images that said that as a Black and as a woman she is not
allowed to exist naturally and freely. Hurston contrasted these community values of one generation with the next.

Nanny Crawford, Janie's grandmother, was a freed slavewoman
who understood marriage as the way to escape poverty and abuse, as
a way to avoid the traditional fate of Black women. Nanny had
suffered the sexual will and whims of the white slaveowner, which
resulted in the birth of an illegitimate child. The baby resembled
the white man so much that his wife violently attacked Nanny and

threatened to have Nanny beaten with one hundred lashes of raw hide on her bare back, "till the blood run down yo' heels."

> "You better git dat kivver offa dat yougun and dat quick!"
> she clashed at me. "Look lak you don't know who is Mistis on
> dis plantation, Madam. But Ah aims to show you . . . Nigger,
> whut's yo' baby doin' wid gray eyes and yaller hair?" She begin
> tuh slap mah jaws ever which a'way. Ah never felt the fust ones
> 'cause Ah wuz too busy gittin de kivver back over mah chile.
> But dem last lick burnt me lak fire. Ah had too many feelin's
> tuh tell which one tuh follow so Ah didn't cry and Ah didn't do
> nothing else. But then she kept astin me how come mah baby
> look white. She asted me dat maybe twenty-five or thirty times
> . . . So Ah told her, "Ah don't know nothin' but what Ah'm told
> tuh do, 'cause Ah ain't nothin' but uh nigger and uh slave."[43]

Nanny then runs away and hides out in the swamp before her body had time to heal because she didn't want her baby to be sold away from her. "De noise uh de owls skeered me, de limbs of dem cypress trees took to crawlin' and movin' round after dark, and two three times Ah heered panthers prowlin' round. But nothin' never hurt me 'cause de Lawd knowed how it was."[44] Nanny's gallant actions amidst fear was the quiet grace of slavewomen, but Janie yearned for something more. The grandmother wanted Janie to have all the material possessions and protective security she herself never had. After Emancipation, Nanny talked about quiet grace as the search for dreams and aspirations. "Ah wanted to preach a great sermon about colored women sittin' on high, but they wasn't no pulpit for me. . . . Ah been waiting a long time Janie, but nothin' Ah been through ain't too much if you just take a stance on high ground lak Ah dreamed."[45]

Nanny's entire moral code has developed in relation to the ethical ambiguities in her experience. Functional prudence is the value center for self-fulfillment. As a slavewoman, Nanny, at an early age had learned to discern suitable courses of action, especially as regards survival. "Ah was born back due in slavery so it wasn't for me to fulfill my dreams of whut a woman oughta be and do. . . . Ah didn't want to be used for a work-ox and a brood-sow and Ah didn't want muh daughter used dat way neither."[46] In order to follow the most ethical course, Janie's grandmother tries to teach her critical forethought and discerning deliberation, which Black women have mastered with an extremely delicate sense of balance down through the years. The virtue of quiet grace is what allows Black women to venture on, to continue taking risks, to push against limits that deny their beingness.

More than anything, Nanny wants Janie to be spared the servile role of Black women in the society.

> Honey, de white man is de rule of everything as fur as Ah been able tuh find out. Maybe it's some place way off in de ocean where de black man is in power, but we don't know nothin' but what we see. So de white man throw down de load and tell de nigger man tuh pick it up because he have to, but he don't tote it. He hand it to his womenfolks. De nigger woman is de mule uh de world so far as Ah can see. Ah been praying fuh it to be different wid you. Lawd, Lawd, Lawd.[47]

Since Nanny believes in marriage as security, she chooses Logan Killicks, a middle age man who has sixty acres, "de onliest organ in town, amongst colored folks," a house bought and paid for, to be Janie's lawful wedded husband. When Janie complains to her grandmother about Logan's dirty body and crusty feet and how, in turn, she does not love him and cannot love him, Nanny sends Janie back to Mr. Killick fully believing that marriage with material possessions is the only way for Black women to forge forward free of the "mule" role.[48]

In the second marriage to Jody Starks, Janie tries again to find her full humanity. But Jody Starks is an ambitious young man, who lives with the illusion of his irresistable maleness, "uh throne in de seat of his pants."[49] Jody sees Janie as a showpiece, a possession, "A pretty doll baby lak you is made to sit on de front porch and rock and fan yo'self."[50] When Janie is twenty-one and has been married to Jody seven years she realizes that her marriage is purely per-functory. "The spirit of the marriage left the bedroom and took to living in the parlor. It was there to shake hands whenever company came to visit, but it never went back inside the bedroom again."[51] It is at this point that Janie accepts, "marriage did not make love. Janie's first dream was dead. So she became a woman."[52] Janie is also confronted with the limitations that marriage placed on her personal freedom. She sees these restrictions in relation to the entire histor-ical and social spectrum of the community.

In contrast to her previous treatment of the female character, Lucy Potts, in *Jonah's Gourd Vine*, Hurston presented Janie as a woman whose success or failure would be measured by the goal of self-actualization. For instance, on the day that Jody slaps Janie

because dinner turned out badly, Hurston revealed the quality of
quiet grace by contrasting Janie's outer actions with her inner
thoughts.

> Janie stood where he left her for unmeasured time and
> thought. She stood there until something fell off the shelf
> inside her. Then she went inside to see what it was. It was her
> image of Jody tumbled down and shattered. But looking at it
> she saw it never was the flesh and blood figure of her dreams.
> Just something she had grabbed up to drape her dreams over.
> In a way she turned her back upon the image where it lay and
> looked further . . . She found that she had a host of thoughts
> she had never expressed to him, and numerous emotions she
> had never let Jody know about. Things packed up and put away
> in parts of her heart where he could never find them. She was
> saving up feelings for some man she had never seen.[53]

As Janie confronts the real feelings which she has concealed under a
conventional code of social behavior, she creates a new code of
values more appropriate to her needs. Mary Helen Washington
contends, "Janie has to resist both male domination and the empty
materialism of white culture in order to get to the horizon."[54]

The third husband, Tea Cake (whose real name is Vergible
Woods), is at least eighteen years younger than Janie. He is a young
Black man, generally dependable, who plays the banjo, hunts and
gives mammoth parties. Of all the men, Janie prefers Tea Cake's
youthful ardor. "Tea Cake makes her feel alive, vital, needed,
wanted, loved and unlimited, and she gives of herself freely. The
horizon with all its infinite possibilities, is back."[55] With Tea Cake,
Janie's soul "crawled out from its hiding place."[56]

The essence of quiet grace in this novel can be explained
thusly:

> It is about the universal quest for the fulfillment of body
> and soul, for it makes clear that material possessions and se-
> curity are not really the stuff out of which good marriages and
> love are made. Born in a racial, masculine environment which
> expected certain stereotyped reactions from women, especially
> if they happened to be black, Janie becomes larger than her
> world, embracing the horizon as the limit, and throwing off the
> shackles of womanhood and society. She attempts to survive
> within society at first, as her two early marriages attest, but
> determines to please herself when tradition fails to satisfy
> her.[57]

June Jordan claims that Hurston revealed the significance of quiet grace in the lives of Black women by writing the prototypical Black novel of affirmation.

> But the book gives us more: the story unrolls a fabulous, written-film of Blacklife freed from the constraints of oppression; here we may learn Black possibilities of ourselves if we could ever escape the hateful and alien context that has so deeply disturbed and multilated our rightful efflorescence—as people.[58]

QUITE GRACE AS TRUTH IN "MOSES, MAN OF THE MOUNTAIN"

Moses, Man of the Mountain (1939), the longest fiction in Hurston's canon, is an allegorical satire concerning the affinities between Voodoo and Christianity.[59] While Hurston's earlier novel, *Jonah's Gourd Vine*, dealt with the common features of these two religions manifested in the life of a Black pastor, this novel delineates the same causal, coalescent relationship by retelling the biblical legend of Moses in the Black esthetic tradition. Moses, associated with the god Damballah, is "the finest hoodoo man in the world." Hurston provided somewhat greater depth of values of the Black community by establishing Moses as an amalgam of the best features of magic art, "the secrets of the deep," and the practices in the inner and outer life of those who are called God's chosen people.

Just as Janie in *Their Eyes Were Watching God* is Hurston's most powerful female character, Moses in this novel is her most powerful male character. Jethro, his father-in-law, tells him, "The great I AM took the soul of the world and wrapped some flesh around it and that made you."[60] Even when Hurston tried to demystify Moses as a person with two beings, one that lives and flourishes in the daylight and stands guard and one that walks and howls at night, she still described him in universal terms. "He was embodying everybody boiled down to a drop."[61] Hemenway says that Hurston's Moses has three distinct roles, "the divinely designated leader of Israel, the possessor of nature's secrets and the most powerful hoodoo doctor of antiquity."[62]

> All across the continent there are the legends of the greatness of Moses, but not because of his beard nor because he brought the laws down Sinai. No, he is revered because he had the power to go to the mountain and to bring them down. Many men could climb mountains. Anyone could bring down

laws that had been handed to them. But who can talk with God
face to face? Who has the power to command God to go to a
peak of a mountain and there demand of Him laws with which
to govern a nation? What other man has ever seen with his eyes
even the back part of God's glory? Who else has ever com-
manded the wind and the hail? The light and darkness? That
calls for power, and that is what Africa sees in Moses to worship.[63]

Hurston used Black speech, to codify into written form, the subtle
dynamics of the metaphorical and proverbial connections between
the exodus of the Hebrews and the African-American trek from
slavery to freedom. She deflated the rigid seriousness of biblical
rhetoric. Just below the surface of this drama is the collective
wisdom revealed in the Black community related to the discrepancy
between professing Christian learnings and practicing a religious
faith.

The basis for the dynamic structure in *Moses, Man of the
Mountain* is that it allows us to see "how Hurston 'invents' a legend
to demonstrate how the traditional legend of Moses might have
been created."[64] Hemenway maintains, "Hurston attempts nothing
less than to kidnap Moses from Judeo-Christian tradition, claiming
that his true birthright is African and that his true constituency is
Afro-American."[65] Hurston placed Moses in both a mythological
and historical past. She juxtaposed the biblical legend with modern
day reality. "Hurston transplanted American Blacks to, and ac-
climatized them within, an Old Testament milieu." For example,
the Hebrews working in Egypt refer to the overseer as "bossman."
In the wilderness when they grow tired of manna and quail, they
yearn for ". . . the nice fresh fish . . . nice sweet-tasting little pan-
fish," that they enjoyed in Egypt.[66] Even the housing in Goshen
resembles the living quarters of chattel slaves on southern plantations.

Zora Neale Hurston retold the legend of Moses with compel-
ling immediacy. She discounted the biblical version of Moses'
origin. She saw it only as a mythical concoction of Miriam, the
daughter of a Hebrew couple, Jochebed and Amran.

According to the Hurston legend, the Egyptian Pharaoh was
concerned with the sweeping growth in population of the Hebrew
people. In order to profit at the expense of humankind, slave labor
was imposed. The monarch also issued an edict that newborn male
children should be killed. When Jochebed gave birth to the male

child, Moses, she made a basket for the child, put it afloat on the
Nile River and asked Miriam to watch. Miriam fell asleep. When she
awoke the "child and his basket were gone, that was all." Thus,
Miriam invented an alibi that spread quickly and became a legend.
Despite the lack of corroborative evidence, Miriam and Jochebed
convinced the Hebrew people of Goshen that the handmaidens of
Pharoah's daughter had taken the child from the ark of bulrushes to
the palace. The princess wanted to raise the Hebrew boy as her own
child. Jochebed, the mother, goes to the palace to offer her services
as a nursemaid for the newly found child but she is told that there is
no new baby to be nursed. By this time the community, like
wildfire, has conceived and added more details in order to lend
credence to the rumor that Moses, a Hebrew child, was living in
Pharoah's palace, and was being raised by Pharoah's daughter.

> Ho, ho! Pharaoh hates Hebrews does he? He passed a
> law to destroy all our sons and he gets a Hebrew child for a
> grandson. Ain't that rich. . . . The crowd talked far into the
> night of the Hebrew victory over Pharaoh and went home.
> They did not question too closely for proof. They wanted to
> believe and they did. It kept them from feeling utterly van-
> quished by Pharaoh. They had something to cherish and chew
> on, if they could say they had a Hebrew in the Palace.[68]

Moses comes of age in Pharaoh's court. He is appointed general of the Army. In order to carry out his grandfather's expansionist
policies, he marries an Ethiopian princess. Eventually, Moses becomes aware of the plight of the Hebrews in Goshen. One day he
sees an Egyptian foreman senselessly beating an already bloody
slave, so Moses kills the Egyptian. He flees from Egypt for fear that
his crime would reveal his true identity which was being seriously
and maliciously questioned in the palace. Moses begins his search
for a country he had never seen. "He was seeing visions of a nation
he had never heard of where there would be equality and opportunity and less difference between top and bottom."[69]

Hurston used Moses' flight speech to make a brief historical
survey of the various stages of quiet grace in the lives of Black
people up to this point in time.

> Moses had crossed over. He was not in Egypt. He had
> crossed over and now he was not an Egyptian. He had crossed
> over. The short sword at his thigh had a jewelled hilt but he had

crossed over and so it was no longer the sign of high birth and power. He had crossed over, so he sat down on a rock near the seashore to rest himself. He had crossed over so he was not of the house of Pharaoh. He did not own a palace because he had crossed over. He did not have an Ethiopian Princess for a wife. He had crossed over. He did not have enemies to strain against his strength and power. He had crossed over. He was subject to no law except the laws of tooth and talon. He had crossed over. The sun was his friend and ancestor in Egypt was arrogant and bitter in Asia. He had crossed over. He felt as empty as a post hole for he was none of the things he had once been. He was a man sitting on a rock. He had crossed over.[70]

The call of Moses to emancipate the people of God is a shift from individualism to a search for truth in the context of community. He had "found a new sympathy for the oppressed of all mankind."[71] Moses is involved in a difficult process, wherein he is "constructing a new identity from the ground up, with no blueprints to predict the final shape of the edifice. Moses' life will be *transformed* into something new when he comes to identify with the oppressed; he truly crosses over into a new and different land."[72]

In a passage remarkably prophetic, Moses passes on to Joshua the moral wisdom he had gained from the community related to the virtue of quiet grace.

> Now one thing I want you to get in your head: You can't have a state of individuals. Everybody just can't be allowed to do as they please. I love liberty and I love freedom so I started off giving everybody a loose rein. But I soon found out that it wouldn't do. A great state is a well-blended mash of something of all the people and all of the none of the people. You understand. The liquor of statecraft is distilled from the mash you got. How can a nation speak with one voice if they are not one? Don't forget now. If you do, you encourage all the stupid but greedy and ambitious to sprout like toadstools and that's the end of right and reason in the state. Coddling and wheedling is not going to stop these destroyers. To a haughty belly, kindness is hard to swallow and harder to digest.[73]

The women in *Moses, Man of the Mountain* are all minor characters. Jochebed, Moses' mother; Miriam, Moses' sister; and Zipporah, Moses' second wife, are all in primary positions but play secondary roles in the unfolding of this legend. The focus throughout is primarily on Moses. The female characters are complementary. They are defined by their affiliation with Moses.

The women in this novel illustrate quiet grace as the search for truth in much subtler forms than Moses. Their struggle for self-actualization is exhibited in much the same manner as Nanny in *Their Eyes Were Watching God*. The Hebrew women, like Black slavewomen, knew that their role was to hide and protect their children from the oppressor. A cry in the night "might force upon them a thousand years of suffering." They fought for their breath and for the boon of shrieking out their agony and suffering. "It was muted by a fear like every other sound in the house."[74] The moral wisdom at work in the lives of slavewomen was consistently more limited, more constricting and more unconscious than the mediating principles directing the life of Moses.

For instance, Miriam feels that she and her brother Aaron should be exalted above all the other people because they were "the very ones that got this thing together and kept it together all down the line." When Moses grows tired of Miriam's assertiveness, he forces her to succumb to his magical powers. The pain is so severe that Miriam begs Moses for permission to die. Hurston as the narrator summed up the moral agency in Miriam's life in this way: "Miriam had lived on hopes where other women lived on memories."[75]

The diminution of the women as minor characters serves as stimulus for the enlargement of Moses. "A mighty thing had happened in the world through the stumblings of a woman who couldn't see where she was going."[76]

QUIET GRACE AS TRUTH IN SERAPH ON THE SUWANEE

Seraph on the Suwanee (1948), Zora Neale Hurston's last published novel, is the only one in which the main characters are white. Some of Hurston's critics charged her with assimilationism, which was one of the trends among Black writers of the period.[77] Assimilationists avoided concentrating on Black characters and partially or totally incorporated the white cultural tradition into their work. However, Hemenway argues, "The peril in deliberately choosing a white subject is considerable. There is nothing which prohibits a black writer from creating successful white characters, black literature is full of brilliant white portraits. But if the novelist consciously seeks to portray whites in order to validate his talent, to prove to the world there are no limits to his genius, the very assumptions of the decision become self-defeating."[78]

"Although Arvay Henson, the novel's heroine, is white, she,

like all Hurston protagonists, searches for self-actualization and love, for life-affirming rather than life-denying experiences," says Howard.[79] Hurston changed the color of her characters in this novel but she did not change the basic habits, attitudes and mode of life. Hurston's portrayal of the characters in *Seraph on the Suwanee* refutes any notions of assimilation: ". . . all the characters in *Seraph* sound exactly like the Eatonville folks sitting on Joe Clarke's front porch."[80]

This last novel of Hurston's continues to follow the moral agency previously established in the earlier works which deal with the painful regeneration one must experience before one possesses the quality of quiet grace. The interrelationship of quiet grace and the search for truth is reinforced by Hurston's development of the feminine psyche of Arvay Henson.

A review of the plot reveals Arvay, a poor white woman of Sawley, Florida, spending most of her life protecting the propositions that support her cherished false assumptions. At age sixteen Arvay renounces the world to become a "foreign" missionary because her older sister marries the man with whom Arvay lives in "mental adultery." At age twenty-one, Jim Meserve, a high-class Irishman, presents Arvay with a proposal for marriage. Arvay tries to discourage Jim with self-induced fainting spells. The more Jim pursues her, the more Arvay tries to discourage him. "Ah, no, this pretty laughing fellow was too far out of her reach. Things as wonderful as this were never meant for nobody like her. This was first-class, and she was born to take other people's leavings."[81]

Finally, after Jim initiates a violent sexual assault, Arvay sublimates and agrees to marry him. Together they prosper as citrus-fruit farmers in Citrabelle, Florida. When the first of their three children is born, Arvay believes that her child's deformity is punishment from God for her adolescent sin of "adultery in the mind." Incident after incident occurs and Arvay continues to cling to a blindfold denial of reality. She wreaks havoc in the marriage, in her parenting and in her life. "Arvay scorned off learning as a source of evil knowledge and thought fondly of ignorance as the foundation of good heartedness and honesty."[82]

Jim grows weary and exasperated with Arvay's patterns of denial. He walks out of the marriage. Soon after, Arvay returns to her home in Sawley to tend to her mother who is terminally ill. It is during this last visit home that Arvay comes to terms with her personhood. She finally breaks free of her shackling past.

In *Seraph on the Suwanee* Hurston presented quiet grace as a quality that belongs only to those who emerge victor in the life-denying battle against self-centered fear. Whatever is "an evil, ill-deformed monstropolous accumulation of time and scum," must be destroyed. Whatever "soaked in so much of doing-without, or soul-starvation, of brutish vacancy of aim, of absent dreams, envy of trifles, ambitions for littleness, smothered cries and trampled love," has to be destroyed. Whatever "caught people and twisted the limbs of their minds"[83] has to be burned to ashes so that real life can begin.

It is possible to conjecture that Zora Neale Hurston's explicit portrayal of sexism in this novel coincides with increasing gender discrimination in her own life during the 1940s. Sexism is mentioned in all of her novels but it emerges in full scale in *Seraph on the Suwanee*.

For instance, in *Jonah's Gourd Vine*, John Pearson's stepfather, Ned, would beat John's mother with a raw hide whip. Ned "uncoiled the whip and standing tiptoe to give himself more force, brought the whip down across Amy's back."[84]

Recurring throughout *Their Eyes Were Watching God* are frequent references to women's honor being readily sacrificed for men's. Jody Starks, Janie's second husband, retorts, "Somebody got to think for women and chillun and chickens and cows, I god, they sho don't think none theirselves." Janie responds, "Ah knows a few things, and womenfolks thinks sometimes too!" Stark replies, "Ah naw they don't. They just think they thinkin'. When Ah sees one thing Ah understand ten. You see ten things and understand one."[85]

In *Seraph*, Hurston fully delineated the propositions, attitudes and behavior that men exhibit in support of their belief in the inherent inferiority of women and their right to dominate over them. Hurston's revealing commentary in *Seraph* is that Jim Meserve, a man blessed with admirable qualities—courage, honesty, loyalty—is also a chauvinist. Jim begins his tirade against women in this manner:

> Women folks don't have no mind to make up no how. They wasn't made for that. Lady folks were just made to laugh and act loving and kind and have a good man to do for them all he's able, and have him as many boy-children as he figgeres he'd like to have, and make him so happy that he is willing to work and fetch in every dad-blamed thing that his wife thinks she would like to have. That's what women are made for.[86]

Joe Kelsey, the Black man who works for Jim, believes women are property. Joe spouts his invectives, "Make 'em knuckle under. From the very first jump, get the bridle in they mouth and ride 'em hard and stop 'em short. They's all alike, Boss. Take 'em and break 'em."[87]

About midway through the novel, Jim becomes irritated with his wife, Arvay, and orders her to strip naked. When she attempts to cover herself, he yells: "Don't you move! You're my damn property, and I want you right where you are, and I want you naked. Stand right there in your tracks until I tell you that you can move." When Jim finally allows Arvay to lie down, he "stretched himself full length upon her, but in the same way that he might have laid himself down on a couch."[88]

In one of Jim's closing protracted speeches to Arvay, he compares her to "an unthankful and unknowing hog under a acorn tree. Eating and grunting with your ears hanging over your eyes and never even looking up to see where the acorns are coming from."[89]

What is recognizable and familiar in all these comments is that gender discrimination is an immutable fact in women's existence. Ostensibly a social-literary critic, Hurston showed how both men and women are captives of their oppression.

CONCLUSION

Zora Neale Hurston used her fiction to embrace affirmatively the culture of the Black community. She showed how Black people are empowered through the collective wisdom transmitted from one generation to the next. The underground treasury of ethics that Hurston identified consists of the voices of Black folks who spoke often in ambiguous and enigmatic proverbs about the virtue of grace in the search for truth. This quality allows one to stand over against critical dilution of her/his personhood. Hurston's work adorns with words, the day-to-day ceremonies of living, which point to lives full of profound wisdom despite observable human failings.[90]

Resources in the Nonfiction of Zora Neale Hurston

In Zora Neale Hurston's nonfiction there is evidence of a third characteristic of moral agency which can be expressed as "unshouted courage," a virtue evolving from the forced responsibility of Black women. Hurston's collections of folklore, as well as her expository discourses, reflect upon the Black community's stamina in dealing with innumerable incidents of unpredictability.

"Unshouted courage" is the quality of steadfastness, akin to fortitude, in the face of formidable oppression. The communal attitude is far more than "grin and bear it." Rather, it involves the ability to "hold on to life" against major oppositions. It is the incentive to facilitate change, to chip away the oppressive structures, bit by bit, to celebrate and rename their experiences in empowering ways. "Unshouted courage" as a virtue is the often unacknowledged inner conviction that keeps one's appetite whet for freedom. The ethical speculation is that courage is the staying power of the Black community wherein individuals act, affirming their humanity, in spite of continued fear of institutionalized aggression.

In the dominant ethical systems, responsibility is often understood as inseparable from free will. A range of choices and the sanctions offered are considered to be prerequisites for genuine moral responsibility. Thus, courage from this vantage point is considered as a virtue only when it is distinguished from spurious, physical fear. Moral actions induced by respect for authority, or that come from unreal apprehended danger, are considered to be utterly worthless, cowardly proceedings.

For instance, Dietrich Bonhoeffer discussed responsibility in terms of deputyship, "being for others," complete surrender of one's self to the other man.[91] H. Richard Niebuhr used the symbol of "man-the-answerer." The four elements in Niebuhr's theory of responsibility are response, interpretation, accountability and social solidarity. "God is acting in all actions upon you. So respond to all actions upon you as to respond to his action."[92] Alice Gardner assumed that each person possesses self-determining power with allowance for equal privileges, a wide range of choices and qualified immunities. For her, courage can only be understood as moral character when one has "the power and determination to follow loyally and reasonably one's own beliefs and principles, irrespective not only of the disapproval of neighbors, but also of painful disturbance in one's own mind."[93]

This notion of courage has proven to be false in the real-lived texture of Black life. Black people live, work and have their being within less gracious boundaries. Often they are compelled to act or refrain from acting in accordance with the external powers and principalities. The Black woman, in particular, is often required to give careful consideration to a will not her own. As the historical custodian in her community and in the society at large, the Black woman is held accountable for many happenings beyond her control. Mignnon H. Anderson dedicates her writing to such courage. "For all of us who lived the misery of being made to be something other than what we were; for all of us now living who picked cotton and bore children unwanted and still find ourselves in strange fields and lying on cold beds, there are changes still due and coming."[94]

Locked into systems of subjugation and exploitation from which they can seldom extricate themselves, Black people live with severely limited ethical choices. Their action guides assert a human validity that is not derived from the white-male-norm. The values and virtues therein teach Blacks the usefulness of prudence, the relativity of truth and how to dispel the threat of death in order to seize life in the present. For Black people the moral element of courage is annexed with the will to live and the dread of greater perpetrations of evil acts against them.

Zora Neale Hurston's folklore collection records the action guides the Black community deemed appropriate within ineradicable systems of oppression.[95] This rich body of accumulated data speaks to some of the ways that Black folk have tried to answer to the wills and whims of those in power, over whom Blacks have no control. The exigencies of circumstances often require Black people to cultivate as a virtue, the ingrown capacity for meeting difficulties with fortitude and resilience. Even when daunted by tribulations, Black people are compelled to act in order to insure their ongoing survival.

> You see we are a polite people and we do not say to our questioner, "Get out of here!" We smile and tell him or her something that satisfies the white person because, knowing so little about us, he doesn't know what he is missing. The Indian resists curiosity by a stony silence. The Negro offers a feather-bed resistance. That is, we let the probe enter, but it never comes out. It gets smothered under a lot of laughter and pleasantries.
> The theory behind our tactics: "The white man is always trying to know into somebody else's business. All right, I'll set something outside the door of my mind for him to play with and handle. He can read my writing but he sho' can't read my mind. I'll put this play toy in his hand, and he will seize it and go away. Then I'll say my say and sing my song."[96]

The central moral emanating from the Black community in such an exchange was an unequivocal call for human equality. The constellation of values that the community upholds taught its members to keep at bay Hurston or anyone else who seemed to disrespect their human beingness. As moral agents in oppressive situations, Black people live with the haunting consequences of the involuntariness of their circumstances. When presented with even a glimpse of choice, oppressed people give answers and responses which allow them to maintain their dignity with all the resiliency and strength they can muster.

The Black community's folklore is the corporate story that enshrines the interlocking complexities of the beliefs, etiology and practices of the community, and also constitutes the community's understanding of, and response to, its own humanity. The oral stories are reappropriations of their past experiences. Brer Fox, Brer Deer, Brer 'Gator, Brer Dawg, Brer Rabbit and the devil always outsmart Ole Massa, his wife and God. In order for Zora Hurston to collect the much desired folklore, she had to shed the superficial vestiges of privilege and voyeur status and stand in solidarity with the group of people who sat on the steps of Joe Clarke's store, exchanging lies and telling stories with the best of them. Hurston had to let go of any hierarchical stance that subordinated, undervalued or threatened the well-being of the teller or the tale. Black people did not want anyone tampering with raw wisdom, reflected and reinforced in their oral traditions.

> Men sat around the store on boxes and benches and passed this world and the next one through their mouths. The right and the wrong, the who, when and why was passed on, and nobody doubted the conclusions. There were no discreet nuances of life on Joe Clarke's porch. There was open kindnesses, anger, hate, love, envy and its kinfolks, but all emotions were naked, and nakedly arrived at. It was a case of "make it and take it." You got what your strengths would bring you.[97]

The moral wisdom within the folklore implies a self-sufficient set of values explaining, legitimizing, and ensuring the continuance of Black life. Hurston came to see that as long as the circumstances and the conditions in which Black folklore originated did not pass away, the Black community would continue to find its strength in the lineaments of its traditional testimonies.[98]

In Zora Neale Hurston's essays the inference of "unshouted courage" continued to be derived from its prominence in the Black community. Alice Walker, in introducing Hurston's nonfiction, as-

serts that the fundamental thesis that Hurston embodied and exhibited in her essays was that one "must struggle every minute of life
to affirm black people's right to a healthy existence."[99] This idea
concurs with the understanding of courage in Paul Tillich's work.
Tillich says that courage is an ethical act when humans affirm their
own being in spite of those elements in their existence which
conflict with their essential self-affirmation.[100]

Zora Neale Hurston's self-contained pieces of non-fictional
prose are quite diverse. Some of them are purely satirical and
entertaining. Others are colloquial in style and avowedly persuasive.
All reveal a fundamental truth—self-fulfillment in a situation of
oppression requires hitting a straight lick with a crooked stick. In
other words, Hurston's journalism, like Black folklore, was a type of
ambiguous featherbed resistance.

Zora Hurston understood the elaborate facades of myths, traditions and rituals erected to couch systems of injustice in America.
"Zora was acutely aware of the predominantly white mass-magazine
audience and of what her editors expected," says Hemenway.[101]
Thus, the indigenous complexity of being a Black-woman-artist
writing for the *Saturday Evening Post*, the *American Mercury* and
the *American Legion Magazine* caused Hurston to combine her
private experiences with various linguistic modes so that her writing
at times appears fairly oblique and non-threatening.

For instance, in her first essay, "How It Feels to Be Colored
Me," published in the *World Tomorrow* in May 1928, Hurston
wrote about "the very day that I became colored." She described the
inner strength that emerged as she "suffered a sea change. . . . I
was not Zora of Orange County anymore, I was now a little colored
girl. I found it out in certain ways. In my heart as well as in the
mirror."[102] And yet, Hurston ended this article with a cosmic,
universal understanding of her identity. "I have no separate feeling
about being an American citizen and colored. I am merely a frag-
ment of the Great Soul that surges with the boundaries."

> Sometimes, I feel discriminated against, but it does not
> make me angry. It merely astonishes me. How *can* any deny
> themselves the pleasure of my company? It's beyond me.[103]

Zora Neale Hurston also used irony, wit and humor to enter-
tain white readers as she reported the Black community's understanding and manifestation of courageous living. In different ways of

saying much the same thing, Hurston's essays are sometimes very belligerent. She took for granted the inseparability of words and action. Her essays are imbued with a conscious hope that language can expose "the weight that racism lays on the whole world."[104]

"The 'Pet' Negro System" is a combative indictment against liberal white "do-gooders" who reduce individual Blacks to indulged, cherished creatures. "The pet Negro, beloved, is someone whom a particular white person or persons wants to have and to do all the things forbidden to other Negroes."[105] Hurston elaborates in explicit detail how certain whites identify certain Blacks as exceptions to the degrading stereotypes assigned to the Black masses. In turn, these whites support their designated Blacks and give money to their causes and underwrite the debts of their separate and so-called equal institutions. Zora Hurston maintained that Blacks also have "pet whites." "It is amusing to see a Negro servant chasing the madam or the boss back on his or her pedestal when they behave in an unbecoming manner. Thereby, he is to a certain extent preserving his own prestige, derived from association with that family."[106] In this essay the emphasis is not so much on the community's courage but it is Zora Hurston's courage to name this evil. As long as the "pet system" exists, white racism reigns supreme.

In considering other essays of Hurston, we find that "High John De Conqueror" and "Negroes Without Self Pity" offered support to the nation during World War II. Hurston writes about the "hope bringers" in the Black community. She describes how laughter and song provide support in times of trials and tribulations.[107]

In 1944, Zora Neale Hurston published an essay, "My Most Humiliating Jim Crow Experience," which happened in New York "instead of the South as one would have expected." Zora returned ill from the Bahama Islands. When she went for her check-up she was examined in "a closet where the soiled towels and uniforms were tossed until called for by the laundry." The white specialist in internal medicine wanted "to get me off the premises as quickly as possible." Hurston ends this article with unfaltering conviction—". . . anything with such a false foundation cannot last. Whom the gods would destroy, they first made mad."[108]

After the war ended, Hurston published "Crazy for this Democracy" in *Negro Digest* (December 1945). This essay reverberates with multiple implications. She discussed the international manifestations of racism. She also wrote about the eternal and irrevocable "First by Birth" status in the mind of the smallest white child.

"By the same means, the smallest dark child is to be convinced of its inferiority, so that it is to be convinced that competition is out of the question, and against all nature and God."[109] Hurston concludes by saying that she is all for trying out democracy and "the only thing that keeps me from pitching headlong into the thing is the presence of numerous Jim Crow laws on the statute books."

> I am all for the repeal of every Jim Crow law in the nation here and now. Not in another generation or so. The Hurstons have already been waiting 80 years for that. I want it here and now. . . . I give my hand, my heart and my head to the total struggle. I am for complete repeal of all Jim Crow laws in the U.S. once and for all, and right now. For the benefit of this nation and as a precedent to the world. . . . Not in some future generation, but repeal *now* and forever!![110]

In 1950, Zora Neale Hurston wrote an essay about the relationship between Black writers and white publishers, "What White Publishers Won't Print." She capsulated the consequences for Black writers who refuse to fit into the false and degrading stereotypes promulgated in Anglo-American popular culture.

One of Hurston's last essays, "Why the Negro Won't Buy Communism," was written at the request of the *American Legion Magazine*. In this article, Hurston took a stand against the "raw flattery" and the "insulting patronage" of the Communist officials toward "pitiable" Blacks.

> The formula was, you can't win Negro, you can't win. Expanded, the poor, dear colored character starts off to be something in the world, but he or she gets trapped by our form of government and down he goes to the lowest depths like bottomless britches. Pity the poor, black brute . . . not his fault at all.[111]

CONCLUSION

All in all, Zora Neale Hurston published two books of folklore and more than fifty essays and articles. The virtue of "unshouted courage" was not her explicit theme but can be frequently explicated from the stance she took on various issues. The central theme in Hurston's early essays (prior to 1948) was courage related to the struggle for racial justice. Testifying to a vision for a just society, Hurston made particular claims on the moral agency of her readers. She encouraged protest against the dehumanization of Black personhood. "If our friends portray us as subhuman varmints, the indifferent majority can only conclude we are hopeless."[112] Even when her essays and articles were heavily edited by the white magazine staff so that they appeared "full of praise and largely devoid of analysis," Hurston's words still unmasked the ideology of oppression in parabolic form.

There are two main criticisms lodged against Zora Neale Hurston's essays: political conservatism and obsessive individualism. I believe, however, that both of these criticisms are inadequate and highly inaccurate when they are evaluated within the context of Hurston's own time. Instead, I find Hurston's publications after 1948 confirming a reactionary position. In the throes of betrayal, Hurston responded in opposite ways from her previous convictions.

Much of the critical commentary tends to minimize the devastating impact of the false charge that she had committed an immoral act with a ten-year-old boy. Hurston was an intensely proud woman. Her whole life was committed to a defiant affirmation of the cultural practices manifested in the Black community. Hemenway's biography documents how Hurston's professional career was spent "trying to show that normality is a function of culture, that an Afro-American culture exists, and that its creators lead lives rich with ideological and esthetic significance."[113] And yet it was a Black court employee who peddled the inaccurate and sensationalized story to the Black press who, in turn, circulated lurid coverage to the Black community. Hurston referred to this betrayal of her as "the *Afro-American* sluice of filth." In the prime of her career, she felt that her world had collapsed, unfairly, unreasonably, in the ugliest possible way. "She was left with nothing to fall back on."[114]

When Hurston did start to write again, she eliminated Black folklore completely from her work. After the case was dropped and the indictment dismissed, Hurston commented that she didn't think that she could even endure the sight of a Black person. Dispirited and broken, Hurston's essays were occasionally suspicious and paranoid. Questioning the motives behind her moral and intellectual lynching, Hurston even wondered if the charges against her in 1948 were part of some kind of Communist frame.

Always struggling to remain solvent, Hurston sold articles and essays to white magazines knowing that they would be heavily edited. She also campaigned for conservative politicians such as Taft, Smathers and Reynolds. "It is the human side of Zora's final years that explains more about her situation than any political analysis can ever do," says Hemenway.[115]

I concur with the critical analyses of established writers such as Alice Walker, Mary Helen Washington, June Jordan, Julius Lester, Larry Neale and Barbara Christian.

> One cannot help but note the similarities between Larsen [Nella] and Hurston's disappearances from the world. Although very different writers, they were both assaulted by the prejudices of the other society. Larsen's writing ability was challenged and Hurston's sex life was used, consciously or unconsciously, as a means of diminishing her effectiveness as a writer and as an anthropologist. Both charges are indicative of the vulnerable position of black women writers. Their sexual morality and intellectual capacity are seen as tentative, not only by their fellow countrymen but by members of their own race as well. Both writers fell prey to the racial and sexual stereotypes inflicted upon the black women.[116]

Across the boundaries of her own experience, Zora Neale Hurston wrote essays about the oppressive and unbearable, about those things that rub Black people raw. Her richness and chaos, her merits and faults bear witness to an "unshouted courage" that can only be lived out in community.

Notes

/1/   Lloyd W. Brown, "Zora Neale Hurston and the Nature of Female Perception," *Obsidian* 4, iii (1978): 39–45; Joyce Jenkins, "To Make A Woman Black: A Critical Analysis of the Women Characters in the Fiction and Folklore of Zora Neale Hurston" (Ph.D. dissertation, Bowling Green State University, 1979); Clyde Taylor, "Black Folk Spirit and the Shape of Black Literature," *Black World* 21 (August 1972): 31–40; Mary Helen Washington, "Black Women Image Makers," *Black World* (August 1974): 10–18.
/2/   Lois W. Banner, *Women in Modern America: A Brief History* (New York: Harcourt Brace Jovanovich, 1974); Caroline Bird, *Born Female* (New York: David McKay Co., Inc., 1968); Elizabeth Janeway, *Man's World, Woman's Place: A Study in Social Mythology* (New York: Dell, 1971); Sheila M. Rothman, *Woman's Proper Place: A History of Changing Ideals and Practices, 1870 to the Present* (New York: Basic Books, 1978); Mary P. Ryan, *Womanhood in America: From Colonial Times to the Present* (New York: New Viewpoints, 1975).
/3/   Toni Cade, ed., *The Black Woman: An Anthology* (New York: Bantam, 1977); Trudier Harris, *From Mammies to Militants: Domestics in Black*

American Literature (Philadelphia: Temple University Press, 1982); Filomina C. Steady, ed., *The Black Woman Cross-Culturally* (Cambridge, Mass.: Schenkman Publishing Co., 1981); Bell Hooks, *Ain't I A Woman: Black Women and Feminism* (Boston: South End Press, 1981); Joyce Ladner, *Tomorrow's Tomorrow: The Black Woman* (New York: Doubleday, 1971).

/4/   Frances Beale, "Double Jeopardy; To Be Black and Female," in *The Black Woman*, ed. Toni Cade (New York: The New American Library, 1970); Bernard Braxton, *Women, Sex and Race* (Washington: Verte Press, 1973); Gwenna Cummings, "Black Women: Often Discussed but Never Understood," in *The Black Power Revolt*, ed. F. B. Barbour (Boston: Extending Horizons Books, 1968).

/5/   Cynthia Fuchs Epstein, "Black and Female: The Double Whammy," *Psychology Today* (August 1973), pp. 57–61; Fletcher Knebel, "Identity: The Black Woman's Burden," *Look*, September 1969, pp. 77–79; Diana Slaughter, "Becoming an Afro-American Woman," *Women in Education, School Review* 80 (special ed., 1972): 299–318; Mel Watkins and Jay David, eds., *To Be a Black Woman: Portraits in Facts and Fiction* (New York: William Morrow, 1971).

/6/   Wade Baskin and Richard Runes, *Dictionary of Black Culture* (New York: Philosophical Library, 1973); George Kent, *Blackness and the Adventure of Western Culture* (Chicago: Third World Press, 1972); Lawrence Levine, *Black Culture and Black Consciousness: Afro-American Folk Thought from Slavery to Freedom* (New York: Oxford University Press, 1977); J. DeOtis Roberts, "Folklore and Religion: The Black Experience," *Journal of Religious Thought* 27 (Summer supplement, 1970): 5–15.

/7/   James Giles, "The Significance of Time in Zora Neale Hurston's *Their Eyes Were Watching God, Negro American Literature Forum* 6 (Summer 1972): 52–53, 60; Lillie P. Howard, "Marriage: Zora Neale Hurston's System of Values," *College Language Association Journal* 21 (December 1977): 256–268; John Oliver Killens, "Another Time When Black Was Beautiful," *Black World* 20 (November 1970): 20–36; Valerie G. Lee, "The Use of Folktalk in Novels by Black Women Writers," *College Language Association Journal* 23 (December 1978): 266–272; James Rambeau, "The Fiction of Zora Neale Hurston," *Markham Review* 5 (Summer 1976): 61–64; Peter Schwalbengerg, "Time As Point of View in Zora Neale Hurston's *Their Eyes Were Watching God*," *Negro American Literature Forum* 10 (1976): 104–105, 107–108.

/8/   Ann Rayson, "The Novels of Zora Neale Hurston," *Studies in Black Literature* 5 (Winter 1974): 1–10; Beatrice Horn, "The Ironic Vision of Four Black Women Novelists: A Study of the Novels of Jessie Fauset, Nella Larsen, Zora Neale Hurston, and Ann Petry" (Ph.D. dissertation, Emory University, 1975); Theresa Love, "Zora Neale Hurston's America," *Papers on Lanugage and Literature* 12 (1976): 423–437.

/9/   Alan Lomax, "Zora Neale Hurston—A Life of Negro Folklore," *Sing Out!* 10 (October–November 1960): 12–13; Hiroko Sata, "Zora Neale Hurston Shiron," *Oberon* 34 (1971): 30–37; Susan Blake, "Modern Black Writers and the Folk Tradition" (Ph.D. dissertation, University of Connecticut, 1976); Clyde Taylor, "Black Folk Spirit and the Shape of Black Literature," *Black World* 21 (August 1974): 31–40.

/10/   Robert Hemenway, *Zora Neale Hurston: A Literary Biography* (Urbana: University of Illinois Press, 1977), p. 224.

/11/   Addison Gayle, Jr., "Strangers in a Strange Land," *Southern Exposure* 3, 1 (1975): 4–7; Daryl Dance, "Following in Zora Neale Hurston's Dust Tracks: Autobiographical Notes by the Author of *Shuckin' and Jivin',*" *Journal of the Folklore Institute* 16 (1979): 120–126; Zora Neale Hurston, "Characteristics of Negro Expression," in *Negro: An Anthology,* ed. Nancy Cunard (New York: Frederick Ungar Publishing Co., 1970).

/12/   Margaret J. Butcher, *The Negro in American Culture, 1956* (New York: Mentor, 1971); Floyd B. Barbour, ed., *The Black Power Revolt* (Boston: Porter Sargent, 1968); Stewart H. Benedict, ed., *Blacklash: Black Protest in Our Time* (New York: Popular Library, 1970); Melvin Drimmer, ed., *Black History Reappraisal* (New York: Doubleday & Co., 1968); Russell Endo and William Strawbridge, eds., *Perspectives on Black America* (Englewood Cliffs, N.J.: Prentice-Hall, 1970); Joanne Grant, ed., *Black Protest History, Documents and Analysis* (New York: St. Martin's Press, 1970); Edward Peeks, *The Long Struggle for Black Power* (New York: Charles Scribner's Sons, 1971); Manning Marable, *Blackwater: Historical Studies in Race, Class Consciousness and Revolution* (Dayton, Oh.: Black Praxis Press, 1981).

/13/   Joyce Jenkins, "To Make a Woman Black"; Gloria Joyce Johnson, "Hurston's Folk: The Critical Significance of Afro-American Folk Traditions in Three Novels and the Autobiography" (Ph.D. dissertation, University of California at Irvine, 1977).

/14/   Zora Neale Hurston, *Their Eyes Were Watching God* (Philadelphia: J. B. Lippincott, 1937; reprint ed., Urbana: University of Illinois Press, 1978), p. 20.

/15/   Karla Holloway, "A Critical Investigation of Literary and Linguistic Structures in the Fiction of Zora Neale Hurston" (Ph.D. dissertation, Michigan State University, 1978).

/16/   See Maya Angelou, *I Know Why the Caged Bird Sings* (New York: Random House, 1969); Elizabeth Janeway, *Powers of the Weak* (New York: Alfred A. Knopf, 1980); June Jordan, *Civil Wars* (Boston: Beacon Press, 1981); Gloria Joseph and Jill Lewis, *Common Differences: Conflicts in Black and White Feminist Perspectives* (Garden City, N.Y.: Anchor Books/Doubleday, 1981); Cherrie Moraga and Gloria Anzaldua, eds., *This Bridge Called My Back: Writings by Radical Women of Color* (Watertown, Mass.: Persephone Press, 1981); Audre Lorde, *Zami: A New Spelling of My Name* (Watertown, Mass.: Persephone Press, 1982); Ntozake Shange, *For Colored Girls Who Have Considered Suicide When the Rainbow is Enuf* (New York: Macmillan Publishing Co., 1975).

/17/   Rambeau, "The Fiction of Zora Neale Hurston," p. 61.

/18/   For an analysis of *Jonah's Gourd Vine,* see Addison Gayle, *The Way of the New World* (Garden City, N.Y.: Doubleday, 1976), pp. 169–175; Arthur P. Davis, *From the Dark Tower* (Washington: Howard University Press, 1974), pp. 113–120; S. P. Fullinwider, *The Mind and Mood of Black America* (Homewood, Ill.: Dorsey Press, 1969), pp. 169–171.

/19/   Larry Neale, Introduction to Zora Neale Hurston, *Jonah's Gourd Vine* (Philadelphia: J. B. Lippincott Co., 1934; reprint ed., New York: Lippincott, 1971), p. 6.

/20/   Hurston to Johnson, April 1934, James Weldon Johnson Collection,

Yale University Library, New Haven.

/21/ Hurston, *Jonah's Gourd Vine*, p. 197.

/22/ Ibid., p. 113.

/23/ Ibid., pp. 84–85.

/24/ Lillie P. Howard, *Zora Neale Hurston* (Boston: Twayne Publishers, 1980), p. 80.

/25/ Hurston, *Jonah's Gourd Vine*, p. 180.

/26/ Ibid., pp. 190–191.

/27/ Ibid., p. 267.

/29/ Howard, *Zora Neale Hurston*, p. 74.

/30/ Hurston, *Jonah's Gourd Vine*, p. 196.

/31/ Hemenway, *Zora Neale Hurston*, p. 190.

/32/ Hurston, *Jonah's Gourd Vine*, p. 209.

/33/ Ibid., p. 204.

/34/ Ibid.

/35/ Hurston, *Jonah's Gourd Vine*, p. 204.

/36/ Jenkins, "To Make a Woman Black," p. 141.

/37/ Howard, *Zora Neale Hurston*, p. 92.

/38/ Lillie P. Howard, "Zora Neale Hurston: A Non-Revolutionary Black Artist" (Ph.D. dissertation, University of New Mexico, 1976); S. Jay Walker, "Zora Neale Hurston's *Their Eyes Were Watching God:* Black Novel of Sexism," *Modern Fiction Studies* 20 (Winter 1974–75): 519–527.

/39/ Holloway, "A Critical Investigation, p. 43; see also, Barbara Christian, *Black Women Novelists: The Development of a Tradition, 1892–1976* (Westport, Conn.: Greenwood Press, 1980), especially chapter one, "From Stereotype to Character."

/40/ Ellease Southerland, "Zora Neale Hurston: The Novelist-Anthropologist's Life/Works," *Black World* 23 (August 1974): 26.

/41/ Hurston, *Their Eyes Were Watching God*, p. 236.

/42/ Mary Helen Washington, "The Black Woman's Search for Identity: Zora Neale Hurston's Work," *Black World* (August 1972): 68–75.

/43/ Hurston, *Their Eyes Were Watching God*, pp. 33–34.

/44/ Ibid., p. 35.

/45/ Hurston, Their Eyes Were Watching God, pp. 31–32.

/46/ Ibid., p. 31.

/47/ Hurston, *Their Eyes Were Watching God*, p. 29.

/48/ Ibid., p. 41: Nanny elaborates her understanding of marriage as security. For her, it has nothing to do with love and loving: "Lawd have mussy! Dat's de very prong all us black women gits hung on. Dis love! Dat's just whut's got us uh pullin' and uh haulin' and sweatin' and doin' from can't see in de mornin' till can't see at night. Dat's how come de ole folks say dat being' uh fool don't kill nobody. It jus' makes you sweat."

/49/ Ibid., p.

/50/ Hurston, *Their Eyes Were Watching God*, p. 49.

/51/ Ibid., p. 111

/52/ Ibid., p. 44.

/53/ Hurston, *Their Eyes Were Watching God*, p. 49.

/54/ Mary Helen Washington, "Black Women Image Makers," p. 16.

/55/ Howard, *Zora Neale Hurston*, p. 105.

/56/   Hurston, *Their Eyes Were Watching God*, p. 192.

/57/   Howard, *Zora Neale Hurston*, p. 108.

/58/   June Jordan, "On Richard Wright and Zora Neale Hurston: Notes Toward a Balancing of Love and Hatred," *Black World* 23 (April 1976): 6.

/59/   See Sir James Frazer, *Folklore in the Old Testament* (New York: Hart Publishing, 1975); Johnanna L. Grimes, "The Function of the Oral Tradition in Selected Afro-American Diction" (Ph.D. dissertation, Northwestern University, 1980); Newbell N. Puckett, *Folk Beliefs of Southern Negroes* (Chapel Hill: University of North Carolina Press, 1926).

/60/   Zora Neale Hurston, *Moses, Man of the Mountain* (Philadelphia: J. B. Lippincott Co., 1939; reprint ed, Chatham, N.J.: The Chatham Bookseller, 1967), p. 137.

/61/   Hurston, *Moses*, p.

/62/   Hemenway, *Zora Neale Hurston*, p. 263.

/63/   Hurston, *Moses*, pp. 7–8.

/64/   Alice Walker, *I Love Myself When I Am Laughing . . . A Zora Neale Hurston Reader*, ed. Alice Walker (Old Westbury, N.Y.: The Feminist Press, 1979), p. 176.

/65/   Hemenway, *Zora Neale Hurston*, p. 257.

/66/   Howard, *Zora Neale Hurston*, p. 116.

/68/   Hurston, *Moses*, pp. 50–51.

/69/   Hurston, *Moses*, p. 100.

/70/   Ibid., p. 103–104.

/71/   Hurston, *Moses*, p. 92.

/72/   Hemenway, *Zora Neale Hurston*, p. 270.

/73/   Hurston, *Moses*, p. 340.

/74/   Hurston, *Moses*, p. 19.

/75/   Hurston, *Moses*, p. 322.

/76/   Ibid., p. 308.

/77/   Robert Hemenway, *The Black Novelist* (Columbus, Oh.: Charles E. Merrill, 1970); Otelia Cromwell, Dow Turner, and Eva B. Dykes, eds., *Readings from Negro Authors* (New York: Harcourt, Brace, 1931); James O. Young, *Black Writers of the Thirties* (Baton Rouge: Louisiana State University Press, 1973).

/78/   Hemenway, *Zora Neale Hurston*, p. 307.

/79/   Howard, *Zora Neale Hurston*, p. 134.

/80/   Washington, "Black Women Image Makers," p. 21.

/81/   Zora Neale Hurston, *Seraph on the Suwanee* (New York: Charles Scribner's Sons, 1948; reprint ed., New York: AMS Press, Inc., 1974), p. 22; see also Worth Tuttle Hedden, "Turpentine and Moonshine," review of *Seraph on the Suwanee*, by Zora Neale Hurston, in *New York Herald Tribune Weekly Book Review*, October, 1948, p. 2.

/82/   Hurston, *Seraph on the Suwanee*, pp. 238–239.

/83/   Hurston, *Seraph on the Suwanee*, p. 269.

/84/   Hurston, *Jonah's Gourd Vine*, p. 22.

/85/   Hurston, *Their Eyes Were Watching God*, p. 62.

/86/   Hurston, *Seraph on the Suwanee*, p. 23.

/87/   Hurston, *Seraph on the Suwanee*, p. 41.

/88/   Ibid., p. 190.

/89/   Ibid., p. 230.

/90/   Discussed by Hemenway, *Zora Neale Hurston*, p. 195.

/91/   Dietrich Bonhoeffer, *Ethics*, ed. Eberhard Bethge, trans. Neville Horton Smith (New York: Macmillan Co., 1965), p. 224: "The structure of responsible life is conditioned by two factors: life is bound to man and to God and a man's own life is free. It is the fact that life is bound to man and to God which sets life in the freedom of a man's own life. Without this bond and without this freedom, there is no responsibility."

/92/   H. Richard Niebuhr, *The Responsible Self* (New York: Harper & Row, 1963), especially pp. 47–68, "The Meaning of Responsibility."

/93/   Alice Gardner, "Courage," in *Encyclopedia of Religion and Ethics*, vol. IV, ed. James Hastings (New York: Charles Scribner's Sons, 1908), pp. 205–206; see also, Albert R. Jonsen, *Responsibility in Modern Religious Ethics* (Washington: Corpus Books, 1968); Moira Roberts, *Responsibility and Practical Freedom* (Cambridge, England: University Press, 1965); Stephen Ross, *The Nature of Moral Responsibility* (Detroit: Wayne State University Press, 1973).

/94/   Mingnon H. Anderson, *Mostly Womenfolk and A Man or Two: A Collection* (Chicago: Third World Press, 1976), p. 8.

/95/   Zora Neale Hurston, *Mules and Men* (Philadelphia: J. B. Lippincott, 1935; reprint ed., New York: Collier, 1970); *Tell My Horse* (Philadelphia: J. B. Lippincott, 1938; reprint ed., Berkeley, Cal.: Turtle Island, 1981); T. C. Chubb, review of *Mules and Men*, by Zora Neale Hurston, *North American Review* 241 (1936): 181; Harold Courlander, review of *Tell My Horse*, by Zora Neale Hurston, *Saturday Review of Literature*, October 1938, p. 6.

/96/   Hurston, *Mules and Men*, pp. 18–19.

/97/   Hurston, *Mules and Men*, pp. 18–19.

/98/   Susan Blake, "Modern Black Writers and the Folk Tradition" (Ph.D. dissertation, University of Connecticut, 1976); Ellease Southerland, "The Influence of Voodoo on the Fiction of Zora Neale Hurston," in *Sturdy Black Bridges*, ed. Roseann Bell, et al. (Garden City, N.Y.: Anchor Press/Doubleday, 1979): Gloria Johnson, "Hurston's Folk."

/99/   Alice Walker, p. 151.

/100/   Paul Tillich, *The Courage to Be* (New Haven: Yale University Press, 1952), p. 3 and especially pp. 178–190, "The Courage to Be as the Key to Being Itself."

/101/   Hemenway, *Zora Neale Hurston*, p. 294.

/102/   "How It Feels to Be Colored Me," reprinted in the *Zora Neale Hurston Reader*, p. 153 (originally published in *World Tomorrow*, May 1928).

/103/   "How It Feels to be Colored Me," *Zora Neale Hurston Reader*, p. 155.

/104/   Ibid., p. 151.

/105/   Ibid., p. 157.

/106/   Ibid., p. 158.

/107/   Hurston discussed a similar understanding in *Mules and Men*, pp. 88–89: "The brother in black puts a laugh in every vacant place in his mind. His laugh has a hundred meanings. It may mean amusement, anger, grief, bewilderment, chagrin, curiosity, simple pleasure or any other of the known or undefined emotions."

/108/   *Zora Neale Hurston Reader,* p. 164.
/109/   Ibid., p. 168.
/110/   Ibid., pp. 167–168.
/111/   Cited in Hemenway, *Zora Neale Hurston,* p. 335.
/112/   Hemenway, *Zora Neale Hurston,* p. 300.
/113/   Hemenway, *Zora Neale Hurston,* p. 332.
/114/   Ibid., p. 321.
/115/   Hemenway, *Zora Neale Hurston,* p. 337. It is important to note that after 1948 none of Hurston's books were published. She completed two novels, "The Lives of Barney Turk" and "The Golden Bench of God," numerous short stories, and had an 800-page manuscript on the life of King Herod ready for publication when she died.
/116/   Christian, 61.

CHAPTER VI

RESOURCES FOR A CONSTRUCTIVE ETHIC IN THE THEOLOGY OF HOWARD THURMAN AND MARTIN LUTHER KING, JR.

As we have seen, Zora Neale Hurston captured the integrity of Black people who buttressed themselves with the community's moral wisdom in their effort to hold on to the essence of their humanity. Hurston wrote about Black consciousness and the political/social awareness within the Black community which were, and are, directly related to its morality and ethics. Through her portrayal of three-dimensional characters, she provided realistic depictions of the essential nature of virtuous living in situations of oppression. The profundity of Hurston's life and work was grounded in the seriousness with which she addressed the Black woman's sensibilities of "invisible dignity," "quiet grace," and "unshouted courage."

So, the question now before us is, what caused this creative, vibrant and astute Black woman to acquiesce into neurotic passivity after the false sodomy charges of 1948? Why did she let go of everything she previously valued? What was missing in the Black woman's wisdom tradition which caused Zora Neale Hurston to sink into unreboundable brokenness when the sex slander was circulated by, to and through the Black community? Hurston's entire life had been grounded in an uncompromising struggle to fulfill her human capacity against incredible odds. In all of her work she adamantly opposed a defensive reactionary posture for Black people. Yet Hurston assumed such a stance as her only recourse in her fight to reclaim her dignity and self-worth. Since the politics of justice was not on the horizon for her and the experience of community was denied to her, were there any resources which would have helped Hurston recover from this traumatic attack against her personhood?

As a Black feminist of faith, I maintain that the cultural and historical support available to Hurston was the balm of the Black religious heritage. By applying the faith claims of Christianity to the nuances and ambiguities of Black life, two of Hurston's contemporaries, Howard Thurman and Martin Luther King, Jr., provide conceptual elements for enhancing the moral agency of Black women. The resources available in the theological vision require an explicit embrace of the ethical themes of *imago dei*, love as grounded in justice, and the irreplaceable nature of community.

Hence, I believe that in the development of an ethic for Black women's lives there must be an appreciation of the contribution of Zora Neale Hurston's life and literature, as well as unequivocal acknowledgement of the Black theological tradition. It is to their resources, contemporaries of Hurston, that I look for further resources.

Thurman: 'Imago Dei' and Mysticism

Howard Thurman's exposition of the sacredness and inherent worth of every human being is uncompromising. The individual personality, as a "child of God," has ultimate significance. The status of *imago dei* has no superior. Any discussion of Thurman's ethics must begin with an understanding of God's grace which comes to humanity, exposing the individual directly to God, so that each person can believe in her divine status.

Being created in the image of God means, for Thurman, that within each individual there is the presence and power of the divine. Only in the concreteness of God's revealed love does each person recognize her worth, purpose and power. A part of every human spirit is the strivings and yearnings to come to itself in its Creator. When the soul feels God's presence, individuals are grasped by the divine essence, which heightens awareness of options and possibilities. This built-in sense of the Creator provides oppressed people with ultimate meaning and the ability to transform circumstances.

Howard Thurman's ethics begins with the divine creative process, wherein the potentiality in every person is aroused, which, in turn, inspires decisive liberating transformation. No matter how restricted moral agents might be, the experiential-mystical element of religion calls on each person to act and to reflect the divine in her actions.

Thurman's most characteristic way of describing moral agency is seen in his description of oppression. When oppressed people experience God, when they experience the essence of what it means to be created in God's image, their spiritual quest for wholeness begins. Those who best know the suffering of injustice and the urgency of freedom must be transformed so that they "can act to shock the oppressor into a state of upheaval and insecurity."[1] God addresses the deepest needs and aspirations of the human spirit, so that those who are oppressed and disinherited can act with ingenuity and dexterity against the judgments of the denigrating environment from the center of their informed hearts. Black women who have experienced enslavement, segregation and discrimination must know that their oppression does not originate with a defect in their personhood but is part of the spiritual ruthlessness in a white, male-oriented society.[2] For Thurman, the awareness of potential is the greatest source of hope. A committed spiritual life is necessary for an accurate sense of moral agency.

> Anyone who permits another to determine the quality of his inner life gives into the hands of the other the keys to his destiny. If a man knows precisely what he can do to you or what epithet he can hurl against you in order to make you lose your temper, your equilibrium, then he can always keep you under subjection.[3]

Despite limiting conditions, Thurman believed that each person can experience integrity and hope through encounters with eternal possibilities.

This understanding of ethics is Thurman's attempt to embrace the religious experience as a source of power. The consciousness that comes with mystical experiences enables individuals to be aware of the humanity of others, even if the external circumstances do not support such.

Smith observes that Thurman's conception of *imago dei* recognizes "the creative capability of personality to grow in the midst of no-growth circumstances; to find faith in the midst of fear, healing in the midst of suffering, love in the midst of hate, hope in the midst of despair, life in the midst of death, and community in the midst of chaos."[4] Thurman's notions of ethics is that the goal of human action according to the distinctive insights of the Judaeo-Christian tradition is to seek "to effect and further harmonious relations in a totally comprehensive climate." Each person, divinely commissioned and led, unites her continuing quest for wholeness with the spatio-temporal realm of life.

> It is in the moment of (mystical) vision there is a sense of community—a unity not only with God but a unity with all of life, particularly with human life. It is in the moment of vision that the mystic discovers that "private values are undergirded and determined by a structure which far transcends the limits of one's individual self." . . . He discovers that he is a person and personality in a profound sense can only be achieved in a milieu of human relations. Personality is something more than mere individuality—it is a fulfillment of the logic of individuality in community.[5]

Speaking confidently from his own experiences, Thurman believed that God always provides resources to meet the harsh demands of life.

> For I believe that there is always something that can be done about anything. What can be done may not alter the situation, but the individual may relate to unalterable situations within the context of his own choosing. In other words, I am saying that a man need not ever be completely and utterly a victim of his cirstances despite the fact, to be repetitive, that he may not be able to change the circumstances. The clue is in the fact that a man can give his assent to his circumstances or he can withhold it, and there are a desert and a sea between the two.[6]

Thurman's ethical orientation can be elaborated in this way:

> If an individual allows his/her worth to be determined by others, or by his/her own inadequate self image, then one loses the freedom, guidance and power which comes from the self. One forfeits one's life to another, and in losing this control a person's condition changes from freedom to slavery, and one's definition changes from human to tool.[7]

Smith summarizes,

> If one does not have any choice, then one does not have responsibility; if one does not have responsibility, then love is

not operative; if love is not operative, then community is impossible.[8]

The primary source of theological ethics, for Thurman, is the religious experience, an intense encounter with God.

King: 'Imago Dei' and Natural Law

In many ways Martin Luther King, Jr.'s understanding of *imago dei* is very similar to Thurman's. Ervin Smith points out that the metaphysical grounding of King's ethics is theistic personalism. "Human personality mirrors divine personality and that divine personality is the infinite expression of the best in human personality."[9] King said, "Every human life is a reflection of the divinity."[10] As people created in God's image, humans are lifted above and separated from all other forms of creation. Each person occupies a particular locus in space and time.

It is important to note that for King, unlike Thurman, the dignity and worth of all human personality are the inalienable rights of human beingness. These rights are unchangeable and universal. "Every person is heir to a legacy of dignity and worth, having rights that are neither conferred by nor derived from the state, they are God-given."[11]

What this means is that King's theological ethics, in contrast to Thurman's, begin with laws that guarantee all humans unqualified freedom, justice and equality. Such laws are unenforceable because they are divine laws written on the human heart, putting each person in relationship with a personal God. Humans are born with a knowledge of what we are to do and not to do.

The significance of this is immense as it allows King to address the dominant oppressive powers. If Christians believe that God created all people in God's own image and that each person has equal value and worth, then the deliberate injury of another person is morally unjustifiable.

Natural laws unfold in history bringing the disconnected aspects of life into a harmonious reality. King wrote, "Every act of injustice mars and defaces the image of God in man."[12] Therefore, theological ethics for King is based on a sense of social responsibility that deals with the inherent value of each human being. The *imago dei* motif gives Black women the divine right "to be treated as ends and never as mere means."[13]

Thurman: Love through Justice and Social Change

Even though Howard Thurman's understanding of ethics involves mysticism, he was a leading protagonist of the demand of religion for social change. According to Thurman, love is the basis of community and community is the arena for moral agency. Thurman argued that only love of self, love between individuals and love of God can shape, empower and sustain social change.[14] The centrality of moral agency is a response to divine love, wherein grace initiates experience of God's love which in turn commission each person to a ministry of love. Thurman advocated a love-ethic which impacts social situations by affirming the inter-relatedness and inter-dependence between each individual. The fullest meaning of love can be known only when human beings, in tune with the infinite, shape a loving reality (community). Thurman's love-ethic calls Black women forth to test and confront all barriers to common unity.

Love as the criteriological mode for Thurman's community of relatedness is manifested in three specific ways.

First, Thurman stressed that love requires reconciliation, a confession of errors and the re-establishment of relationships with those who have natural claims upon individuals but who have caused conflictual rifts within the oppressed community. In the first dimension, love restores unity within the infrastructures of Black life. Parents and children, as well as all those who are not related by blood or marriage but who make up the aggregate of the Black community, must take the initiative to break down the barriers which divide them. By dealing with the root causes of hostility among family members and neighbors, Thurman believed that Black people would recognize new forms of mutual responsibility to each other. Inherent in human-family interrelationships is Thurman's vision of wholeness that brings into harmonious relationship those within the insular community who are alienated from the core of life.

Thurman spelled out the nature of this second dimension of love as the way to reclaim those persons from within the insular community who function as cohorts with the malevolent social structures. Thurman wrote, "There are always those who seem to be willing to put their special knowledge at the disposal of the dominant group to facilitate the tightening of the chains. They are given position, often prominence, and above all a guarantee of economic security and status."[15] This second type of love does not mean condoning ruthless behavior but recognizing with respect and reverence the *imago dei* in every personality.

The community creatively intersects the renouncement of evil deeds with a pronouncement of forgiveness for the doers of such deeds. In overcoming enmity with love, those who betray the trust and violate their allegiance to the justice struggle of the Black community, make amends which release them from the penalties of ostracism and they are accepted back into the community as "children of God."

The third type of love expounded in Thurman's ethics is a "common sharing of mutual worth and value"[16] in the wider human community. Thurman believed that the oppressor and the oppressed are within the same ethical field. Each must be seen in the context of a common humanity. For instance, the "white necessity" to maintain privileges of supremacy must be eradicated. The "male necessity" to protect privileges of superiority also must be broken down. When the heavy weight of status is sloughed off, "each person meets the other where he is and there treats him as if he were where he ought to be. Here we emerge into an area where love operates, revealing a universal characteristic unbounded by special limited circumstances."[17]

Thurman worked with an understanding that hate, fear and deceptions are contradictions to life. They attack self-worth and freedom, rendering the status of outsider to those who are treated in inhumane ways. Moreover, these contradictions rot the spirit.[18] Love, however, was Thurman's underlying unity for life. It embraces the truth about God's intention for creation. Love transforms all people, places, and things which fend off wholeness. It provides the Black woman with confidence to be bold and defiant, to risk all and stand by the truth, no matter what the cost.

KING: LOVE AND JUSTICE

Martin Luther King, Jr.'s conception of theological ethics, like Thurman's, was love centered. However, King's theology required him to give much greater significance in his ethics to the *relationship* of love and justice than Thurman's more concentrated love motif.

For Martin Luther King, all of life is interrrelated, 'an inescapable network of mutuality,' wherein love serves as the binding force. Agapic love gives natural human relations divine significance and value.[19] *Agape* is understanding and creative, redemptive goodwill for all people. ". . . Agape is the love of God operating in the human heart. At this level . . . we love every man because God loves him."[20] In fact, agape is unconditional love. It is applied both to God's love for humans, and to human's reciprocal love for God, which necessarily extends to love of one's neighbor.

> *Agape* is disinterested love. It is love in which the indi-
> vidual seeks not his own good, but the good of his neighbor. (I
> Cor. 10:24)
> *Agape* does not begin by discriminating between worthy
> and unworthy people, or any qualities people possess. It be-
> gins by loving others *for their sake*. It is entirely "neighbor-
> regarding concern for others," which discovers the neighbor in
> every man it meets. Therefore, *agape* makes no distinction
> between friend and enemy; it is directed toward both. . . .
> Consequently, the best way to assure oneself that love is disin-
> terested is to have love for the enemy-neighbor from whom you
> can expect no good in return, but only hostility and persecu-
> tion.
> Another basic point about *agape* is that it springs forth
> from the *need* of the other person—his need for belonging to
> the best in the human family. The Samaritan who helped the
> Jew on the Jericho Road was "good" because he responded to
> human need that he was presented with.[21]

One of the fundamental theological assumptions in King's agapic love is the connection made between love and community, which he phrased as "the solidarity of the human family." Jesus' saying, "Love your enemies," forces the enemies to see themselves as they are and begin to change. This commandment of love ex-cludes casuistic interpretations. It allows whole communities and nations to practice the "turn-the-other-cheek" love ethic of the Sermon on the Mount (Matt.: 5–7).

King's love is active, dynamic and determined. It breaks through a stagnant, complacent, standardized Christian ethic. Love generates the motive and drive for justice. It is self-giving, expecting nothing in return. Reinhold Niebuhr argues that it is easy for love to become the screen which hides injustices.[22] Love is often used to maintain the status quo. But for King, love could never be con-nected to injustice. God in Christ is the paradigm of *agape* love.

King also believed that life is fundamentally social in character and thus love can exist only in communication between people, never in total isolation of the individual. The realization of neigh-borly love in "the least of these my brethren" is a decisive criterion for King: all people are brothers and sisters. *Agape* is inclusive, uniting all humankind in corporate community.

In elaborating King's understanding of *agape*, Smith and Zepp point out the following:

> King speaks of *agape* as "live in action," "love seeking to preserve and create community," "a willingness to go to any length to restore community," and as "the only cement that can hold this broken community together." He relates *agape* to the cross of Jesus Christ and finds there "eternal expression of the length to which God will go to restore broken community.[23]

King concluded that love is an absolute norm of human behavior and the ultimate goal of human society.

Justice in King's thought follows closely the principle of agapaic love. Justice is more than the absence of brutality and regenerated evil. Christian love is always in search of vehicles that will convert love into actions of justice and morality. According to King, justice is twofold: (1) ultimate referent, God's cosmic law of moral justice and righteousness; (2) penultimate referent, political, social and civil laws of society. The ultimate justice refers to those inalienable rights due every human being precisely because of the *imago dei*. Love manifested in penultimate justice involves those aspects of human rights that can be achieved by legislation, such as those originally formulated in the Declaration of Independence and the Bill of Rights of the Constitution. This type of justice demands frontal attacks on racism, poverty, exploitation and all forms of discrimination. In his attempt to explain more clearly this dual meaning of justice, King said, "It may be true that the law can't make a man love me but it can keep him from lynching me." In *Strength to Love*, King elaborated this idea further: Morality cannot be legislated but behavior can be regulated. Judicial decrees may not change the heart, but they can restrain the heartless."[24] King suggested that the penultimate "man-made" laws should be regulated by the law-enforcement agencies of society, with the intent of humanizing social conditions. Therefore, for King the penultimate laws should insure "free access to public accommodations and transportation, the right to equality in education, employment, housing, health, as well as freedom of religion, assembly, protection against deprivation of life, liberty, and property without due process of law, trial by jury, for all people, regardless of race, sex or class."

Thurman: Community and Inter-relatedness

In discussing the previous ethical themes we find that for both Thurman and King everything moves toward community. Thurman emphasized the cruciality of the mystical experience which grounds love but then moved on to state explicitly the need for harmonious common unity.[25] Thurman's basic proposition is that "all life is one, arising out of a common center—God."[26] The conception of moral agency is set in the context of basic interrelationship and the need for community. All people who have experienced God's love and know what it means to be created in God's own image are related and aligned with actualizing the potentiality of all persons (and nature). Therefore, the Black woman's receptivity and responsive action, her mystical experience and her praxis, are dialectically one.[27]

Segundo Galilea agrees with Thurman's position that morality and responsibility move from mystical autonomy to unity in community.

> Authentic Christian contemplation, passing through the desert, transforms contemplatives into prophets and heroes of commitment and militants into mystics. Christianity achieves the synthesis of the politician and the mystic, the militant and the contemplative, and abolishes the false antithesis between the religious-contemplative and the militantly committed. Authentic contemplation through the encounter with the absolute of God leads to the absolute of one's neighbor.[28]

Individual religious experiences serve as conduits which call isolated individuals to move toward each other into inclusive community. In order to bring to fruition a future, full of God's promises, each person must realize his/her kinship under God with all others. Thurman explains, "We are all related either positively or negatively to some immediate social unit which provides the other-than-self reference which in turn undergirds the sense of self. Such a primary group confers *persona* upon the individual; it fashions and fortifies the character structure."[29] Thurman, as we have seen, believed that the maintenance and furtherance of life at its highest level require a move from false self-centeredness to community relatedness. Participation in the unfolding promises of God means that Black women gather with all others as common people under God.

Thus, from the standpoint of Thurman's ethics the mystical experience awakens and makes explicit what is already there in the

depths of each person. Each woman is then called to move toward
the common ground of relatedness, in order to translate the formulation of God's love into the actual phenomena of her human
existence. It is important to note that this aspect of Thurman's ethics
concurs with what Paul Tillich proposed in *Systematic Theology*.
Human relations alone "cannot conquer loneliness, self seclusion,
and hostility. . . . Relatedness needs the vertical dimension in order
to actualize itself in the horizontal dimension."[31] It is apparent that
for Thurman the mystical experience, love and community relatedness are part of the same continuum. Inclusive community is non-
spatial. It is qualitative.[32]

Luther Smith summarizes the essence of Howard Thurman's
theological ethics in this manner:

> Thurman's greatest legacy may be his vision of inclusive
> community: a community based on reconciliation, which rec-
> ognizes and celebrates the underlying unity of life and the
> inter-dependence of all life forms. Justice and a sense of innate
> equality are ruling principles for this community, and love-
> ethic establishes and maintains the community's creative
> character. Personal identity is affirmed while unity is sought
> with one's fellows. Thurman's inclusive community harbors all
> races, classes, faith claims, and ethnic groups, for in the eyes of
> God every human is His beloved child. Differences among
> people are not ignored or depreciated, though their impor-
> tance does not overshadow the bond of kinship between indi-
> viduals. And because of this bond, differences can be appreci-
> ated rather than feared, for the variety of truth perspectives
> they bring to understanding. In cultural pluralism persons
> come to know the many faces of God, and what God is doing
> through diverse ways. Hopefully, this will give individuals a
> proper sense of self and neighbor such that one does not fall
> into destructive righteousness. Inclusive community confirms
> what Thurman understands as God's will for human rela-
> tionships.[33]

King: Beloved Community, Pragmatism and a Praxis of Resistance

Martin Luther King, Jr.'s theological ethics emphasized even
more strongly than Thurman's a commitment to the actualization of
an inclusive human community. King's conception of the "beloved
community" is described as "the mutually cooperative and volun-

tary venture of man to assume a semblance of responsibility for his brother."[34]

In many of his writings King challenged Christians to become "extremist for the extension of justice," so that Blacks and whites could work together transforming a segregated society into a genuine integrated community. In the Spring of 1963, King and large numbers of his supporters were jailed in Birmingham, Alabama when they participated in a non-violent campaign to end segregation at lunch counters and in hiring practices. King's "Letter from the Birmingham Jail" was a response to the Black clergy who refused to participate in the campaign and to the white clergy who strongly opposed King by issuing a statement urging Blacks not to support the civil rights demonstrations. In the epistle from jail, King once more expressed his conviction concerning the total interrelatedness of all of life.

King believed that the civil government has a responsibility to sanction and uphold law and order for all its citizens. Whenever government creates laws which are out of harmony with the law of God and natural law, the government forfeits its authority. When the government and its laws do not uplift "the solidarity of the human family" but instead unjustly degrade members of the society, then Christians have no alternative but to engage in direct action in order to defy oppressive and unjust authority. "One has not only a legal but a moral responsibility to disobey unjust laws,"[35] said King. To cooperate passively with an unjust system makes the oppressed as evil as the oppressors.[36] Thus, Black people are called to actualize their moral selves by realizing the indivisibility of human existance.

> We are caught in an inescapable network of mutuality, tied into a single garment of destiny. Whatever affects one directly affects all indirectly. We are made to live together because of the inter-related structure of reality.[37]

Pragmatism was Martin Luther King's means to achieve the "beloved community." One should not conclude that King stressed the priority of love and justice as fixed verifications in and of themselves. King knew that Blacks lacked the physical and material resources to sustain a long-term violent rebellion; yet he never wavered in his insistence to find the most effective strategies in the actualization of an integrated society.

Being fond of Hegel's dialectics, King insisted on seeing the whole of complex issues. He was always in search of the emergent truth between the usefulness, workability, and practicality of strategies and tactics as well as the doctrines and moral criteria that would shape a reconciled Christian community. In considering moral agency, King often quoted the pragmatic Biblical formula: "Be ye therefore wise as serpents, and harmless as doves." He was committed to actualizing his vision of a thoroughly integrated society by assessing realistically institutional powers.

In varying degrees, King's ethical decisions arose from his cautious weighing of the consequences of direct action and the general welfare of the oppressed people with the hope of invoking the ultimate principles of love and justice in wholistic community. "This process was not a static-deductive relation," argues Enoch Oglesby, "but a dynamic interplay between King's ethics and theology as he sought to respond to the pull of contemporary events."[38]

For Martin Luther King, pragmatism was a ready-made factor in the non-violent Civil Rights Movement. King knew that in conflict, the opposition would bring in the National Guards, state patrols, county and city "peace" officers. King also opposed violence in principle:

> . . . It is better to be the recipient of violence than the inflicter of it, since the latter only multiplies the existence of violence and bitterness in the universe, while the former may develop a sense of shame in the opponent, and thereby bring about a transformation and change of heart.[39]

Committed to the norms of love and justice, King worked toward a destiny for this society wherein humankind would not end in utter ruin through bombs and missiles.

King's solidaristic approach to human existence helped him galvanize masses of people into non-violent direct action so that they could advance against the social structures of sin and oppression. King believed in bringing people of all races, classes, nations, religions and ethnic groups together so that they could create and foster situations of tension which were so crisis-packed that doors to negotiation would inevitably open. Prior to direct action, King always tried to negotiate with those who were responsible for obstructing justice. Embracing the dignity of all human personality, he did not seek to defeat or to humiliate the opponents, but to convert the enforcers of social stagnation to his side through friendship and understanding. However, when those who maintain oppressive power structures refuse to be prodded around the negotiation table, then those from oppressed communities are left with no alternative but to engage in constructive forms of coercion. The dramatization of injustice must be done in such a way that even "the most recalcitrant elements" are forced to admit that change is necessary. Overt, collective pressure is indispensable. Mass-action movement is a palpable force that exposes the callous and cynical codes of evil. "Injustice anywhere is a threat to justice everywhere."[40]

As a negotiator, King was aware that the normative factor must be considered in relation to the probable effects of direct nonviolent action upon the economic and political situation at any given time. King stressed that tactics must merge with the larger principles of love and justice in the sphere of practical action. Even when bombings, intimidations, discrimination, disfranchisement, and various "Gestapolike pressures" are exploding all around, the opposition to injustice must be one of self-discipline, organized, and peaceful resistance. When one is faced with physical violence en masse, it would be impractical and disastrous to precipitate a violent confrontation with the dominant group which has both the resources and the techniques to win.

For instance, during the summer of 1957 when Congress whittled down the general civil rights legislation to a single item of the right to vote, King's pragmatism allowed him to accept the much-compromised bill without despair for the future. Some members of the Black community were demanding "all or nothing" and considered King a "dupe" and a "sellout" for compromising. But King understood that without a compromise, there would be no bill passed.

Another pragmatic development of far-reaching importance in community building was when King agreed to a "package deal": (1) he would pay his fine for breaking the Alabama anti-boycott law; (2) all other cases against the eighty-nine Black boycott leaders would be dropped; and (3) all cases against white "bombers" would be dropped. King accepted this as possibly the best way out of a difficult situation. When asked why he agreed to such a settlement, King replied, "It would have been a needless waste of time and money to continue the case. We decided the best thing to do was pay the fine and move on to another phase of the battle."[41]

On still another occasion, the Montgomery court found King guilty for refusing to obey a policeman. The penalty was ten dollars, and costs of court, totalling fourteen days in jail. King refused to pay the fine, but agreed to go to jail and serve out the time. His statement to the Judge; "Your Honor . . . I could not in all good conscience pay a fine for an act that I did not commit and above all for brutal treatment that I did not deserve."[42] Through such examples we find that King always balanced his theory of pragmatism with his fundamental commitment to an inclusive human community.

In each of the above situations there are three basic strategic principles at work: assessing the character and logistics of the situation; naming the primary evil to be dramatized; and identifying the meaning of non-cooperation with evil. King considered these as means moving toward the achievement of the "beloved community." He wrote,

> It is true that as we struggle for freedom in America, we will have to boycott at times. But we must remember . . . that a boycott is not an end in itself. . . . But the end is reconciliation; the end is redemption; the end is the creation of the beloved community.[43]

As members of the "beloved community," Black women are responsible, along with others who care, for collecting the facts to determine whether injustice exists, whether a law, an historical situation, existing social relations elevate or debase human beingness. Moral agents must evaluate every situation as to whether it contributes to or impedes the growth of human personality and genuine community. Their task is to determine whether inalienable rights are granted or denied. Ethical living requires an intolerance of civil arrangements that result in the horrors of racism, gender discrimination, economic exploitation and widespread cruelty. The interdependency of the "beloved community" projects a "constructive equality of oneness." "Whatever affects one directly affects all indirectly."[44]

Paul Garber says that the significance of King's legacy is that

> King was a working theologian who practiced what he preached. He was, perhaps, the best model for a new style of theologian, working not in leisure on the fringes of significant social movements, but in the midst of a people struggling to be free, struggling along with them, and declaring to them the ultimate significance of what they were doing together.[45]

CONCLUSION

Taking seriously the theological tradition of the Black Church means that Black women can enhance their experiential moral wisdom. Neither Howard Thurman nor Martin Luther King, Jr. reflect directly on the Black woman's experience, but emergent in their theologies is the strong affirmation of the dignity of all Black people grounded in God, precisely the starting point of Hurston's vision. This theme resonates with Zora Neale Hurston's deepest conviction and what she mirrored as a portrayer of Black life. Hurston insisted that Black women seek the realization of their dignity as persons. This dignity is a birthright, a non-negotiable need.

Implicit, not yet explicit, in Hurston's literary vision (i.e. her love of Black life, her sense of the value of community, her search for truth, etc.) is the theological vision: human beings are united in a bond of divine love which enables them to live justly; and the overarching mandate calls for all people to live cooperatively as faithful disciples in an inclusive human community. As a Black-woman-artist, Hurston lived in a world wherein Thurman's concept of harmonious common unity was not yet her reality, and King's mass-base-politics could not be envisioned. The lack of objective conditions for experiencing this reality were not apparent to Hurston and are not yet characteristic of the moral situation of the vast majority of Black women.

Hurston's suspicion of the Black religious tradition is valid. Black male theologians continue to ignore the victimization of gender discrimination. However, in this chapter, I signal three basic theological themes in the ethics of Thurman and King that can sustain the politics of justice, which Black women need. What Hurston was denied, Black women of today must have. Black women intellectuals must transform the tradition so as to enable Black women, who celebrate Black life, to make a reaffirmation of their spiritual roots.

The triple jeopardy of Black women's lives and the lack of ability to control the ongoing dynamics of oppression mean that the mystical ground of dignity and the need for love and community in struggle really must be made explicit in our contemporary times. In order to sustain the living out of 'invisible dignity,' 'quiet grace' and 'unshouted courage' Black women today must embrace the formal features of the theological ethics of Thurman and King because they provide moral resources for the great struggle that *still lies ahead.*

Remembering the words of our women who came before us, we must walk the path of the struggle, not by ourselves, but we must walk it. Not to do so is to die forever.[46]

Notes

/1/   Howard Thurman, *Jesus and the Disinherited* (Nashville: Abingdon-Cokebury Press, 1949), p. 21.

/2/   Thurman, *Jesus and the Disinherited*, p. 28.

/3/   Luther Smith, Jr., *Howard Thurman: The Mystic as Prophet* (Washington, D.C.: University Press of America, 1981), p. 54.

/4/   Thurman, *Disciplines of the Spirit*, pp. 104–05. Detail discussion of moral agency: Hans Gerth and C. Wright Mills, *Character and Social Structure* (New York: Harbinger Books, 1953); Romano Guardini, *The Virtues: On the Forms of Moral Life* (Chicago: Henry Regnery, 1967); James M. Gustafson, "Moral Discernment in the Christian Life," in Gene H. Outka and Paul Ramsey, eds. *Norm and Context in Christian Ethics* (New York: Charles Scribner's Sons, 1968).

/5/   Howard Thurman, "Mysticism and Social Change," *Eden Theological Seminary Bulletin*, IV (Spring Quarter, 1939), p. 27.

/6/   Howard Thurman, "What Can We Believe In?" reprinted from *Journal of Religion and Health*, 12 (April 1973), p. 117.

/7/   Howard THurman, *With Head and Heart: Autobiography* (New York: Harcourt Brace Jovanovich, 1979), p. 165. See also, Emil Brunner, *The Divine Imperative, a Study in Christian Ethics,* translated by Olive Wyon (New York: The Macmillan Co., 1937), esp. pp. 130–39; Rudolph Otto, *Mysticism East and West: A Comparative Analysis of the Nature of Mysticism,* translated by Berthan L. Bracev and Richenda C. Payne (New York: Macmillan Co., 1932).

/8/   Luther Smith, Howard Thurman, p. 51.

/9/   Erwin Smith, *The Ethics of Martin Luther King, Jr.* (New York: The Edwin Mellen Press, 1981), p. 151.

/10/   Martin Luther King, Jr., *Where Do We Go From Here: Chaos or Community?* (New York: Harper & Row, 1968), p. 84.

/11/   Martin Luther King, Jr., *Why We Can't Wait*. See also, Lonnie Edmonson and Archie Logan, "Martin Luther King, Jr.: Theology in Context," *Duke Divinity School Review* 40 (Spring 1975); Enoch H. Oglesby, "Ethical and Educational Implications of Black Theology," *Religious Education* 69 (July 1974): 403–12; John W. Rathbun, "Martin Luther King: Theology of Social Action," *American Quarterly* 20 (Spring 1968): 38–53; Mohan Lal Sharma, "Martin Luther King: Modern America's Greatest Theologian of Social Action," *Journal of Negro History* 53 (July 1968): 257–63.

/12/   King, *Where Do We Go From Here*, p. 99.

/13/   Ibid., p. 97.

/14/   Thurman's love ethic is discussion in detail in *Jesus and the Disinherited*, pp. 89–109.

/15/   Thurman, *Jesus and the Disinherited*, p. 100.

/16/   Ibid., p. 105.

/17/   Howard Thurman, *The Luminous Darkness: Personal Interpretation of the Anatomy of Segregation and the Gound of Hope* (New York: Harper & Row, 1965), pp. 42–44. See also, *The Search for Common Ground: An Inquiry in the Basis of Man's Experience of Community* (New York: Harper & Row, 1971).

/18/   Howard Thurman, *Deep Is the Hunger: Meditations for Apostles of Sensitiveness* (Richmond, Ind.: Friends United Press, 1951), p. 39.

/19/   For further discussion, see Gene H. Outka, *Agape: An Ethical Analysis* (New Haven, Conn.: Yale University Press, 1972); Paul Tillich, *Love, Power and Justice: Ontological Analyses and Ethical Applications* (New York: Oxford University Press, 1954); Raymond L. Whitehead, *Love and Struggle in Mao's Thought* (Maryknoll, N.Y.: Orbis Books, 1977).

/20/   Martin Luther King, Jr., *Strength To Love* (New York: Harper & Row, 1963), p. 44.

/21/   Martin Luther King, Jr., *Stride Toward Freedom: The Montgomery Story* (New York: Harper & Row, 1958), pp. 104–05.

/22/   R. Davis and Robert C. Good, *Reinhold Niebuhr on Politics* (New York: Charles Scribner & Sons, 1960), p. 107.

/23/   Kenneth L. Smith and Ira Zepp, *Search for the Beloved Community* (Valley Forge, Pa.: Judson Press, 1974), p. 64.

/24/   King, Strength To Love, p. 22.

/25/   Abraham Heschel concludes that the prophets in Israel developed their God consciousness in the same manner that Thurman describes. Heschel writes, "An analysis of prophetic utterances shows that the fundamental experience of the prophet is a fellowship with the feelings of God, a *sympathy with the divine pathos*, a communion with the divine consciousness which comes about through the prophet's reflection of, or participation in, the divine pathos. The typical prophetic state of mind is one being taken up into the heart of the divine pathos." In Volume II Heschel continues asserting that the encounter with God awakens the prophet to God's concern for the welfare of the people. *The Prophets*, Vols. I & II (New York: Harper & Row, 1962), pp. 26 and 263.

/26/   Thurman, *Deep is the Hunger*, p. 109. This concept is also discussed in Thurman's *Footprints of a Dream: The Story of the Church for the Fellowship of All Peoples* (New York: Harper & Brothers, 1959); *Meditations of the Heart* (New York: Harper & Row, 1953).

/27/   Howard Thurman, "Good News for the Underprivileged," *Religion in Life*, Summer Issue (1935): 403–409; *Disciplines of the Spirit* (New York: Harper & Row, 1963); *The Greatest of These* (Mills College, Calif.: Eucalyptus Press, 1944); also, Joachim Wach, *Types of Religious Experience, Christian and Non-Christian* (Chicago: University of Chicago Press, 1951).

/28/   Segundo Galilea, "Liberation as an Encounter with Politics and Contemplation," in *The Mystical and Political Dimensions of the Christian Faith*, eds. Claude Geffre and Gustavo Gutierrez (New York: Herder and Herder, 1974), p. 28.

/29/   Thurman, "Mysticism and Social Change," p. 53. See also Howard Thurman, *Mysticism and the Experience of Love* (Wallingford, Pa.: Pendle

Hill, 1961); Rufus Jones, *Social Law in the Spiritual World: Studies in Human and Divine Inter-Relationship* (Philadelphia: John C. Winston Co., 1904; Walter T. Stace, *The Teachings of the Mystics* (New York: New American Library, 1960).

/31/ Paul Tillich discusses this same understanding of receptivity and human relations in *Systematic Theology*, III (Chicago: University of Chicago Press, 1951–63), esp. pp. 231–35.

/32/ Howard Thurman, *The Creative Encounter: An Interpretation of Religion and the Social Witness* (Richmond, Ind.: Friends United Press, 1954), p. 20; see also Thurman's *The Centering Moment* (New York: Harper & Row, 1969); *The Inward Journey* (Richmond, Ind.: Friends United Press, 1961); "Mysticism and Jesus," Lecture V given at the University of the Redlands, May 1973; "Mysticism and Ethics," *The Journal of Religious Thought*, Summer Supplement (1970): 23–30; "Mysticism and Social Action," the Lawrence lecture on Religion and Society (First Unitarian Church of Berkeley), 13 October 1978.

/33/ Luther Smith, p. 176.

/34/ Martin Luther King, Jr., "The Ethical Demands of Integration," *Religion and Labor* (May 1963), p. 7.

/35/ King, *Why We Can't Wait* (New York: Harper & Row, 1963), p. 87.

/36/ Elaborated in detail in ibid., pp. 77–100.

/37/ Martin Luther King, Jr., *Trumpet of Conscience* (New York: Harper & Row, 1968), p. 68.

/38/ Enoch H. Oglesby, "Martin Luther King, Jr., Liberation Ethics in a Christian Context," *Journal of the Interdenominational Theological Center*, Spring 1977, p. 34.

/39/ King, *Stride Toward Freedom*, pp. 98–99. For detailed discussion of pragmatism and ethics, see: Saul D. Alinsky, *Rules for Radicals: Practical and Primer for Realistic Radicals* (New York: Random House, 1971); John Dewey, *Ethics*, rev. ed. (New York: H. Holt & Co., 1938); Rao K. Ramakrishna, *Ghandi and Pragmatism: An Intercultural Study* (Calcultta: Oxford & IBH Pub. Co., 1968).

/40/ King, *Why We Can't Wait*, p. 78.

/41/ L. D. Reddick, *Crusader Without Violence (New York: Harper & Brothers, 1959), p. 210. See also: Richard B. Gregg, The Power of Nonviolence*, 2nd rev. ed. (New York: Schocken Books, 1966), esp. pp. 15–42; William Robert Miller, *Nonviolence: A Christian Interpretation* (New York: Association Press, 1964); G. Ramachandran and T. K. Mahadevan, *Nonviolence after Ghandi: A Study of Martin Luther King, Jr.* (New Dehli: Ghandi Peace Foundation, 1968).

/42/ Reddick, *Crusader Without Violence*, p. 212.

/43/ Cited in William R. Miller, *Martin Luther King, Jr.: His Life, Martyrdom and Meaning for the World* (New York: Avon Books, 1968), p. 66.

/44/ King, *Where Do We Go From Here?*, p. 181. See Donald H. Smith, "An Exegesis of Martin Luther King's Social "Philosophy," *Phylon* 31 (Spring 1970): 89–97; Warren E. Steinkraus, "Martin Luther King's Personalism and Nonviolence," *Journal of the History of Ideas* 34 (January–March 1973): 97–111; Hanes Walton, Jr., *The Political Philosphy of Martin Luther King, Jr.* (Conn.: Greenwood Press, 1971).

/45/   Paul Garber, "King was a Black Theologian," *Journal of the Inter-denominational Theological Center* 2 (Spring 1975): 100–13.

/46/   This paraphrased statement is taken from an article by Geraldine L. Wilson, "The Self/Group Actualization of Black Women," in *The Black Woman*, ed. La Frances Rodgers-Rose (Beverly Hills, Ca.: Sage Publications, 1980), pp. 301–14.

SELECTED BIBLIOGRAPHY

Aptheker, Bettina. *Woman's Legacy: Essays on Race, Sex, and Class in American History.* Amherst: The University of Massachusetts, 1982.

Barnett, Ida B. Wells. *Crusade for Justice: The Autobiography of Ida B. Wells,* ed. A. M. Duster. Chicago: The University of Chicago Press, 1970.

Ben-Jochannan, Yosef. *The Black Man's Religion.* New York: Alkebu-lan Books, Associates, 1974.

Bennett, Lerone, Jr. *Black Power, U.S.A.: The Human Side of Reconstruction, 1867–1977.* Chicago: Johnson Publishing Co., 1967.

Blassingame, John W. *The Slave Community: Plantation Life in the Antebellum South.* New York: Oxford University Press, 1972.

Blaustein, Albert P. and Clarence C. Ferguson. *Desegregation and the Law.* New Brunswick, N.J.: Rutgers University Press, 1957.

Boesak, Allan A. *Farewell to Innocence: A Socio-Ethical Study on Black Theology.* Maryknoll, N.Y.: Orbis Books, 1977.

Bonhoeffer, Dietrich. *Ethics,* ed. Eberhard Bethge; trans. Neville Horton Smith. New York: Macmillan Co., 1965.

Brown, Hallie Quinn. *Homespun Heroines and Other Women of Distinction.* Xenia, Ohio: The Aldine Pub Co., 1926.

Bullock, Henry A. *A History of Negro Education in the South from 1619 to the Present.* Cambridge: Harvard University Press, 1967.

Cade, Toni, ed. *The Black Woman: An Anthology.* New York: Bantam, 1977.

Camejo, Peter. *Racism, Revolution and Reaction 1861–1877: The Rise and Fall of Radical Reconstruction.* New York: Monad Press, 1976.

Childress, Alice. *Like One of the Family: Conversations from a Domestic Life.* New York: Independence Pub., 1955.

Christian, Barbara. *Black Women Novelists: The Development of a Tradition, 1892–1976.* Westport, Conn.: Greenwood Press, 1980.

Cone, Cecil W. *The Identity Crisis in Black Theology.* Nashville: AMEC, 1975.

Cone, James H. *Black Theology and Black Power.* New York: Seabury Press, 1969.

———. *A Black Theology of Liberation.* Philadelphia: Lippincott Co., 1970.

———. *God of the Oppressed.* New York: Seabury Press, 1975.

────── and Gayraud Wilmore, eds. *Black Theology: A Documentary History, 1966–1979*. Maryknoll, N.Y.: Orbis Press, 1979.

Cooper, Anna Julia. *A Voice from the South, by a Black Woman of the South*. Westport, Conn.: Greenwood Press, 1976; orig. pub. 1892.

Dalfiume, Richard. *Desegregation of the U.S. Armed Forces—Fighting on Two Fronts, 1939–1953*. Columbia, Missouri: University of Missouri Press, 1969.

Davis, Angela Y. *Women, Race & Class*. New York: Random House, 1981.

Davis, Arthur P. *From the Dark Tower: Afro-American Writers, 1900–1960*. Washington, D.C.: Howard University Press, 1974.

Deats, Paul, Jr., ed. *Toward a Discipline of Social Ethics*. Boston: Boston University Press, 1972.

DeNevis, Donald P. and Doris A. Holmes, ed. *Racism at the Turn of the Century: Documentary Perspectives, 1870–1910.* : Leswing Press, 1973.

DuBois, W.E.B. *Black Reconstruction in America, 1860–1880*. New York: Russell & Russell, 1935; rpt. New York: Atheneum, 1969.

Dubois, Silvia. *Silvia Dubois (now 116 years old): a biografy of the slav who whipt her mistress and gand her freedom*. Ringos, N.J.: C. W. Larison, 1883; rpt. Westport, Conn.: Greenwood Press, 1983.

Gayle, Addison, Jr. *The Way of the New World: The Black Novel in America*. Garden City, N.Y.: Doubleday & Co., 1973.

Geffre, Claude and Gustavo Gutierrez, eds. *The Mystical and Political Dimensions of the Christian Faith*. New York: Herder and Herder, 1974.

Greene, Lorenzo and Carter G. Woodson. *The Negro Wage Earner*. Washington, D.C.: Association for the Study of Negro Life and History, 1930.

Gustafson, James M., ed. *On Being Responsible: Issues in Personal Ethics*. London: SCM Press, 1969.

Harley, Sharon and Rosalyn Tarborg-Penn, eds. *The Afro-American Woman, Struggles and Images*. Port Washington, N.Y.: Kennikat Press, 1978.

Harris, Trudier. *From Mammies to Militants: Domestics in Black American Literature*. Philadelphia: Temple University Press, 1982.

Hemenway, Robert. *Zora Neale Hurston, A Literary Biography*. Urbana: University of Illinois Press, 1977.

Henri, Floretti. *Black Migration: Movement North, 1900–1920*. New York: Doubleday/Anchor, 1975.

Heyward, I. Carter. *The Redemption of God: A Theology of Mutual Relation*. Washington, D.C.: University Press of America, Inc., 1982.

Hull, Gloria T., Patricia Bell Scott and Barbara Smith. *All the Women Are White, All the Black Are Men, But Some of Us Are Brave: Black Women's Studies*. Old Westbury, N.Y.: Feminist Press, 1982.

Hurston, Zora Neale. *Dust Tracks On A Road*. Philadelphia: Lippincott Co., 1942; rpt. New York: Lippincott, 1971.

————. *Jonah's Gourd Vine*. Philadelphia: Lippincott Co., 1934; rpt. New York: Lippincott, 1971.

————. *Moses, Man of the Mountain*. Philadelphia: Lippincott Co., 1939; rpt. Chatham, N.J.: The Chatham Bookseller, 1967.

————. *Mules and Men*. Philadelphia: Lippincott Co., 1935; rpt. New York: Harper & Row, 1970.

————. *Seraph on the Suwanee*. New York: Charles Scribner's Sons, 1948; rpt. New York: AMS Press, Inc., 1974.

————. *Tell My Horse*. Philadelphia: Lippincott Co., 1938; rpt. Berkeley: Turtle Island, 1981.

————. *Their Eyes Were Watching God*. Philadelphia: Lippincott Co., 1937; rpt. Urbana: University of Illinois Press, 1978.

————. *The Sanctified Church*. Berkeley: Turtle Island, 1981.

Jackson, Kenneth T. *The Ku Klux Klan in the City, 1915–1930*. New York: Oxford University Press, 1967.

Jordan, June. *Civil Wars*. Boston: Beacon Press, 1981.

Joseph, Gloria I. and Jill Lewis. *Common Differences: Conflicts in Black and White Feminist Perspectives*. Garden City, N.Y.: Anchor Press/Doubleday, 1981.

King, Martin Luther, Jr. *The Measure of a Man*. Philadelphia: United Church Press, 1958.

————. *Strength to Love*. New York: Harper & Row, 1963.

————. *Stride Toward Freedom*. New York: Harper & Row, 1958.

————. *Where Do We Go From Here: Chaos or Community?* New York: Harper & Row, 1967.

————. *Why We Can't Wait*. New York: Harper & Row, 1964.

Ladner, Joyce. *Tomorrow's Tomorrow, The Black Woman*. Garden City, N.Y.: Doubleday, 1971.

Lehmann, Paul. *Ethics in a Christian Context*. New York: Harper & Row, 1963.

Lerner, Gerda, ed. *Black Women in White America: A Documentary History*. New York: Random House, 1972.

Levine, Lawrence W. *Black Culture and Black Consciousness: Afro-American Folk Thought from Slavery to Freedom*. New York: Oxford University Press, 1977.

Lewis, David L. *King: A Critical Biography*. New York: Praeger, 1970.

Loewenberg, Bert and Ruth Bogin, ed. *Black Women in Nineteenth Century American Life*. University Park: Penn State University Press, 1972.

Long, Edward L., Jr. *A Survey of Recent Christian Ethics*. New York: Oxford University Press, 1982.

Lynch, Hollis R. *The Black Urban Condition: A Documentary History, 1866–1971*. New York: Thomas Y. Crowell Co., 1973.

MacMurray, John. *The Self as Agent*. London: Faber and Faber, 1957.

Marable, Manning. *Blackwater, Historical Studies in Race, Class Consciousness, and Revolution*. Dayton, Ohio: Black Praxis Press, 1982.

Moraga, Cherrie and Gloria Anzaldua, eds. *This Bridge Called My Back: Writings by Radical Women of Color*. Watertown, Mass.: Persephone Press, 1981.

Moses, Wilson J. *Black Messiahs and Uncle Toms: Social and Literary Manipulations of a Religious Myth*. University Park: Penn State University Press, 1982.

Niebuhr, H. Richard. *The Responsible Self*. New York: Harper & Row, 1963.

Niebuhr, Reinhold. *Moral Man and Immoral Society*. New York: Charles Scribner's Sons, 1960.

Noble, Jeanne. *Beautiful, Also, Are the Souls of My Black Sisters: A History of the Black Woman in America*. Englewood Cliffs, N.J.: Prentice-Hall, Inc., 1978.

Oglesby, Enoch H. *Ethics and Theology from the Other Side: Sounds of Moral Struggle*. Washington, D.C.: University Press of America, 1979.

Puckett, Newbell Niles. *Folk Beliefs of Southern Negroes*. Chapel Hill: University of North Carolina Press, 1926.

Ransom, Roger and Richard Sutch. *One Kind of Freedom: The Economic Consequences of Emancipation*. New York: Cambridge University Press, 1977.

Reid, Inez. *"Together" Black Women*. New York: Emerson Hall, 1971.

Rodgers-Rose, La Frances, ed. *The Black Woman*. Beverly Hills, Calif.: Sage Publications, 1980.

Rothman, Sheila M. *Woman's Proper Place: A History of Changing Ideals and Practices, 1870 to the Present*. New York: Basic Books, 1978.

Scott, Ann Firor. *The Southern Lady: From Pedestal to Politics, 1830–1930*. Chicago: University of Chicago Press, 1970.

Sellers, James. *Theological Ethics*. New York: Macmillan Co., 1966.

Smith, Erwin. *The Ethics of Martin Luther King, Jr*. New York: The Edwin Mellen Press, 1981.

Smith, Luther E., Jr. *Howard Thurman: The Mystic as Prophet*. Washington, D.C.: University Press of America, 1981.

Smith, Kenneth L. and Ira G. Zepp. *Search for the Beloved Community: The Thinking of Martin Luther King, Jr*. Valley Forge, Pa.: Judson Press, 1974.

Stack, Carolyn. *All Our Kin: Strategies for Survival in a Black Community*. New York: Harper & Row, 1974.

Staples, Robert. *The Black Woman in America: Sex, Marriage and the Family*. Chicago: Nelson-Hall Publishers, 1973.

Steady, Filomina Chioma. *The Black Woman Cross-Culturally*. Cambridge: Schenkman Publishing Co., 1981.

Sullivan, John Edward. *The Image of God: The Doctrine of St. Augustine and its Influence*. Dubuque, Iowa: Priory Press, 1963.

Terrell, Mary Church. *A Colored Woman in a White World*. Washington, D.C.: Ransdell, 1940.

Thurman, Howard. *The Centering Moment*. New York: Harper & Row, 1969.

———. *The Creative Encounter: An Interpretation of Religion and the Social Witness*. New York: Harper & Brothers, 1954.

———. *Deep Is the Hunger*. New York: Harper & Row, 1951.

———. *Deep River and the Negro Spiritual Speaks of Life and Death*. Richmond, Ind.: Friends United Press, 1975.

———. *Disciplines of the Spirit*. New York: Harper & Row, 1963.

———. *The Growing Edge*. New York: Harper & Row, 1956.

———. *The Inward Journey*. New York: Harper & Row, 1961.

———. *Jesus and the Disinherited*. Nashville: Abingdon-Cokesbury Press, 1949.

———. *The Luminous Darkness: A Personal Interpretation of the Anatomy of Segregation and the Ground of Hope*. Harper & Row, 1965.

———. *The Search for Common Ground: An Inquiry into the Basis of Man's Experience of Community*. New York: Harper & Row, 1971.

———. *With Head and Heart: The Autobiography of Howard Thurman*. New York: Harcourt Brace Jovanovich, 1975.

Tillich, Paul. *Love, Power and Justice: Ontological and Ethical Applications*. New York: University of Oxford Press (Galaxy Books), 1954.

———. *The Courage to Be*. New Haven: Yale University Press, 1952.

U.S. Department of Commerce, Bureau of the Census. *The Social and Economic Status of the Black Population in the United States: An Historical Overview, 1790–1978*. Washington, D.C.: U.S. Government Printing Office, 1974.

U.S. Department of Labor, Women's Bureau. *Minority Women Workers: Statistical Overview*. Washington, D.C.: U.S. Government Printing Office, 1977.

Walker, Alice, ed. *I Love Myself When I Am Laughing . . . And Then Again When I Am Looking Mean and Impressive: A Zora Neale Hurston Reader*. Old Westbury, N.Y.: The Feminist Press, 1979.

Wallace, Phyllis A. *Black Women in the Labor Force*. Boston: MIT Press, 1980.

Walton, Hanes, Jr. *The Political Philosophy of Martin Luther King, Jr.* Westport, Conn.: Greenwood Press, 1971.

Washington, Joseph R. *Black Religion: The Negro and Christianity in the United States*. Boston: Beacon Press, 1964.

Wilmore, Gayraud. *Black Religion and Black Radicalism*. New York: Anchor Books, 1973.

Woodson, Carter G. *The Negro Church*. Washington, D.C.: Associated Press, rpt. 1972.